CISTERCIAN STUDIES SE

Adalbert de Vogüé

Reading Saint Benedict

Reflections on the Rule

CISTERCIAN STUDIES SERIES: NUMBER ONE HUNDRED FIFTY ONE

Reading Saint Benedict

Reflections on the Rule

by

Adalbert de Vogüé

Monk of La Pierre-qui-Vire

translated by Colette Friedlander ocso

Cistercian Publications
Kalamazoo, Michigan

A translation of
Ce que dit saint Benoît: Une lecture de la Règle. Vie Monastique 25
Abbaye de Bellefontaine, 1991

*The work of Cistercian Publications is made possible in part
by support from Western Michigan University to
The Institute of Cistercian Studies*

Library of Congress Cataloguing in Publication Data
Vogüé, Adalbert de.
    [Ce que dit saint Benoît. English]
    Reading Saint Benedict : reflections on the Rule / by
Adalbert de Vogüé ; translated by Colette Friedlander.
        p.   cm. — (Cistercian studies series ; no. 151.)
    ISBN 0–87907–651–8 (alk. paper). — ISBN 0–87907–751–4
(pbk. : alk. paper)
    1. Benedict, Saint, Abbot of Monte Cassino. Regula.
2. Benedictines—Rules.   I. Benedict, Saint, Abbot of Monte
Cassino. Regula.   II. Title.   III. Series.
BX3004.A2 1994
255′.106—dc20   93–27072
                                                        CIP

Printed in the United States of America

In memory of my novice master,
Father Placid

Table of Contents

To Novices

BROTHER OR SISTER novice, this book has been written for you. Its purpose is to help you read the Rule of Saint Benedict. When I entered the monastery forty-five years ago, our novice master, to whom this volume is dedicated, would ask us to put down in writing each day the thoughts suggested to us by the section of the Rule read to the community. Together with all the monks, we would hear this passage in Latin during chapter after Prime, then again in French at the evening meal; it fell on our ears three times a year. As for our personal reading, we were asked to write those few lines of commentary in order to make it less absent-minded or superficial. The purpose was not to penetrate all the secrets of the ancient text, but to ensure that we had given it at least some attention. I remember having thus gone through the Rule twice, putting down my comments day after day, with no other means at my disposal than my perfectly ignorant mind. The third time, following my novice master's advice, I used Dom Delatte's commentary and drew some light from it.

That is how my interest in the Rule began. After almost a half-century, having considered it in manifold ways and from many a viewpoint, I would like to return in this little volume to the simple everyday reading of my novitiate days. If I can be of help to you in turn, just as Delatte helped me, I shall be very happy.

The thoughts suggested by such a text are numberless, especially when one has spent a whole lifetime listening to it. I have had to choose. In this brief commentary, I have aimed at what seemed most necessary to me. In order to understand what Saint Benedict is saying, we must first and foremost heed what fills his mind and his heart: the Word of God, Scripture. I have constantly tried to bring out this scriptural warp of the Rule. Following in Saint Benedict's footsteps, we must prefer nothing to Christ who speaks in the Old Testament as in the New.

Second to this paramount spotlight, another seemed to me indispensable: the Rule of the Master. Written in the neighborhood of Rome in the first quarter of the sixth century, this work, three times as long as our Rule, provides it first, with most of its spiritual part (Prol.–7), then with a guiding thread which it usually follows almost until its conclusion (8–66). We are exceptionally lucky thus to have in hand the draft which Benedict used in writing up his own work. Might he have written this text himself—a text so seriously defective in some respects, but so remarkable in many others during the early half of his career? The use he made of it evidences his interest and invites us to compare it constantly with what he himself says: as we see how the saint uses this model, sometimes copying it, sometimes omitting, adding, or modifying, we witness the genesis of our Rule and we gain a better understanding of its author's intentions.

This is why you will constantly find parallels between Benedict and the Master in this commentary. Without going into much detail, I have attempted to indicate at least briefly the backdrop which the Master's work provides for Saint Benedict's. The relevance of such a comparison seems obvious to me: instead of reading the Rule laid out flat, as it were, we see it in three dimensions, standing out against this background. Often the Master's text explains Benedict's. In particular, it allows us time and time again to understand the link between chapters in Benedict's text, in which conciseness has entailed the obliteration of many connections.

Having thus found in this commentary some initial guidance as regards Benedict's relation to the Master, you may, if you feel so inclined, directly approach the long and strange Rule from which our own originated. Many readers of this surprising work wonder whether we are dealing with actual legislation aimed at real-life communities. Many passages seem artificial, as though they had been written in an armchair. In order to reconcile this utopic impression with other data which indicate a practical thrust, it is useful to remember that the RM (to introduce this usual abbreviation immediately) was designed to be read constantly in the refectory. Its scope was thus didactic as well as directive. The speeches, long or short, which it puts in the mouth of the abbot and brothers were obviously not meant to be repeated verbatim on every occasion. Their purpose was rather to indicate once and for all the meaning of the institutions and actions established or prescribed by the Rule.

In addition to the Master, I have rather often mentioned some other ancient writers, beginning with the one to whom Benedict, directly or through his forerunner, owes the most: John Cassian. Once again, confronting Benedict's text with its sources and parallels is singularly enlightening. Emerging from its isolation, it ceases to appear as an erratic block and takes its place within the great living tradition of monasticism.

While providing such insights into earlier or contemporary literature, I have especially tried to bring out the structure of the text itself. If I were to succeed in conveying or in developing a taste for this sort of analysis, I would feel that I had truly been of service. Seeing how a text is put together, what the author's starting point is, what he is aiming at and how he arrives there is a simple investigation, within everyone's reach, and is both necessary and enlightening. Nothing can better contribute to fostering that attention to the written word which is a prerequisite to all fruitful reading.

This brings me to an important recommendation. Above all, do not read this commentary before or immediately after the text. Begin by reading and re-reading the text itself, taking time to listen to what it says to you and to perceive the echos it awakens in you. Such immediate first contact is irreplaceable. Only afterwards can you find it helpful to enrich your understanding and control your reactions by resorting to someone else's knowledge. A commentary is designed to aid personal study, not to replace it.

You will perhaps be disappointed to find few answers to the questions which the modern reader of the Rule constantly asks: how much of this old text are we to retain today? Which of its elements are obsolete and which remain valid? I am fully aware that these are legitimate and urgent questions, but I do not feel qualified to answer them. It is up to each superior to determine, along with his or her brothers or sisters, what portion of the Rule is applicable in community. As for its impact on the personal life of the monk or nun: each person must hear what God is saying to him or her day after day through this word, inspired by his own word, coming down through the centuries. A commentator can do no more than hint unobtrusively at his own experience regarding this or that point. It is my personal conviction that in some areas the Rule can and should be followed more exactly than it presently is. In my view, true fidelity lies ahead of us, in a courageous and intelligent effort to rediscover some fundamental observance which the wear and tear of time has eliminated.

A word concerning the translation of the Rule which you find in this book. I must warn you that it is an unattractive one. Based on the text of the *Sources chrétiennes* edition with hardly any changes, it follows the Latin closely without concealing any of its grammatical inconsistencies, verbal repetitions, or other literary failings. The resulting impression is unpleasant, but not necessarily unprofitable: by keeping the work at its modest cultural level, such a translation—in fact, nearly a transposition—gives a truer picture. But I would not want you to be repelled or bothered by it. If this is the case, do not hesitate to use another translation.

I have divided this rugged text into sections according to the traditional distribution which provides for a reading of the entire Rule in four months' time, one section a day. In a few cases, however, I have modified the accepted division slightly to make it coincide with the actual articulations of the Rule. Such a reform of the traditional distribution would be desirable, as it does not always agree with the articulations of the text.

In conclusion, I would like to wish you the grace of patiently reading the Rule. Not all of it is interesting at first glance. In an ancient text like this, many things apparently mean nothing to us. We must learn to wait, to pay attention to what we have trouble understanding, to come to grasp a language and concerns which are not ours. You will notice that this commentary makes little distinction between what we find meaningful today and the rest. It assumes that everything is interesting provided we are capable of taking an interest in it. We must leave ourselves behind and listen to another's voice if we are to receive something. In return for this attentive, patient, and respectful openness, the Rule, like the Gospel from which it derives, will be for you what it has been for so many monks and nuns to this day: a treasure as new as it is old.

DAILY READING OF THE RULE

New divisions are indicated by an asterisk.

Prol.	1	7.	49	26.	1	51.	1
	8		51	27.	1	52.	1
	22*		55	28.	1	53.	1
	35*		56	29.	1		16
	39		59	30.	1	54.	1
	45		60	31.	1	55.	1
1.	1		62		13		16*
	6		67*	32.	1	56.	1
2.	1	8.	1	33.	1	57.	1
	11	9.	1	34.	1	58.	1
	16	10.	1	35.	1	59.	1
	23	11.	1	36.	1	60.	1
	30	12.	1	37.	1	61.	1
	37*	13.	1	38.	1		11*
3.	1		12	39.	1	62.	1
	13	14.	1	40.	1	63.	1
4.	1	15.	1	41.	1		10
	20*	16.	1	42.	1	64.	1
	44	17.	1	43.	1		7
	62*	18.	1		13	65.	1
5.	1		7	44.	1		11
	14		12	45.	1	66.	1
6.	1		20	46.	1	67.	1
7.	1	19.	1	47.	1	68.	1
	10	20.	1	48.	1	69.	1
	14*	21.	1		10	70.	1
	26*	22.	1		22	71.	1
	31	23.	1	49.	1	72.	1
	34	24.	1	50.	1	73.	1
	35	25.	1				
	44						

PRINCIPAL ABBREVIATIONS

Augustine

| *Ordo* | *Ordo monasterii* (Rule) |
| *Praec.* | *Praeceptum* (Rule) |

Basil

LR	Long Rules (Greek)
SR	Short Rules (Greek)
Reg.	*Regula* (Latin version by Rufinus)

Caesarius of Arles

| *Reg. uirg.* | Rule for virgins |

Gregory the Great

| *In I Reg.* | Commentary on the Book of Kings |

Horsiesius

| *Lib.* | *Liber* (Testament) |

Pachomius

Praec.	*Praecepta* (Rule)
Inst.	*Instituta* (Rule)
Iud.	*Iudicia* (Rule)

Rules of the Fathers

| *RIVF* | Rule of the Four Fathers |
| *2RF* | Second Rule of the Fathers |

Lives of Saint Pachomius

G[1]	Greek Life
SBo	Coptic Life
Vitae Patrum V	Apophthegms, systematic collection (latin version by Pelagius and John)

See the full Table of Abbreviations, pp. 339–348.

Prologue

THIS TEXT is a summary of the Master's long series of introductions. The Master presents the three pillars of monastic life one by one, beginning with a Prologue full of mysterious resonances in which we are invited to listen to the *Rule* as to God's genuine word. Then, following a wide-ranging, three-part piece of baptismal catechetics, he unveils his purpose of founding a school of the Lord's service, a *monastery*. Finally, after a picturesque description of the various kinds of monks, he introduces the teacher of this school, the *abbot*.

Benedict has retained only the second of these three successive presentations: the definition of the monastery as a school alone remains at the end of his Prologue, which is simply the last section of the Master's baptismal catechesis. As for the invitation to listen to the Rule, only an echo of it survives in Benedict's first words: 'Listen, my son'. Finally, the initial presentation of the abbot has disappeared completely, for after listing the kinds of monks Benedict goes straight to an abbatial directory.

Our whole Prologue thus leads up to its last paragraph, where Benedict decides along with the Master to 'establish a school for the Lord's service'. To introduce this key passage, the Master paraphrased two brief pieces from the Psalter: a few verses from Psalm 33 and the very short Psalm 14.[1] Benedict has retained this double paraphrase, which lends our text its structure. In order to understand that text, we must remember the catechetical custom underlying it: the bishop taught the newly baptized to pray the *Our Father* and the psalms. These two great christian prayers were taught them in turn, through homilies in which the meaning of the Lord's Prayer was explained to them first, then that of two psalms or psalm sections chosen for their brevity. Starting from this custom of the Church, the Master began by evoking baptism through his parable of the spring, then went on to a commentary on the *Our Father* with its seven petitions. After these first two parts of the baptismal catechesis, only traces of which remain at the beginning of our Prologue, we will hear the third, which Benedict has reproduced almost entirely.

[1] Listen, my son, to the master's instructions, and bend the ear of your heart. This is advice from a father who loves you; welcome it willingly, and assiduously put it into practice. [2] Thus you will return through your laborious obedience to him from whom you had drifted through your slothful disobedience. [3] This message of mine is for you, then, whoever you may be, who, giving up your own will in order to serve under the true king, Christ the Lord, take up the strong and noble weapons of obedience. [4] First of all, every time you begin a good work, pray to him most earnestly to bring it to perfection, [5] so that he who in his goodness has already deigned to count us as his sons may never have to grieve over our evil actions. [6] With his good gifts which are in us, we must obey him at all times, not only that he may never become the angry father who disinherits his sons, [7] but also that the dread Lord, enraged by our sins, may not

---

[1]Psalms follow the Septugint/Vulgate enumeration here, as in the Rule of Saint Benedict.

punish us forever as most foul servants for refusing to follow him to glory.

Before beginning to recopy the Master's commentary on the psalms, as he will do in the last three verses, Benedict sums up his forerunner's earlier passages in a few lines. 'Listening' to the Rule and 'putting it into practice' in order to walk toward God—this was already the initial message of the Master in his Prologue. As for 'praying instantly' for divine grace, this was also recommended by the Master in his commentary on the Lord's Prayer.

But Benedict adds to these remnants of his chief source some even more precise reminiscences of an *Admonition to a spiritual son* ascribed to Saint Basil. This is a characteristic process which we will encounter many a time throughout the Rule. Benedict's mind is full of what he has read, not only in Sacred Scripture, but also in the writings of the monastic Fathers. Thanks to this reading, he is able to complete and correct the Master. The first author he joins with him, as we can see here, is the great Basil, that 'holy Father' whose Rule he will mention with veneration in his epilogue.

Yet this archeology of the text matters less than the call which rings out from it. Like Basil and the inspired scribes of the Book of Proverbs, Benedict experiences himself as a 'father' as well as a 'master' (*magister*). He shares these two qualities with God, who speaks through him. At the end of the passage we will meet God the 'father' and 'Lord' (*dominus*) once more, but this time kindness will have given way to wrath. Entry into monastic life thus stands between a loving call and a fearsome judgment.

Not only at the offset but throughout, that life consists in listening to God's voice, that is, in obeying him. Obedience and disobedience, obedience and self-will, obeying or acting as a foul servant, these three successive pairs mark the great alternative with which the Christian and the monk constantly find themselves confronted. Disobedience is an accomplished fact in Adam, obedience an accomplished fact in Christ. We must live out this contrast between the two heads of humankind, as delineated by Saint Paul (Rm 5:12–21), by going once and for all and day after day from the disobedience of Adam to the obedience of Christ.

This is an immense task; it would be out of proportion with our human strength, if prayer did not allow us to receive God's help in perfecting it. Christ is not only the king who commands and the guide whom we must attempt to follow. In him we have the grace of baptism, which makes us sons and heirs apparent, destined to share his glory. This gift and this promise of life demand that we act in a way which is beyond us, but simultaneously they ground the possibility of obtaining everything through prayer.

> [8] Let us get up then, at long last, for the Scriptures rouse us when they say: 'It is high time for us to arise from sleep'. [9] Let us open our eyes to the light that comes from God and listen with attentive ears to the divine voice that every day calls out this charge: [10] 'If you hear his voice today, do not harden your hearts'. [11] And again: 'You that have ears to hear, listen to what the Spirit says to the churches'. [12] And what does he say? 'Come and listen to me, sons; I will teach you the fear of the Lord. [13] Run while you have the light of life, that the darkness of death may not overtake you.'

Of the five scriptural passages quoted here, only the next to last (Ps 33:12: 'Come and listen to me, sons; I will teach you the fear of the Lord') is chosen for its own sake: it introduces the psalm quotation which will unfold in the next paragraph. Before quoting continuously four verses from Psalm 33, the Master and Benedict here offer the verse preceding them as an invitation to listen to what follows.

This preliminary call by the Psalmist is itself prepared by three quotations and rounded off by yet another one. In the series thus formed, the Old and New Testaments alternate regularly: from Paul (Rm 13:11) to the Psalter (Ps 94:8), and from Revelation (Rv 2:7) back to the Psalmist (Ps 33:12), ending with the Gospel (Jn 12:35). As in the Mass readings which this sequence calls to mind, the Lord's voice—that is, the voice of Christ and of his Spirit—may be perceived uniformly throughout. Through the Old Testament as well as through the New, it is he who speaks.

Scripture thus enters the stage both explicitly and massively. Its importance is paramount in the monk's life. It is both 'light from God' and 'voice from heaven'—one and the same element through which the Lord touches all our spiritual senses.

We are thus asked first of all to awaken, then to open wide our eyes and ears. The first word we hear is taken from that very Psalm 94 which the Rule has us sing at the beginning of the nocturns, immediately after rising. Benedict, who adds this quotation to the Master's series, is probably thinking of the daily invitatory of Vigils.

The summons to listen obviously recalls the opening words of the Prologue. Those words referred to the Rule; now we are dealing with Scripture. The Rule's only ambition is to lead us to Scripture. Behind the author of the Rule, both 'father and master', stood the figure of the Lord. Here again he speaks in this double capacity, calling us 'sons' and announcing that he will 'teach' us. For the Master as for Benedict after him, Christ is a father. And his teaching mission will be proclaimed at the end of the Prologue, where the monastery will be defined as a 'school' for his '*magisterium*'. As for that fear of the Lord which he teaches us, the chapter on humility will reveal its meaning and importance.

As was the case previously with the words from Revelation, the gospel quotation which ends the passage is put by John himself on Christ's lips. Instead of the usual reading ('Walk'), our Rules, along with other patristic texts, have

'Run'. As we shall see, this verb connotes action for our authors. More than just listening is involved. We must also act, put into practice. In the Gospel, Jesus called himself the 'light' whose presence his Jewish hearers had to turn to good account in view of their conversion. By specifying 'light *of life*', with its correlative 'darkness *of death*', our Rules apply Christ's words to the Christian's condition: the time clause with which Jesus' summons ends is meant to convey the urgency of conversion in the present life, before death makes it impossible. We are thus brought back to the Apostle's initial message: 'It is high time for us to arise from sleep'.

> [14] And seeking his workman in a multitude of people to whom he calls out, the Lord again says: [15] 'Is there anyone here who yearns for life and wishes to see good days?' [16] If you hear this and your answer is 'I do!' God then directs these words to you: [17] 'If you desire true and eternal life, keep your tongue free from vicious talk and your lips from all deceit; turn away from evil and do good; seek peace and pursue it. [18] And once you have done this, my eyes will be upon you and my ears will listen for your prayers; and even before you call to me, I will say to you: Here I am!' [19] What, dear brothers, is more delightful than this voice of the Lord calling to us? [20] See how the Lord in his love shows us the way of life. [21] Thus, girding our loins with faith and the performance of good works, let us set out on his ways, with the Gospel for our guide, that we may deserve to see him who has called us to his kingdom.

This is not the first time that these verses from Psalm 33 are offered to Christians as a program for life here below with a view to gaining eternal life. Saint Peter had already quoted the passage in nearly identical form to his asian neophytes (1 P 3:10–12). The Rule thus goes back to the roots of monastic life: the monk's vocation is none other than that of the baptized Christian, called by God to 'receive a blessing as his inheritance', as Peter says, or to 'true and eternal life', in the words of the Master and Saint Benedict.

First quoted verbatim (Prol 15 and 17), then paraphrased and completed by two phrases from Isaiah (Prol 18; cf. Is 58:9 and 65:24), this psalm text (Ps 33:13–16) takes on the appearance of a dialogue between man and God. God issues a call to life, then indicates how we must behave in order to attain it. After hearing the Lord's first words, a human person answers the call. Finally, the author-preacher highlights the divine invitation and himself invites the hearers to set out in order to reach the goal.

As in the preceding passage, the New Testament constantly surfaces next to the Old. In the very first words we can make out the parable of the workmen in the vineyard (Mt 20:1–16), and the crowd where the Lord searches for his man reminds us of the multitude of the called who follow the broad way, in contrast to the small number of chosen who take the narrow way (Mt 22:14; 7:13–14). Then the 'life' of which the Psalmist speaks is called 'true and eternal', an obvious reference to the everlasting life promised by Christ (Mt 19:16). Likewise, the expression 'way of life', though found in the Psalter (Ps 15:10), reminds us again of the narrow way of the Gospel which leads to life (Mt 7:14). As for the last sentence, everything in it exudes the New Testament: not only the 'loins girded with faith', an allusion to the pauline armor (Eph 6:14–15), but also and explicitly the 'guide' that is the Gospel, and finally the description of God as 'he who has called us to his kingdom' (1 Th 2:12), where we hope to 'see' him (Mt 5:8). The Rule thus has us listen to Psalm 33 with christian ears. Underlying its very general moral agenda is the Gospel in every detail.

At the beginning of the last sentence, the 'faith-good works' pair again recalls the previous paragraph. Just as we have been asked not only to 'hear' but also to 'run', that is to act, here too faith is coupled with action. No doubt in order to form this very important binomial, the Master and Benedict modify Saint Paul's armor slightly. According to the letter to the Ephesians, the loins (*lumbos*, as here) are girded with 'truth'; faith is compared to a shield, not to a belt. Perhaps our authors were remembering the shoot of Jesse (Is 11:5): 'faith shall be the girdle of his loins (*renum*)'. But in a letter to the Emperor Justinian (519), Hormisdas, a contemporary pope, had already recommended that he 'gird his loins (*lumbos*) with the energy of faith'.

These details in wording matter less, however, than the magnificent hope which vibrates through the two previous sentences ('What . . . is more delightful . . . the way of life') and which reappears in the last words of the paragraph ('to see him who has called us to his kingdom'). Unlike the Letter of Peter, our Rules stop at the positive promise contained in the psalm and do not go on to the threat which follows it (Ps 33:17; 1 P 3:12). The somber image of the enraged father and lord, conjured up at the beginning of the Prologue, has now disappeared. As becomes Christians, people who are saved, monks have eyes and ears for nothing but the everlasting bliss to which they know themselves to be destined. Today, as in Benedict's time, there is no greater happiness on earth than to live in that hope.

22 If we wish to dwell in the tent of this kingdom, we will never arrive unless we run there by doing good deeds. 23 But let us ask the Lord with the Prophet: 'Who will dwell in your tent, Lord; who will find rest upon your holy mountain?' 24 After this question, brothers, let us listen well to what the Lord says in reply, for he shows us the way to his tent 25 by saying: 'One who walks without blemish and is just in all his dealing; 26 who speaks the truth in his heart and has not practiced deceit with his tongue; 27 who has not wronged a fellowman in any way, nor listened to slanders against his neighbor'; 28 who

when the evil one, the devil, suggested something to him, flung both him and his promptings far from the sight of his heart, and catching hold of his young— the thoughts he inspired—dashed them against Christ. [29] Those people who fear the Lord do not become elated over their good deeds; judging that the Lord's power, not their own, brings about the good in them, [30] they praise the Lord working in them, and say with the Prophet: 'Not to us, Lord, not to us, but to your name alone give glory!', [31] just as Paul the Apostle also refused to take credit for his preaching and declared: 'By God's grace I am what I am'. [32] And again he said: 'He who boasts, let him boast in the Lord'. [33] That is why the Lord says in the Gospel: 'Whoever hears these words of mine and does them is like a wise man who built his house upon rock; [34] the floods came and the winds blew and beat against the house, but it did not fall, for it was founded on rock'.

This section devoted to Psalm 14 is very similar to the preceding one. Like the passage from Psalm 33 just quoted, the short psalm reproduced here contains a promise of happiness and a catalogue of good actions, which remind a christian reader of eternal bliss and of the demands of the Gospel. Again as before, the pericope contains a question and an answer, which the Rule presents in dialogue form. Again as before, the psalm text is first quoted verbatim (Prol 25–27 = Ps 14:2–3), then paraphrased (Prol 29–33; cf. Ps 14:4–5). Finally, like the first, this second psalm commentary combines other scriptural quotations or allusions with the text being commented upon, and they are lined up in an order intended to bring the liturgy to mind: Saint Paul follows on the Old Testament and is followed by the Gospel.

Again, therefore, the christianization of the Psalter is obvious. Christ is called by name moreover in the middle of the passage (Prol 28), before being referred to by his title of Lord (Prol 33). He is the rock against which evil thoughts are smashed, and also the rock upon which the Christian's spiritual home is built.

The first sentence is both a clip linking the two psalm quotations together and a summary of what follows. From it it is clear that to 'run' means to 'act well'. Let us note next that this time the initial question is asked not by God but by man. And the divine answer goes into more detail than did Psalm 33, with which it has in common the condemnation of deceit.

Like the simple quotation, the paraphrased text is also longer than that of Psalm 33. This paraphrase is not without subtlety. The Psalmist said of the just man: 'Before him [literally: before his sight] the wicked man is reduced to nothingness'. Seeing in this wicked man the 'fiend', that is, the devil, the Master and Benedict want the monk to 'reduce him to nothingness' by casting him far from the 'sight' of his heart. In practice, this concerns the evil suggestions of temptation. 'Happy is he who seizes your children and dashes them against the rock' (Ps 136:9): the object of this terrible curse is no longer Babylon but Satan, whose offspring are evil thoughts. According to an interpretation common in the writings of the Fathers, the rock here is Christ, as Saint Paul stated (1 Co 10:4).

The Psalmist then says that the just man 'magnifies (*magnificat*) those who fear the Lord'. But in the Psalter with which the Master and Benedict were acquainted, just as in the one used by their contemporary Saint Germanus of Paris, the verb is in the plural (*magnificant*). Thus 'those who fear the Lord magnify him'. On the basis of this reading, the psalm text is understood as calling for humility: the person who behaves rightly ascribes all the good he does to the grace of God, in the line of a passage from the 'prophet' David (Ps 113:9) and of two others from the Apostle Paul (1 Co 15:10; 2 Co 10:17). This acknowledgment of divine grace goes further than the one at the beginning of the

Prologue, where God was simply asked to 'bring to perfection' the good work undertaken (Prol 4). Now all of human action is referred to its transcendent cause, for we obey God only 'with his good gifts which are in us' (Prol 6).

Omitting three sentences of the text (Ps 14:4–5) which the Master had reproduced without comment, Benedict goes on to the conclusion. The verses omitted deal with false oaths, loaning money at usury, and bribes offered to judges, none of which normally has any place in a monk's life. In contrast, the psalm's final statement—'He who does these things shall never be shaken'—recalls to every christian ear the conclusion of the Sermon on the Mount (Mt 7:33–34), and this is why the Rule substitutes these words of Jesus for those of the Psalter. In the Master's text the transition from the latter to the former was explicit. Elliptically and somewhat obscurely, Benedict presents the gospel text as the continuation of the psalm he has just commented on. For both monastic authors, in any case, it is clear that the agenda delineated by the Psalmist, modest though it is, is identified with the loftiest demands of the Gospel.

> [35] With this conclusion, the Lord waits for us to respond daily to his holy teachings by our actions. [36] This is why our life span has been lengthened by way of a truce, that we may amend our misdeeds, [37] as the Apostle says: 'Do you not know that the patience of God is leading you to repent?' [38] And indeed the Lord assures us in his kindness: 'I do not wish the death of the sinner, but that he turn back to me and live'.

Following on the Sermon on the Mount, Matthew notes the feeling of the crowds 'when Jesus had finished this discourse' (Mt 7:28). Benedict's first words allude to this sentence. Psalm 14 has just been identified with the great gospel discourse. Once it is over, the Lord expects our actions to answer his precepts. The dialogue is to continue:

the ultimate response expected is no longer verbal but factual.

According to the Rule of the Master, the Lord waits *in silence*. Benedict omits this touch, but it helps us understand the rather somber note taken on by the passage which follows; God's present silence is fraught with menace. One day the just judge will break it in order to pass sentence, and then he will say: 'This you did, and I remained silent' (7:30, quoting Ps 49:21).

Given this fearsome prospect of judgment, life appears as a reprieve granted us so that we may mend our ways, an opportunity for penance (Rm 2:4), a time for conversion (Ezk 33:11). We thus revert to a consideration of sin and its terrible consequences, contemplated at the beginning of the Prologue (Prol 6–7), then somewhat lost sight of in the rush toward happiness aroused by the call of the two psalms. At the same time the theme of life's shortness and of the urgent need to act before it is too late surfaces once more (Prol 13).

> [39] Brothers, now that we have asked the Lord who will dwell in his tent, we have heard the instruction for dwelling in it, but only if we fulfill the obligations of those who live there. [40] We must, then, prepare our hearts and bodies for the battle of holy obedience to his instructions. [41] What is not possible to us by nature, let us ask the Lord to supply through the help of his grace. [42] And if, fleeing the torments of hell, we wish to reach eternal life [43] then—while there is still time, while we are in this body and have time to accomplish all these things by the light of life— [44] we must run and do now what will profit us forever.

After the reflections suggested by the epilogue of the Sermon on the Mount, here we find the conclusion of Psalm 14. It brings us back to the psalm's positive vision. Turned as it is toward eternal life, it makes only a brief mention of hell and its torments, which we are to flee. Beyond Psalm 14, the entire commentary on both psalms, including the introduction, is summed up in these lines, where we once more come across man's action and God's, the powerlessness of nature and the help of grace, our resort to prayer to obtain grace, and finally the urgency of striving in the limited time allotted us.

[45] We must therefore establish a school for the Lord's service. [46] In drawing up its regulations, we hope to set down nothing harsh, nothing burdensome. [47] If, however, a concern for equity prompts us to a little strictness in order to amend faults and to safeguard love, [48] do not be daunted immediately by fear and run away from the road that leads to salvation, which is bound to be narrow at the outset. [49] But as we progress in religious life and in faith, 'our hearts shall open up and we shall run on the path of God's commandments', overflowing with the inexpressible delight of love. [50] Never swerving from his instructions, then, but persevering in observing his teaching in the monastery until death, we shall through patience share in the sufferings of Christ that we may deserve also to share in his kingdom. Amen.

This conclusion to the Prologue is of paramount importance, for it sets out in a few lines the project which the entire Rule will elaborate. As we remarked earlier, the Master had already brought in the essential point of his second introduction—the decision to establish a 'school of the Lord', that is, a 'monastery'— at the end of his psalm commentary. The Master's text is reproduced at the beginning and end of the present paragraph (Prol 45 and 50). Between these two passages borrowed from his forerunner, Benedict inserts an original one (Prol 46–49) in which he specifies his own notion of the monastic school. Both authors define with equal clarity in their respective Rules what it is that they intend to establish.

For the Master, the 'school of the Lord's service' or, as he says more simply elsewhere, the 'Lord's school' has its foundation charter in the words of the Gospel: 'Place my yoke upon your shoulders and learn from me' (Mt 11:29). It is the natural place for baptized human beings who have become children of God and disciples of Christ. Once the Church, our mother, has provided us with this new birth in Baptism, the task of the monastic school is to educate us in the life of perfection according to the Gospel. The baptistery leads to the monastery. In the monastery, we do nothing our whole life long but listen to Christ and obey his lessons. For Christ is its sole teacher, represented by a visible schoolmaster: the abbot.

As the last sentence says, 'persevering in Christ's teaching until death' presupposes that we 'share in his sufferings through patience'. We are reminded of the early Christians who persevered in the teaching of the apostles and of Christ (Ac 2:42; 2 Jn 9), of Saint Peter or Saint Paul calling us to take part in the sufferings of Jesus in order to be allowed to share his glory (1 P 4:13; Rm 8:17). The vision delineated by the Rule of the Master is magnificent, but apparently stern: life here below seems to be no more than one long passion with Christ; the happiness of the kingdom is reserved for the hereafter.

In making this program his own, Benedict judged it necessary to complete and qualify it. In his view, the present life is not merely a painful preparation for the joy of the kingdom. It has its share of 'delight' (*dulcedo*), which is even termed 'inexpressible', and this foretaste of heavenly bliss is due to the love with which we carry out God's commandments.

Before coming to this statement, which immediately precedes the Master's last words and acts as an advance corrective, Benedict meditates on the project for a school which his senior had begun by delineating. Because it is a school of Christ, which answers Christ's call (Mt 11:29), it will have to manifest the characteristics indicated immediately afterwards by Jesus himself: 'My yoke is sweet (*suave*) and my load is light' (Mt 11:30). In other words, 'nothing harsh, nothing burdensome' should be found there. But this maxim of Jesus does not stand alone. Elsewhere in the same Gospel, he speaks of the two ways which human beings follow, a broad way along which the great number moves forward toward perdition, and a narrow way, chosen by a few, which leads to life (Mt 7:13–14). A certain stringency, something 'strict', is thus equally required of Christ's school.

How can these contrasting traits—mildness and lightness on one hand, stringent demands on the other—be reconciled? Along with many other patristic writers, Benedict raises the question, and like several of them he seeks an answer in love. Without diminishing the objective demands of God's law, love makes them subjectively mild and light, for nothing is painful to those who love. The fulfillment which love brings amid the strictest observances finds its symbol in the 'overflowing heart' of which the Psalmist speaks (Ps 118:32). Thus the Psalter reconciles the two apparently conflicting statements of the Gospel.

Yet this solution of the problem through love cannot disregard time. We arrive at it only as we progress. By taking time into account this way, Benedict is led to correct the Gospel materially. Christ had presented the way of salvation as narrow from end to end. According to the Rule, it is so only at the beginning. But this apparent change does not affect the substance of the gospel teaching, for the widening takes place within: the human heart finds fulfillment, while God's precepts retain their full strictness.

Starting from the words 'to establish a school', Benedict's meditation on the Master's text thus opens onto the dimension of time, where it meets the perspective of 'persevering until death' set out by the other Rule. Several important notions have slipped in between the two sections of the

Master's sentence, notions whose echoes we will soon perceive: 'equity', 'amending faults and safeguarding love', the concern not to frighten the weak who might run away, the dynamic character of religious life (*conversatio*) which involves 'advancing' and 'running' toward perfection. In conclusion, let us note the mystical touch added by the term 'inexpressible', used by Benedict to describe the 'delight of love'; Saint Paul applies the same adjective to the groans of the Spirit in the hearts of the children of God (Rm 8:26).

I

The kinds of monks

IN THE RULE of the Master, this chapter ends with a wide-ranging presentation on the abbot, the third element that goes to make up cenobitism. Lacking this final piece, which he did away with, Benedict retained the enumeration of the three pillars of monasticism in community in his initial definition of cenobites: monastery, rule, abbot. The abbot, mentioned here for the first time, is at last introduced with a word.

In describing the different kinds of monks, the Master and Benedict follow Cassian (*Conf.* 18.4–8), who in turn drew his inspiration from Saint Jerome (*Ep.* 22.34–36). What those writers said of the monks of Egypt is here extended by our two legislators to all of monasticism throughout the world. The first three kinds of monks are to be found in all descriptions. The fourth alone is proper to our two Rules.

[1] There are clearly four kinds of monks. [2] First, there are the cenobites, that is to say, those who live in monasteries, where they serve under a rule and an abbot.

[3] Second, there is the kind called anchorites or hermits, who are no longer in the first fervor of religious life; but through the test of living in a monastery for a long time, [4] they have learned to fight against the devil; thanks to

the help and guidance of many, [5] they have built up their strength and go from the battle line of their brothers to the single combat of the desert. Self-reliant now, without the support of another, they are ready with God's help to grapple single-handed with the vices of flesh and mind.

Cenobites (from a Greek term which means 'living in common') are mentioned first for several reasons. First, because the entire Rule will deal with them. Secondly, because the anchorites are drawn from their ranks and presuppose their existence. Finally because, according to Cassian, they appeared first historically: cenobitism is supposedly no more than a continuation of the early Church, where the faithful owned everything in common and were of one heart and one soul; this cenobitic tradition, unbroken since the time of the apostles, was assumed to have given rise in the third century to the first anchorites such as Saint Anthony.

The neatly turned definition of cenobites presents them first of all as forming communities ('monasteries'), then indicates the two authorities by which they are ruled: a law and a person, a rule and an abbot. The verb which characterizes their way of life means something more than 'to serve', by which we translate it. Literally, cenobites 'do battle' under their abbot, just as the postulant, according to Benedict, wishes to 'do battle' under Christ the king (Prol 3). But by the days of the late roman empire, *militare* meant any kind of public service, military or not.

The anchorites or hermits, two words which call to mind retreat far from the world and into the desert, appear more explicitly as warriors. The image of combat reflects back from this description onto the cenobites, among whom they have been trained to struggle. This is a valuable touch which reveals a major aspect of cenobitism: antagonism with the devil, who stirs up the 'vices of flesh and mind'.

All of monastic life aims at freeing human beings, through divine grace, from these enemies of God.

Cenobites and hermits thus resemble a battleline from which lone combatants emerge. This warlike metaphor is the only one used by the Master and Benedict. Cassian added another contrast: that between the 'active life' and the 'contemplative life', that is, between purifying asceticism, for which a community setting is essential at first, and continual union with God, which is fostered by the solitary life. From both perspectives, eremitism appears as a continuation of cenobitism, one which cultivates more intensely some of the latter's sacrifices and values. From this viewpoint, *anachoresis* is beyond cenobitism. It calls for and transcends previous community formation.

According to our two Rules, as already according to Cassian, these two ways of life are less opposed than they are interdependent: cenobitism is a preparation for the solitary life, and the latter actualizes some of the former's potentialities. This tradition, egyptian in origin, differs sharply from the views of Saint Basil, who approved of community life to the exclusion of solitude. In contrast to basilian cenobitism, Benedict's remains open. In practice, these two forms of authentic monasticism have developed in a mutually fruitful symbiosis. Eremitism needs a cenobitic foundation, but cenobitism lacks something when the anchoritic life does not confront it with its model of extreme renunciation and unceasing conversation with God alone.

⁶ Third, there are the sarabaites, the most detestable kind of monks, who with no experience to guide them, no rule to try them as gold is tried in a furnace, have a character as soft as lead. ⁷ Still loyal to the world by their actions, they clearly lie to God by their tonsure. ⁸ Two or three together, or even alone, without a sheperd, they pen themselves up in their own sheepfolds, not the Lord's. Their law is what they like to do, whatever strikes

their fancy. [9] Anything they believe in and choose, they call holy; anything they dislike, they consider forbidden.

[10] Fourth and finally, there is the kind of monks called gyrovagues, who spend their entire lives drifting from region to region, staying as guests for three or four days in different monasteries; [11] always on the move, they never settle down, they are slaves to their own wills and to the temptations of gluttony, and are worse in every way than sarabaites.

[12] It is better to keep silent than to speak of the wretched way of life of all these people. [13] Let us pass them by, then, and with the help of the Lord, proceed to organize that most valiant kind, the cenobites.

'Sarabaites' is a coptic term which means 'separated from monasteries'. The Master and Benedict borrowed it from Cassian, according to whom these separatists, supposedly, broke away from the ancient cenobitic tree at a late date, after the praiseworthy exodus of the first hermits. The author of the *Conferences* saw in them a reappearance of the spirit of Ananias and Sapphira, who were cut off from the early Church for having kept their possessions on the sly. In striking them down, Saint Peter had taxed the couple with 'lying to God' (Ac 5:3–4). The same blame is here leveled at their epigones, whose behavior does not accord with their monastic tonsures any more than the goods set aside by the couple were in accord with their statements of renunciation.

Another scriptural reminiscence surfaces just before this, when Benedict notes that the sarabaites have not been 'tried as gold in a furnace' (Ws 3:6), thus crediting the cenobitic rule with the purifying effect of fire. Sarabaites differ from anchorites primarily by this absence of regular formation, although they resemble them outwardly because they live alone. Moreover, they lack that shepherd commissioned by Christ, the abbot, and that authentic sheepfold of the Lord, the monastery (cf. Jn 10:16). These deficiencies result in their canonizing their every wish; this is described by the Master and Benedict in terms which again echo Cassian (*Conf.* 18.3.2).

'Gyrovagues', a compound noun which evokes circling and wandering, was doubtless a rather common term in late Latin, for it can be found in the correspondence of a seventh-century gallic bishop, Didier of Cahors, as well as in modern Italian. Such vagrants were not unknown in the East, but they do not appear in the picture of the kinds of monks painted by Jerome and Cassian. It is the Master who must be credited with making them into a fourth kind, one against which he takes manifold precautions in his chapters on hospitality. At this juncture, he spends several pages ridiculing them. Benedict cuts down this endless satire to a paragraph even shorter than the two preceding it, eager as he is to address his subject: the organization of cenobitism, to which he applies, as he previously did to the 'weapons of obedience', the qualifier *fortissimum* ('very powerful' or 'valiant').

II

What the abbot must be

IMMEDIATELY after introducing the abbot to the brothers, the Master addresses him, telling him what he must be. Dealing first with the superior is a characteristic feature of the tradition derived from Egypt and Lérins. We find it in Horsiesius and the Four Fathers, as well as in the Oriental Rule, whereas Basil, Augustine, and others speak of the superior only later on or even in closing. It goes hand in hand with a hierarchical notion of the cenobium favoring the vertical relationship of obedience to God, who is represented in the monastery by a leader analogous to the bishop in the Church.

Divided as it is into two symmetrical parts, the Master's chapter follows a layout which is both rigorous and flexible. In Benedict's text, this neat order is clouded by a series of omissions and additions which reveal personal concerns. The introductory section which we will now read has not, however, been significantly modified:

> [1] The abbot who is worthy of governing a monastery must always remember what his title signifies and verify the superior's name by his actions. [2] For he is believed to hold the place of Christ in the monastery, since he is addressed by a title of Christ, [3] as the Apostle indicates:

'You have received the spirit of adoption of sons by which we exclaim, A*bb*a, father'.

4 Therefore, the abbot must never teach or decree or command anything that would deviate from the Lord's instructions; 5 on the contrary, everything he teaches and commands should, like the leaven of divine justice, permeate the minds of his disciples. 6 Let the abbot always remember that at the fearful judgment of God not only his teaching but also his disciples' obedience will come under scrutiny. 7 And the abbot must be aware that the shepherd will bear the blame wherever the father of the household finds that the sheep have yielded no profit. 8 On the other hand, if the shepherd has used all his zeal in serving a restive and disobedient flock, always striving to cure their unhealthy ways, 9 their shepherd will be acquitted at the Lord's judgment and, like the Prophet, he will say to the Lord: 'I have not hidden your justice in my heart; I have proclaimed your truth and your salvation. But they spurned and rejected me'. 10 Then at last the sheep that have rebelled against his care will be punished by the overwhelming power of death.

In the monastery, the superior's name is 'abbot' (*abbas*). This aramaic term which Jesus used in speaking to his Father (Mk 14:36) was applied in Syriac and later in Greek to those monks who by reason of their age and authority were acknowledged as spiritual fathers. Coptic monasticism adopted it, and we find it even in the earliest monastic texts written in Latin.

According to Saint Paul (Rm 8:15; cf. Gal 4:6), Jesus' cry of agony, 'Abba, Father!' is repeated by the Holy Spirit in the hearts of Christians. We rightly believe today that this cry is addressed to the Father of our Lord Jesus Christ, to the first person of the Trinity. In the view of the Master and Benedict, however, it is addressed to Christ himself, regarded as our father. Thus, according to them, the title of abbot makes its bearer into a representative *of Christ*.

Surprising though it may be in our eyes, this interpretation of Saint Paul's text is obvious to the Master, since he sees Christ as 'our Father', the one we invoke in the Lord's Prayer. Faith in the God-man, questioned by the Arians, had become as an indirect consequence so vital to these sixth-century italian monks that they almost went so far as to stop at him and forget his Father. Though not pushed to such lengths, the theme of the fatherhood of Christ, to which we are no longer accustomed, comes up often in the best patristic writings. It is solidly grounded in Saint John—who parallels our relationship to the Son with that of the Son to his Father—as well as in Saint Paul, for whom Christ is the second Adam, the father of regenerated humankind.

'Representing Christ' had been the role proper to the bishop since Saint Cyprian. By extending it to the abbot, the Master and Benedict imply that the monastery is a kind of Church in which the teaching of one of the apostles' successors continues to breed brotherly communion, as in the days immediately following Pentecost (Ac 2:42). In fact, teaching God's law and seeing that it is observed is the first task assigned the abbot by the present chapter. It calls to mind the yeast in the dough (Mt 13:33) and places a heavy burden of responsibility upon the abbot: he is accountable for all of the brothers' activity, shaped as it is by his leadership.

We have just said 'brothers', but the Master and Benedict say 'disciples'. This word recalls the Gospel. Jesus was surrounded by disciples, the closest of whom were called the apostles or the Twelve. He was regarded as the master *par excellence*, who taught in God's name. By using these same words, our Rules are referring to this circle of disciples around Jesus. They define the monastery as a 'school' because, although the term does not appear in the Gospels, it is nonetheless the exact definition of the group of Twelve surrounding Christ. The monastic school is the continuation of that group, and one of its members holds the place of the invisible master, Christ.

The abbot is thus enjoined to model his instructions strictly on those of Christ, on pain of punishment by Him at the last day. Conjuring up that fearful judgment gives rise to several scriptural reminiscences. Two of them are explicit (Ps 39:11, Is 1:2), but others remain latent. The judgment of the shepherd reminds us of the end of the Epistle of Saint Peter (1 P 5:1–4), and the 'overwhelming power of death' (*praeualens mors*) comes from the Old Latin version of the Prophets (Is 25:8). The ancient version of the Psalter which says of the wicked that 'death shall be their shepherd' (Ps 48:15) may also hover in the background: instead of the Good Shepherd and his representative, that sinister herdsman will hold sway over them.

> [11] Therefore, anyone who receives the name of abbot is to lead his disciples by a twofold teaching, [12] that is, he must point out to them all that is good and holy more by actions than by words. Thus he shall propose the commandments of the Lord to receptive disciples with words, but demonstrate God's instructions to the hard-hearted and the simple-minded by his actions. [13] Conversely, if he teaches his disciples that something is forbidden, then let him show by his actions that it should not be done, 'lest after preaching to others, he himself be found reprobate', [14] and God some day call to him in his sin: 'How is it that you repeat my just commands and mouth my covenant, when you hate discipline and toss my words behind you?' [15] And also this: 'You who saw a splinter in your brother's eye never noticed the beam in your own'.

Like the introductory section, this first development of the Master is reproduced almost without change by Benedict. It distinguishes between two kinds of teaching: by word and example, the second being especially suited to

the uncouth. The two methods must be combined, whether
we are dealing with the divine commandments or with
their antithesis.

The exposition begins with a reminder of the meaning
of 'abbot'. The first and true abbot, we remember from
the beginning of the chapter, is Christ; the superior of
the monastery is no more than his lieutenant. The entire
abbatial mission stems from this. Besides this reference
to their own text, the Master and Benedict call on three
scriptural passages: a phrase from Saint Paul (1 Co 9:27),
another from the psalms (Ps 49:16–17) and a sentence from
the Gospel (Mt 7:3). The final progression from the Old
Testament to the New recalls the Prologue.

> [16] The abbot should avoid all favoritism in the monastery.
> [17] He is not to love one more than another, unless he
> finds someone better in good actions and obedience.
> [18] A man born free is not to be given higher rank than
> a slave who enters religion, except for some other good
> reason. [19] If the abbot so decides, and as justice de-
> mands, he shall do thus as regards anyone's rank: other-
> wise, everyone is to keep to his regular place, [20] because
> 'whether slave or free, we are all one in Christ' and share
> alike in bearing arms in the service of the one Lord, for
> 'God shows no partiality among persons'. [21] Only in this
> are we distinguished in his sight: if we are found better
> than others in good works and in humility. [22] Therefore,
> the abbot is to show equal charity to everyone and apply
> the same discipline to all according to their merits.

The previous paragraph noted the differences between
dispositions and consequently recommended diversity in
teaching methods. Here we go from the differences between persons to the equal treatment the abbot must mete
out to them. This is the case at any rate in the Master's text,
for Benedict qualifies and tones down this duty of treating
everyone alike. He does so by first setting aside the case

in which a 'good reason' justifies unequal treatment (18b–19), then by eliminating a sentence from the Master which reminded us that God makes his creation available to the wicked as well as to the good (RM 2:21; cf. Mt 5:45) and finally by adding 'according to their merits' at the end of the passage.

Benedict, who is more sensitive to the differences between persons than the Master and concerned with avoiding equalitarianism, also shows for the first time his preoccupation with the order according to which the brethren rank within the community (19). In actual fact, he parts with the Master on this point by placing them according to their date of entry, while allowing the abbot to make justified exceptions. These departures from the order of seniority are targeted here.

Let us note two other small but significant additions: the mention of obedience (17) and humility (21). These words, lacking in the Master's text, reveal Benedict's particular regard for both these virtues.

In the monastery the cleavage between free men and slaves is abrogated. This revolution is grounded in the New Testament but goes beyond it. In proclaiming that all are one in Christ (Gal 3:28) and that there is no partiality among persons on God's part (Rm 2:11; cf. Eph 6:8–9), Saint Paul was simply putting forth views based on faith, devoid of any immediate impact on social reality. It was to be up to monasticism to turn these mystical principles into structural laws governing the community.

[23] In his teaching, the abbot must always observe the Apostle's recommendation, in which he says: 'Use argument, appeal, reproof', [24] that is, he must vary with circumstances, threatening and coaxing by turns, stern as a master, tender as a father. [25] With the undisciplined and restless, he will use firm argument; with the obedient and docile and patient, he will appeal for greater

progress; but as for the negligent and disdainful, we charge him to use reproof and rebuke.

26 And let him not gloss over the sins of those who err, but cut them out at the root while he can, as soon as they begin to sprout, remembering the fate of Eli, priest of Shiloh. 27 He is to admonish upright and perceptive spirits with words a first and a second time, 28 but curb those who are evil or stubborn, arrogant or disobedient by blows or some other physical punishment at the first offense, knowing that it is written, 'The fool cannot be corrected with words'; 29 and again, 'Strike your son with a rod and you will free his soul from death'.

In beginning his second part, the Master goes back to the necessary diversity in the abbot's teaching according to the differences in the monks' dispositions, and he illustrates this idea by a phrase from Saint Paul (2 Tm 4:2) which he quotes and comments on. Benedict, whose interest for this theme we have noted, reproduces the passage more or less as it stands (23–25), confining himself to adding, in v. 25, the adjective 'firm' and the words 'and rebuke'; these additions show his concern for effective correction.

Unlike this borrowed passage, the continuation of Benedict's text is original. He omits two paragraphs from the Master and replaces them with personal reflections. Omissions and additions follow the same lines. The suppressed passage first invited the abbot to join example with word by making himself humble, like the child Christ set up as a model for the apostles; then it again recommended that he show equal charity to all, combining the shades proper to a father's affection and to a mother's. Among the reasons Benedict might have had for striking out these suggestions, the most obvious is his acute sense of the differences between persons and the uneasiness which all uniform treatment consequently aroused in him. In fact, his addition is the exact opposite of the passage he eliminated: far from acting in identical fashion towards all, the abbot is again exhorted to vary his conduct. Following on the three kinds of minds distinguished earlier, a new two-part distinction is added.

Besides, this time the subject of the directions regarding diversity is the manner of exercising correction. This is another of Benedict's characteristic concerns. He fears that the abbot will be overcome by Eli's weakness (1 S 2–4) and advises him to punish certain people immediately. He knows that God 'glosses over sins' in order to give people time to repent (Ws 11:24) and that the Gospel directs that the guilty be warned several times before sanctions are imposed on them (Mt 18:15–17), but he does not consider such reprieves applicable to minds too crude to benefit from them. An inspired saying (Pr 29:19) establishes the uselessness of warnings in such cases. It suggests resorting to the rod, something formally prescribed by another maxim, at least as far as children are concerned (Pr 23:14). Benedict adds the 'physical punishment' mentioned by Saint Paul (1 Co 9:27) to the thrashing recommended by the Old Testament: like nearly all the Fathers, he doubtless has in mind the practice of fasting.

[30] The abbot must always remember what he is, remember what he is called, and be aware that 'more will be expected of one to whom more has been entrusted'.

[31] And let him know what a difficult and demanding burden he has undertaken: directing souls and serving a variety of temperaments, coaxing, reproving and encouraging them as appropriate to each of them; [32] and he must so accomodate and adapt himself to each one's character and intelligence that he will not only keep the flock entrusted to his care from dwindling, but will rejoice in the increase of a good flock. [33] Above all, he must not neglect or treat lightly the salvation of the souls entrusted to him, by showing more concern for the fleeting and temporal things of this world, [34] but let him constantly reflect that he has undertaken to direct souls,

for whom he must also give an account. [35] And that he may not plead lack of resources as an excuse, he is to remember what is written: 'Seek first the kingdom of God and his justice, and all these things will be given you as well', [36] and again, 'Those who fear him lack nothing'.

Only the first sentence of this long passage comes from the Master. He begins his conclusion with it, repeating the initial words of the chapter. And as in the introduction to the chapter, this reminder of the meaning of 'abbot' is accompanied by a phrase announcing the judgment (Lk 12:48); the end of the text will be permeated with the thought.

Benedict interrupts this barely initiated development by inserting two original paragraphs. One goes back once more to diversity of treatment, the other recommends, in more novel fashion, that the temporal be subordinated to the spiritual. The common expression 'directing souls' connects the two notes. Borrowed as it is from a sentence of the Master's which we will encounter at the beginning of the next passage, it shows that here Benedict is engaged in meditating on his forerunner's text, as he had done at the end of the Prologue: 'directing souls' requires both adaptation to different dispositions and freedom from earthly concerns. Moreover, each of the two notes refers more or less directly to the general theme of the Master's conclusion, that of judgment; the first does so by speaking of gains and losses in the flock entrusted to the abbot (cf. 7 and 30), the second by mentioning the 'account' he will have to give.

Like all authority according to the Gospel, the abbatial office is a service, and if it is impossible to serve two masters, serving a multitude cannot be easy. As for the priority of spiritual concerns, Benedict grounds it in both the New Testament (Mt 6:33) and the Old (Ps 33:10). Moreover, 'always keep in mind the account to be given' is a maxim from Augustine's Rule (*Praec.* VIII.3) which Benedict combines with the words borrowed from the Master mentioned earlier ('directing souls').

> [37] And let him know that anyone undertaking the charge of souls must prepare to account for them. [38] Whatever the number of brothers he has in his care, let him be certain that on judgment day he will have to submit a reckoning to the Lord for all their souls—and indeed for his own as well. [39] In this way, while always fearful of the future examination of the shepherd about the sheep entrusted to him and careful about the state of others' accounts, he becomes concerned also about his own, [40] and while helping others to amend by his warnings, he achieves the amendment of his own vices.

After making his two additions, Benedict comes back to the Master's conclusion; but he omits nearly half of it. The Letter to the Hebrews had already said of those in charge within the Church: 'They remain watchful, with the prospect of the account they will have to give for souls' (Heb 13:17). The Master had these words in mind in his first sentence. Similar echoes of them can be found in Augustine's Rule and in the Testament of Horsiesius. Like the Master and Benedict, Horsiesius warned the superiors of the pachomian Congregation that they would have to account in turn for themselves and for their subjects (*Lib.* 10–11). Our authors, however, add a valuable corollary: responsible as he is for the sheep, the shepherd benefits personally from his efforts at their improvement.

These, the chapter's last words, are most significant. 'To achieve the amendment of his own vices' is the finest hope the abbot can entertain on earth. Like anchorites (1:5), cenobites and their leader are constantly fighting 'the vices of body and mind'. In solitude or in community, monastic life is nothing more than a struggle to purify the soul in view of giving it over completely to God.

III

Summoning the brothers for counsel

AT THE END of his second chapter, the Master added to the abbot's spiritual directory an appendix dealing with the temporal management of the monastery: in such matters, the abbot must avail himself of the brothers' advice. This mere appendix to the Master's treatise on the abbot becomes a separate chapter in Benedict's Rule; the latter moreover shows his interest in the question by completely rewriting his forerunner's text, as he was to do in the legislative part of the Rule (8–66). In the spiritual field he was content to reproduce the Master with a few changes, but when it came to practical matters he went to the trouble of doing a personal job.

[1] As often as anything important is to be done in the monastery, the abbot shall call the whole community together and himself explain what the matter is. [2] After hearing the advice of the brothers, let him ponder it and follow what he judges the wiser course. [3] The reason why we have said all should be called for counsel is that the Lord often reveals what is better to the younger.

[4] The brothers, for their part, are to express their opinions with all humility, and not presume to defend their own views obstinately. [5] The decision is rather the abbot's to make: when he has determined what is more

prudent, all shall obey. 6 However, granted that it is proper for disciples to obey their master, so it is becoming for the master on his part to settle everything justly and with foresight.

According to the Master, all temporal business was to be examined in council. In Benedict's Rule the temporal nature of the matters dealt with emerges less clearly, and, in addition, a new distinction is introduced: the community is not to be summoned for all business, but only for 'important' things. Moreover, the Rule takes the greatest care to reserve all initiative as regards the proceedings to the abbot, as well as any and all power of decision. This plenary authority of the superior is nothing new, but Benedict defined it more clearly than the Master had.

All the brothers, both junior and senior, are to be summoned. The Master justified such universal consultation by putting forward reasons of common sense and fairness: hearing multiple opinions is useful, and the monastery's property belongs to all the members. Benedict's sole motivation is a purely spiritual one: 'The Lord often reveals what is better to the younger'. We are reminded of the words of Jesus, giving thanks to the Father for having 'revealed these things to the little ones' (Mt 11:25).

The recommendations addressed to the brothers on the manner of giving their opinion and to the abbot on his duty to decide well are equally new. Concern with the way things are done is characteristic of the benedictine Rule; the Master is usually content, as in this instance, with saying what is to be done. It is no surprise, moreover, that the right way of giving one's opinion is marked by humility and obedience, for these two virtues had already been the subject of additions on Benedict's part in the previous chapter.

As for the recommendation directed at the abbot, Benedict formulates it in terms borrowed from the Master's treatise on silence, which we will encounter later (6:6). But instead of teaching the brothers a lesson, as it does in that chapter, the phrase is used here to lecture the abbot. Benedict's Rule is much more concerned than his forerunner's with the superior's shortcomings. The present passage offers us a first example of this.

> [7] Accordingly, in every instance, all are to follow the rule as their teacher, and no one shall rashly deviate from it. [8] In the monastery no one is to follow his own heart's desire, [9] nor shall anyone presume to contend with his abbot defiantly, or outside the monastery. [10] Should anyone presume to do so, let him be subjected to the punishments of the rule. [11] For his part, however, the abbot must fear God and keep the rule in everything he does, knowing beyond any doubt that he will have to give an account of all his judgements to God, the most just of judges.
>
> [12] If less important business is to be transacted for the good of the monastery, he shall take counsel with the seniors only, [13] as it is written: 'Do everything with counsel and you will not be sorry afterward'.

Obedience on the brothers' part and the appropriateness of the abbot's decisions: both come down to following the Rule. In referring to the latter, Benedict reiterates his symmetrical exhortations addressed in turn to the monks and to the superior. The monks are not to follow their self-will, which the beginning of the Prologue had already called on them to give up. The monk is not dispensed from obeying either the Rule or the abbot, whether in the monastery or outside (the words 'or outside the monastery' have doubtless been displaced). In this connection, Benedict resorts for the first time to the legal vocabulary familiar to him: 'presume' (*praesumere*) and 'be subjected to the punishments of the rule' (*regulari disciplinae subiacere*) will appear again and again in the legislative part of his work. In contrast, the exhortation addressed to the abbot echoes the terms used by the Master in the conclusion to the previous chapter (2:37–38): the evocation of divine judgment and accountability can readily be recognized.

The limited council of seniors, regulated by the last sentence, is an innovation with regard to the Master's text, which provided only for general meetings. Knowingly or not, Benedict here follows Basil, or at least the longer version of his Rules (*LR* 48 and *SR* 104), written later than the shorter text translated into Latin by Rufinus. In the same connection, Basil had already called on the first half of the composite quotation found here (Pr 31:3 according to the Old Latin version), whereas the second half (Si 32:24) is unique to Benedict.

This chapter is of considerable interest. We knew that cenobites lived in community, under a rule and an abbot. We now witness the interaction of the three terms. The abbot consults the community, the community obeys the abbot, and both submit to the rule. The abbot is not only the shepherd of souls described in the previous chapter, but also the leader of a group of men who live here below. As to the first duty his norm is Scripture; as to the second, he is guided by the rule. In him spiritual and temporal authority are combined. Two powers are not found in the monastery, as in the Church and the world, but one alone. Simple and total, monasticism requires this merging of the two orders, and because of this the word of God can give form to the entire existence of both individuals and group. Although this is not very democratic, it does not operate without consultation. Under the one authority by which it is ruled, its supreme law is to avoid all dissension.

IV

The tools of good works

FOLLOWING THE ABBOT'S directory, the Master drew up for him a list of seventy-seven precepts which made up 'the holy craft he is to teach his disciples'. What we find here is this catalogue of maxims, slightly modified by Benedict. The name of 'tools for good works' which he gives them is itself inspired by the Master, who called the virtues by means of which the holy craft is practiced 'spiritual tools'.

This series of seventy-four maxims serves as a transition between the treatise on the abbot, with its appendix on the council, and the chapters in which the monk's three great virtues will be described. On several occasions, we will come across sketches of these later expositions on obedience, silence, and humility. Specifically monastic touches are, however, quite rare; the chapter on the whole remains at the level of general christian morality. In this regard, the passage recalls the Prologue and its basic catechesis rooted in the psalms. Once again the Master and Benedict remind us that the monk, like every Christian, is subject first of all to the universal demands of the word of God.

[1] First of all, 'love the Lord God with your whole heart, your whole soul and all your strength', [2] then 'love your neighbor as yourself'.

3 Then the following: 'You are not to kill, 4 not to commit adultery, 5 you are not to steal 6 nor to covet; 7 you are not to bear false witness'. 8 Honor everyone, 9 and 'never do to another what you do not want done to yourself'.

10 Renounce yourself in order to follow Christ. 11 Discipline your body; 12 do not seek delicacies, 13 but love fasting. 14 Feed the poor, 15 clothe the naked, 16 visit the sick 17 and bury the dead, 18 go to help the troubled 19 and console the sorrowing.

The two great commandments of love (Mk 12:30–31; Lk 10:27–28), the six articles of the Ten Commandments reiterated by the New Testament (Mt 19:18–19; Lk 18:20; Rm 13:9), the golden rule from the Sermon on the Mount (Mt 7:12; cf. Tb 4:16): this opening, also found in the Latin version of the *Didachè*, is assuredly the appropriate beginning for a form of life designed for disciples of Christ. The double command to love God and neighbor is here placed at the beginning, whereas the ladder of humility, as we will see, leads up to charity as to a summit. These two apparently conflicting perspectives are grounded in different scriptural texts. The Master and Benedict are now following the Old Testament and the Gospel, whereas later they will have in mind the glorification of love by Saint John and Saint Paul.

One of the Ten Commandments has been modified by Benedict. Instead of 'honor your father and your mother', as prescribed by the Rule of the Master, the benedictine text reads: 'honor everyone'. This precept, which can also claim roots in Scripture (1 P 2:17), is no doubt in Benedict's mind a maxim dealing with hospitality (cf. 53:2). The correction can be explained by the fear of encouraging relations with one's family which might be detrimental to monastic life. Did Christ not separate his disciples from their parents, sometimes very abruptly? It is because of him, as we will see, that we must honor everyone, particularly guests.

'Renounce yourself in order to follow Christ' (Mt 16:24), which undoubtedly brings us into the New Testament, comes before 'discipline your body'. That this pauline maxim (1 Co 9:27) is aimed especially at limitations in the area of food, according to the interpretation customary among the Fathers, is indicated by what comes next: 'do not seek delicacies', and especially 'love fasting'. These restrictions on eating lead in turn to the next series, where we are asked to feed the poor and to provide for the other needs of those in want. The underlying idea, clearly brought out by one of the Master's sources, is that we give others what we deprive ourselves of. As in the Gospel, fasting and almsgiving go hand in hand.

The first three works of charity are obviously suggested by the scene of the last judgment, in which Christ identifies himself with those who suffer hunger, lack of clothing or illness (Mt 25:3–5). The next recalls the charity of Tobias (Tb 1:20). At the end, Benedict does away with 'consent to lend' and 'give to the destitute', two maxims from the Master which are hardly applicable to the individual monk. Here as earlier, and as was already the case in the Prologue, the benedictine Rule modifies an agenda originally aimed at all Christians in order to bring it closer to the conditions peculiar to monastic life.

Taken as a whole, this second series of ten maxims (10–19) is constructed on the model of the word of the Lord which introduces it. Just as we must renounce ourselves in order to follow Christ, we subtract from our food, as Saint Paul did, to help the unfortunate, as the Gospel demands. A word from the New Testament commanding a pair of negative and positive acts which are themselves suggested by other scriptural texts: this structure may be found again in the series which we will now read.

[20] Make yourself a stranger to the world's ways, [21] prefer nothing to the love of Christ. [22] You are not to act in

anger, 23 or set aside a time for wrath. 24 Do not entertain deceit in your heart, 25 do not give a false greeting of peace 26 or forsake charity. 27 Bind yourself to no oath lest it prove false, 28 speak the truth with heart and tongue.

29 Do not repay one bad turn with another, 30 do not injure anyone, but moreover bear injuries patiently, 31 love your enemies; 32 when you are cursed, do not answer by cursing but rather by blessing; 32 endure persecution for the sake of justice.

33 Do not be proud, 34 nor given to wine, 35 refrain from too much eating 36 or sleeping, 37 and from laziness; 38 do not grumble 39 or speak ill of others.

41 Place your hope in God. 42 If you notice some good in yourself, give credit to God, not to yourself; 43 as for the evil, be certain that it is always your own and acknowledge it.

This time, the renunciation/commitment couplet which heads the series consists of the first two maxims. 'Make yourself a stranger to the world's ways' echoes Saint Paul's words (2 Tm 2:4), while the invitation to love Christ above all is a rendering of Jesus' warning: 'Whoever loves his father or his mother . . . his son or his daughter more than me is not worthy of me' (Mt 10:37). 'Prefer nothing to the love of Christ' is, moreover, a famous maxim, popularized in particular by Saint Cyprian. In the specific form found here, the Master has no doubt borrowed it, along with its neighbors and a good number of others later on, from one of his favorite sources, the Passion of Saints Julian and Basilissa.

As was the case earlier (10–19), this double principle of renunciation and love is followed by a series of negative and positive attitudes, but this time the latter are few in number. Moreover, renunciation and charity take on new faces. Mortification is no longer aimed at sensuality but at aggressive urges, whether visible or veiled; love no longer consists in helping the needy but in bearing patiently with one's opponents.

The scriptural reference also changes. Instead of the last judgment scene, the backdrop here is the Sermon on the Mount: anger, swearing and retaliation are forbidden (Mt 5:22, 34, 39) and we are invited to love our enemies (Mt 5:44; Lk 6:28) and to bless those who curse us (Lk 6:29), all in the same order as in the words of Jesus. Moreover, 'persecution for the sake of justice' recalls the last of the Beatitudes (Mt 5:10). These echoes of the gospel discourse are complemented in the letters of Peter (1 P 3:9, 14) and Paul (1 Co 4:12). As for the maxims on deceit and truth, they call to mind among others two passages from the Psalms quoted in the Prologue (Prol 17 and 26). Items not drawn directly from the Bible are rare; one invites us to bear injuries rather than cause them, following a famous saying of Cyprian's.

Before the item on charity, Benedict, as was his wont, omits three maxims of the Master's suited less to monks than to seculars. Two of them prescribed honoring one's commitments; but the monk has none but the promises which bind him to God. As for 'Do not delight in speaking ill of others', Benedict was doubtless appalled, in spite of the scriptural reference (Pr 20:13), at seeing scandalmongering tolerated up to a point. He transfers the item to the end of the next series (34–40) and turns it into an absolute prohibition.

This series of seven negative precepts begins, as usual, with a biblical reminiscence: 'Do not be proud, nor given to wine' comes from the portrait of the *episkopos* in Saint Paul (Tt 1:7). Several of the failings then proscribed are also formulated in scriptural terms (Si 37:32; Rm 12:11; Ws 1:11).

In conclusion, three maxims broach the important question of grace. In the midst of the moral obligations just listed, our eyes must remain set on God. Our hope is in him, and we credit him with the good we see in ourselves, while we hold ourselves responsible for the evil. This acknowledgment of divine aid, which recalls the end of the commentary on Psalm 14 in the Prologue, is made much more assertive by Benedict than it was in the Master. In accordance with the augustinian leanings then prevalent in Gaul as in Rome, our Rule insists on man's guilt and on his inability to act rightly on his own strength. At the end, two of the Master's maxims are omitted. The first suggested that good desires can arise without God's intervention. The second allotted production of the means of subsistence to both Providence and human industry.

[44] Live in fear of judgment day, [45] have a great horror of hell, [46] yearn for everlasting life with all your spiritual desire, [47] keep death before your eyes every day as an imminent event. [48] Hour by hour keep careful watch over all you do, [49] be certain wherever you may be that God's gaze is upon you. [50] As soon as wrongful thoughts come into your heart, dash them against Christ and disclose them to a senior who is a spiritual person. [51] Guard your lips from harmful and wicked speech, [52] do not love to speak a great deal [53] and speak no foolish chatter, nothing that provokes laughter, [54] do not love prolonged or boisterous laughter.

[55] Listen readily to holy reading, [56] prostrate yourself frequently in prayer, [57] confess your past sins to God in prayer every day, with tears and sighs, [58] and change from these evil ways in the future. [59] Do not gratify the desires of the flesh, [60] hate the urgings of self-will, [61] obey the orders of the abbot in everything, even if his own conduct—which God forbid—be at odds with what he says, remembering the commandment of the Lord: 'Do what they say; as for what they do, do not do it'.

The structure of this passage is quite clear. In considering the last things, we are prompted to exercise constant control over our behavior: actions, thoughts, speech, and laughter. Sinful human speech thus eliminated is replaced by the word of God, which leads to prayer, repentance, and conversion. Likewise, obedience is substituted for the desires of the flesh and for self-will.

The last two items recall the agenda consisting in renunciation of self-will and obedience to Christ defined at the beginning of the Prologue. But the section as a whole should be compared especially with a later passage: the first step of the ladder of humility, which will likewise inculcate control over all our actions and all our being under God's gaze in view of the last things. That great passage in Chapter 7, which similarly cautions us against the desires of the flesh and against self-will, will lead us, as here, to put aside all personal will in order to give ourselves over unreservedly to obedience (second and third steps of humility).

The beginning of the section outlines a retrograde progression: from the judgment and its sequel, unhappy or happy, we go back to death, and from there to the present life. The thought of the hereafter was dear to the monks of old, as it should be to every disciple of Christ. Saint Anthony and Cassian, to name but two of them, had already prescribed the daily expectation of death as a sovereign remedy against all forms of passion.

As for the yearning for everlasting life, Benedict significantly modifies its formulation. According to the Master, we are to yearn for 'everlasting life and the holy Jerusalem'. The benedictine text replaces these last words by 'with all one's spiritual desire'. We know, thanks to Saint Paul, that the Spirit has its own desire, similar to that of the flesh and opposite to it (Gal 5:17). Benedict, who paid more attention than the Master to the inner aspect of behavior, shows an interest in this movement of the Spirit in us. He will mention it once more in the chapter on Lent, asking the monks to 'look forward to holy Easter'—that passage from death to life—'with the joy of spiritual longing' (49:7).

Another maxim gives rise to a noteworthy addition. After advising us to dash wrongful thoughts against the rock of Christ—this advice comes from the Master and is reminiscent of the Prologue (Prol 28; cf. Ps 136:9)—Benedict adds: 'and disclose them to a senior who is a spiritual person'. We will come upon this confession of sins to the seniors again further on (46:5), and will see then what the qualifying adjective 'spiritual' means. Here let us be content with noting this fresh allusion to the Holy Spirit.

Like the previous ones, this paragraph on the last things and on the present life refers implicitly to Scripture in more than one of its items. General concepts such as judgment, hell, and everlasting life aside, specific texts form the basis for the maxims on God's universal gaze (Pr 15:3; Ps 13:2), moderation in speech (Pr 10:18) and foolish chatter (Mt 12:36).

The same is true, in the two following paragraphs, of frequent prayer (1 Th 5:17, etc.), confession of sins in prayer (Mt 6:12), and resisting the promptings of the flesh (Gal 5:16), which go hand in hand with self-will (Si 18:30; cf. Gal 5:17). The formal quotation from the Gospel which concludes the entire passage (Mt 23:3) along with the preceding words ('even if . . .'), a personal addition of Benedict's, revealing his keen concern with remedying the abbot's failings—a concern we have already noted.

In this section in which everything is important, let us simply, by way of conclusion, note the sequence: reading-prayer-compunction-correction. In Benedict's time reading, even personal reading, was done out loud oftener than is the case today. It was necessary to listen 'readily', attentively, in order to benefit from it. The divine word which replaces empty human speech calls for prayer in response. Ancient monasticism's whole method of prayer is contained in those two items, whose order is irreversible: as always in the economy of salvation, the initiative belongs to God. Before speaking to him, we must listen to him.

Besides being 'frequent', prayer must normally be brief in order to remain intense, as Benedict, following Cassian, will later teach us. In the Rule of the Master, the monks 'prostrate themselves' in prayer, but we cannot be certain that Benedict gives *incumbere* that down-to-earth connotation. The verb may simply mean that one 'devotes oneself' to prayer. In any case, prayer is ordinarily accompanied by confession, tears, and sighs. Numberless accounts show that this was the usual content of prayer in ancient times. Springing as it did from an acute consciousness of sin, it consisted first and foremost in pleading for forgiveness. This is a prayer born of humility, which recalls that of the publican. Touched to the point of tears, the heart turns wholly to God. Through prayer and compunction, the divine voice heard in reading attains its goal, which is conversion.

62 Do not aspire to be called holy before you really are, but first be holy that you may more truly be called so. 63 Carry out God's commandments every day by your actions; 64 love chastity.

65 Harbor neither hatred towards anyone, 66 nor jealousy, 67 and do not act out of envy. 68 Do not love quarreling. 69 Shun arrogance. 70 Respect the elders 71 and love the young. 72 Pray for your enemies out of love for Christ. 73 Make peace with your opponent before the sun goes down.

74 And never lose hope in God's mercy.

75 These, then, are the tools of the spiritual craft. 76 If we use them without ceasing day and night and return them on judgment day, our wages will be the reward the Lord has promised: 77 'What the eye has not seen nor the ear heard, God has prepared for those who love him'.

78 The workshop where we are to toil faithfully at all these tasks is the enclosure of the monastery and stability in the community.

Over half of these final thirteen maxims deal with fraternal relations and are related to the section on patience, inspired by the Sermon on the Mount, which we read earlier. Following two items which recommend conformity of being with appearance and of actions with the divine precepts, 'love chastity' (Jdt 15:11) brings to mind 'love fasting'. These two forms of asceticism are related; they are not to be endured as deprivations, but loved as liberations.

'Harbor no hatred towards anyone', which is based on the Old Testament (Lv 19:17; Dt 23:8) and prescribed by the *Didachè*, appears to be simply an imperfect hint at the great commandment of love of neighbor. In actual fact, however, we are dealing with a very reliable overall test of true charity, particular aspects of which are detailed in the next three items.

'Shun arrogance' heralds the cardinal chapter on humility, whereas the next two maxims on the mutual feelings of the young and the elders are a preview of the rules on rank and fraternal relations (63:1–9). These three items are unique to Benedict, who also adds prayer for one's enemies (Mt 5:44). Nothing is closer to his heart, as we will see, than good relations between brothers, for which the Master showed remarkably little concern. This is why, taking advantage of two maxims on concord (68 and 73), he inserts this brief personal exposition between them; he begins by banning the cause of all quarreling—that is, pride—and ends by directing us to pray for our opponents even before we have made peace with them, as we must do 'before the sun goes down' (cf. Eph 4:26). We are reminded of the solemn recitation of the *Our Father* at Matins and Vespers for the mutual forgiveness of offences (13:12–13).

The last item is one of the finest. In it, Benedict replaces 'God' by 'God's mercy'. Beyond the maxims on hope in God and on the gift of grace which we came across halfway through the chapter, this conclusion brings us back to the great commandment with which our catalogue began. The

first tool was to love God; the last consists in never doubt-
ing his love.

The Master's next to last maxim—'Obey all the good
wholeheartedly'—is omitted. Before ending his Rule, Benedict will add a chapter on this matter of mutual obedience.
On the whole, his catalogue of 'tools' is barely shorter than
the Master's. By contrast, the Master's conclusion is greatly
abridged. Having replaced a long depiction of heaven by a
mere sentence from Saint Paul (1 Cor 2:9) and then omitted
two lists of virtues and vices, Benedict simply retains a
considerably simplified description of the monastery as
a 'workshop' where the spiritual craft is practised. His
last words recall the conclusion of the Prologue, but the
Master's 'perseverance' is replaced here by a new term,
'stability', whose importance will emerge at the end of
the Rule.

V

Obedience

FOLLOWING THE PIECEMEAL agenda we have just sur-
veyed, here we find ample expositions on the three virtues
peculiar to the cenobite: obedience, stillness, and humility.
The trio originated with Cassian, whose description of humility begins with expressions of obedience and ends with
practices related to silence (*Inst.* 4.39.2). His portrait of the
humble monk forms the basis for our Rule's great chapter
on humility, represented by a ladder on which obedience
occurs towards the beginning and stillness towards the
end. The three virtues are thus intimately related: one of
them includes the other two.

The Master's chapter on obedience is five and a half times
longer than Benedict's. He begins with the outward forms
of obedience, which can be fairly speedy; he then develops at length the contrast between the 'wide road' of the
sarabaites, who do not obey, and the 'narrow road' of cenobitic obedience, which goes so far as to imitate martyrdom.
Finally he turns to the interior aspect: the monk must obey
joyfully. Each of these three parts provides Benedict with
some of his material. His text, like that of his forerunner,
begins with the outward spectacle of the obedient monk
(1–9); then the narrow way is conjured up (10–13), and
finally the inner face of obedience (14–19).

[1] The first step of humility is obedience without delay. [2] It becomes those who hold nothing dearer than Christ. [3] Because of the holy service they have professed, or because of the dread of hell and the glory of everlasting life, [4] as soon as a superior commands them something, as if the command came from God himself, they cannot suffer the slightest delay in accomplishing it. [5] The Lord is speaking of them when he says: 'No sooner did his ear hear than he obeyed me'. [6] Again, he tells teachers: 'Whoever listens to you, listens to me'. [7] Such people as these, then, immediately putting aside their own concerns and abandoning their own will, [8] laying down whatever they have in hand and leaving it unfinished, follow the voice of authority in their actions with the ready step of obedience. [9] As though at the same moment, then, the instruction given by the master and the work performed by the disciple—both actions together are swiftly completed as one, with the speed which the fear of God inspires.

[10] Those who are impelled by the desire of advancing toward everlasting life [11] take the narrow road of which the Lord says: 'Narrow is the road that leads to life': [12] no longer living by their own judgment nor giving in to their whims and appetites, but rather walking according to another's decisions and directions, living in monasteries, they choose to have an abbot over them. [13] Such people unquestionably conform to the saying of the Lord, in which he says: 'I have come not to do my own will, but the will of him who sent me'.

The opening sentence will be contradicted in the chapter on humility, where the first of the twelve steps on the ladder is not obedience but fear of God. Here the Master, followed by Benedict, no doubt had in mind Cassian's description, in which the first of the ten signs of humility consisted in obeying.

'To hold nothing dearer than Christ', which echoes one of the maxims found in the previous chapter, is, according to the Master, a trait peculiar to the small number of 'perfect' brothers who obey with no delay whatever. As for the greater number, the Master allowed less speedy obedience and asked the abbot to be kind enough to reiterate his commands. Benedict does away with this distinction and puts before all the ideal of immediate obedience.

The three motives indicated next combine consideration of the last things with that of the 'service' professed by the monk. This recalls the definition of the monastery as a school at the end of the Prologue. As for the scriptural quotations, the first (Ps 17:45) says in veiled terms what the second (Lk 10:16) openly states: we obey Christ in person. This same connection, obedience with Christ, appears in the next, long sentence in which obedient monks are depicted using traits borrowed from the Gospel: at Jesus' call, the first disciples 'immediately lay down' their nets to 'follow' him (Mt 4:18–22). This evangelical model is coupled with that of the egyptian cenobites whose lightning obedience at any and every signal (*Inst.* 4.12) had been extolled by Cassian, as had their faith, which perceived God's voice in the superior's (*Inst.* 4.10 and 24).

Between this first paragraph and the next, Benedict omitted several pages from the Master. He kept only a few lines of the latter's long dissertation on the 'two roads', and these are carefully chosen on account of their importance. Two scriptural texts illustrate them: one likens obedience to the narrow way of the Gospel (Mt 7:14), the other holds up the obedience of Jesus himself as an example for the monk (Jn 6:38).

Thus Christ says in turn 'Whoever listens to you listens to me', and 'I have come not to do my own will, but the will of him who sent me'. According to the first of these statements, he is the one who commands; according to the second, the one who obeys. Monastic obedience derives its incomparable value from this twofold root. It is both obedience *to Christ* and obedience *in the image of Christ*.

By obeying him we imitate him. We make his will our own and we participate in his submission to the Father. Obedience is at the heart of Redemption.

> [14] This very obedience, however, will be acceptable to God and agreeable to men only if compliance with what is commanded is not cringing or sluggish or half-hearted, but free from any grumbling or any reaction of unwillingness, [15] for the obedience shown to superiors is given to God, since he himself said: 'Whoever listens to you, listens to me'. [16] And the disciples' obedience must be given gladly, for 'God loves a cheerful giver'. [17] For if a disciple obeys grudgingly and grumbles, not only aloud but also in his heart, [18] then, even though he carries out the order, his action will not be accepted with favor by God, who sees that he is grumbling in his heart. [19] He will have no reward for service of this kind; on the contrary, he will incur punishment for grumbling, unless he changes for the better and makes amends.

This last passage answers the first: we go from the outside to the inside; obedience must be not only immediate, but also joyful. Thus it will be 'acceptable to God and agreeable to men'. This last phrase is aimed primarily at superiors, whom the rest of the sentence once more parallels with God, but it can also mean those who obey.

In order to demand such an inner quality of obedience, the text points out that it is given to God, who sees into human hearts (cf. Ps 7:10). As in the first paragraph, this relation to God is grounded on the words of Christ (Lk 10:16). Moreover, according to Saint Paul, 'God loves a cheerful giver' (2 Co 9:7), and Ecclesiasticus had already recommended that we give 'gladly', with a 'joyful' countenance (Si 35:10–11).

As for grumbling, the 'punishment' with which Benedict threatens it is no doubt that which struck Israel in the desert (1 Co 10:10), but the end of the sentence ('change for the better and make amends') also calls to mind the Rule's penal code and the penalties it inflicts. Benedict hated grumbling above all else, as we will see. Moreover, while eliminating some of the Master's repetitions from this passage, he did not abbreviate it as he did the two preceding ones. This preferential treatment shows once more the importance he attached to the inner quality of behavior.

VI

Stillness

[1] Let us do as the Prophet says: 'I said, I shall keep watch over my ways that I may never sin with my tongue. I have put a guard on my mouth. I was silent and was humbled, and I refrained even from good words'. [2] Here the Prophet indicates that, since there are times when good words are to be left unsaid out of esteem for silence, evil speech must be curbed all the more because of the punishment due for sin. [3] Thus, no matter how good or holy or edifying the talk involved, the permission to speak should seldom be granted mature disciples, so that they may observe a stillness marked by seriousness, [4] because it is written: 'In speaking a great deal you will not avoid sin'; [5] and elsewhere, 'The tongue holds sway over life and death'. [6] Speaking and teaching are the master's task; silence and listening become the disciple.

[7] Therefore, any requests to a superior should be made with all humility and respectful submission. [8] As for idle jesting and empty chatter and talk leading to laughter, we sentence them to perpetual imprisonment in all places, and we do not permit a disciple to open his mouth in order to engage in words of that kind.

BENEDICT DEALS with this virtue more summarily than with the one before it. Of his forerunner's two long chapters on silence, he reproduces only the last paragraph of the first (1–6) and the last sentence of the second (8); everything between is summed up in a few words (7). All in all, the benedictine text amounts to less than one-tenth of the Master's.

To start with, Benedict does away with a general exposition on anthropology and asceticism, in which mastery of one's gaze and thoughts preceded that of speech. Retaining only the latter, he begins abruptly with a psalm quotation (Ps 38:2–3), to be followed by two Proverbs (Pr 10:19; 18:21). The conclusion of the Master's first chapter ends this first paragraph of Benedict (1–6).

Our authors thus draw a distinction between good words, from which the Psalmist declared he abstained, and evil ones. Although the order of the text leaves something to be desired in Benedict's Rule as in the Master's, both seem to think that the motivations for silence are of two kinds. First and foremost, we must avoid sin, and to achieve this we must speak sparingly. Then we must behave as disciples, and to achieve this we must keep silent and listen. The first motivation is general, while the second is peculiar to disciples, indeed to 'perfect' disciples. In that last word we recognize the distinction already made by the Master in the previous chapter: when it comes to silence, as when obedience is involved, perfect or imperfect monks are subject to fairly strict rules.

In principle, then, speech is reserved to the one teaching. As we may recall, the monastery is a school in which the students listen to the teacher. Stillness is understood and motivated in the same way as obedience. Both virtues are necessary because of the structure of monastic society, where the invisible Lord lets himself be represented by the superior. Through the superior, we listen to God.

'Humility and respectful submission.' These words, in which Benedict sums up nearly all of the Master's second chapter, take on a new meaning in his text. In the other Rule, humility consisted in bending one's head before the abbot while addressing him, and in showing respect by remaining silent in his presence. Modulating these exercises was a complicated casuistry according to whether the disciple was perfect or imperfect, was speaking of spiritual or secular matters, or happened to be in the abbot's presence or far away from him. Benedict seems to have had something else in mind. He shifts from the plane of gestures and observances, to which the Master confined himself, to that of interpersonal relationships. Here, as in the chapter on counsel (3:4), his concern is the complete submission, humble and deep, with which the monk must speak to his superior. This is a matter not of observing a ritual, but of preserving peace of souls and order in the community.

Avoiding sin and practising humility: these two motives doubtless do not exhaust the meaning of silence. It holds other riches, particularly the possibility of conversing with God. Some of these uniquely religious elements will appear later in the Rule. Let us content ourselves here with stressing the fact that for Benedict as for the Master 'stillness' consists not only in the spirit of silence but in its actual practice. *Taciturnitas* amounts to *silentium* (42:9).

The final sentence, borrowed almost verbatim from the Master, absolutely condemns idle speech (Mt 12:36) and anything inducing laughter (Lk 6:25), whether words or gestures. This double prohibition, which we have already come across in the preceding chapter, may appear stringent. In the eyes of the monks of old, it simply followed from the Gospel. This is one of the points on which our way of thinking as modern Christians and monks finds it most difficult to concur with that of our Fathers—most difficult, but also most profitable.

VII

Humility

THIS CHAPTER, which is longer and more important than any other, does not simply describe one of the monk's great virtues. Because that virtue, as we have seen, encompasses the other two, the chapter contains the whole of the Rule's spiritual teaching. Moreover, this description of humility is drawn from a passage in Cassian (*Inst.* 4.39) which outlined the monk's journey toward perfection, from initial fear of God to the love which drives away fear. Integrated as they are into the present chapter, this starting point and conclusion really give the treatment found in the Master and Benedict the scope of a synthesis. The image of a twelve-step ladder, which serves as its framework, is presented by our authors in a preamble:

[1] Brothers, divine Scripture calls to us saying: 'Whoever exalts himself shall be humbled, and whoever humbles himself shall be exalted'. [2] In saying this, it shows us that every exaltation is a kind of pride. [3] The Prophet indicates that he shuns this by saying: 'Lord, my heart is not exalted, and my eyes are not lifted up. I have not walked in the ways of the great nor gone after marvels beyond me.' [4] But what would happen 'if I had not a humble spirit, if I had exalted my soul? You would treat me as a child weaned from its mother.'

⁵ Accordingly, brothers, if we want to reach the summit of supreme humility, and if we want to attain speedily that exaltation in heaven to which we climb by the humility of this present life, ⁶ then by our ascending actions we must set up that ladder on which Jacob in a dream saw angels descending and ascending. ⁷ Without doubt, this descent and ascent can signify only, according to us, that exaltation makes us descend and humility makes us ascend. 8 As for the ladder erected, it is our life here below. When our hearts have been humbled, the Lord will raise it to heaven. ⁹ We may say that our body and soul are the sides of this ladder. Into these sides, the divine call has fitted the various steps of humility and good conduct that we may ascend them.

The words of Christ which open the chapter can be read three times in the New Testament. Their purpose there is to instil now modesty which makes us agreeable to men (Lk 14:11), now the spirit of service which must impel God's representatives (Mt 23:12), now the attitude appropriate to the sinners we all are before the Lord (Lk 18:14). Quoted here in the form given by Saint Luke, this keyword of the Gospel has two parts, both of which will be briefly commented on by means of texts from the Old Testament. The first, on the humbling of the proud, is paraphrased by the Psalmist: the soul that gives itself over to pride shall be weaned from God (Ps 130:1–2). The second, on the exaltation of the humble, is explained by Jacob's dream: a ladder rises up to heaven (Gn 28:12). In both these Old Testament passages, humility appears under a twofold aspect, interior and exterior. The Psalmist speaks of both 'heart' and 'eyes'; Jacob's ladder has two sides, symbols of body and soul. Benedict and especially the Master note the predominantly interior or bodily aspect of certain steps.

The gospel maxim will therefore be illustrated by the image from Genesis. Giving these scriptural texts their broadest and strongest meaning, our authors draw from them a vision of all of christian life, both here below and in the hereafter. We abase ourselves in this world in order to be exalted in the next. The ladder is a figure of our entire present life, viewed as an ascent towards heaven. This is why the Master very logically concludes his chapter with a description of heaven, while Benedict, wishing to abridge the text, stops at the spiritual summit attained on earth, which is charity.

To ascend to heaven is a uniquely christian ambition. The author of Genesis did not contemplate it: the beings Jacob saw going up and down the ladder were angels, not human beings. In order to give humankind the unheard-of hope of going to God, nothing less was needed than the ascension of the Son of God made man. It is in his wake and by his grace, obtained through his abasement, that we dare to start up the ladder and to aspire to see the transcendent God.

Like the gospel quotation, the image of the ladder is unique to the Master and Benedict. It is not found in the underlying passage from the *Institutes*. Cassian did, to be sure, outline a journey which went from fear to charity by way of outward renunciation and humility, but its ten 'signs' did not constitute a progression. Though carefully ordered—three traits relating to obedience and two to patience, then three concerning self-effacement and two connected with stillness—they were not set out as a methodical and complete agenda, but merely as a list of examples liable to be expanded and ordered differently.

By transposing this description of the humble monk within the framework of his graduated ladder, the Master, followed by Benedict, gave it a progressive and systematic appearance which should probably not be taken too seriously. Like Cassian's signs, to which they correspond, the steps of our Rules are not so much rungs to be climbed one after the other as signs of virtue which can and should appear simultaneously.

In contrast to this central block, made up of steps 2–11, the first step has a clearly initial and basic character. This is because the Master has borrowed it not from the list of the ten signs of humility, but from the preliminary stage constituted, in Cassian's view, by 'fear of the Lord'. Originally external to humility, this religious fear was inserted into it by our Rules, giving the great monastic virtue a primordial orientation towards God. Cassian's signs concerned only humility toward one's neighbor. By adding a first step relative to the Lord and a twelfth which has the same direct connection with the divine Master, our Rules envelop humility towards human beings within a gaze turned towards God.

> [10] The first step of humility, then, is that placing the fear of God always before our eyes, we always shun forgetfulness, [11] and constantly remember everything God has commanded, constantly going over in our mind how hell burns all those who despise God on account of their sins, as well as everlasting life prepared for those who fear God. [12] And guarding himself at every moment from sins and vices of thought or tongue, of hand or foot, of self-will or fleshly desire, [13] man must be persuaded that God is looking at him from heaven at every moment, that the deity's glance sees his actions everywhere and that angels report on them at every hour.

Just as Chapter 7 is disproportionate in size, so the first step likewise differs entirely in length from those following it. Together with the twelfth, it amounts to a picture of humility with regard to God which is barely less ample and less detailed than that of humility with regard to human beings contained in the ten intermediate steps.

The details of this great fresco are nearly all drawn from a passage of the 'tools for good works' (4:44–60): awaiting the last things, watching over our own conduct, believing that we are always in God's sight, controlling our thoughts and words, renouncing fleshly desires and self-will—all of these have already been found there as separate items. But the phrase 'fear of God' under which these elements are grouped here echoes Cassian. More specifically, Cassian spoke of the 'fear of the Lord' (*Inst.* 4.39.1) which, according to Scripture, is the beginning of wisdom (Ps 110:10; Pr 9:10). Our authors substitute 'God' for 'the Lord' because they have in mind another expression from the psalms: 'keeping the fear of God before one's eyes' (Ps 35:2).

According to Cassian, this initial fear, in permeating the soul, gives rise to the outer renunciation of all ownership, and the latter leads to the inner renunciation which is humility. These two steps, the first of which corresponds to entering the monastery and the second to monastic life itself, imitate Christ's successive abasements: the deprivation of the Incarnation and the humiliation of the Cross (Ph 2:6–8). Omitting the stage of renouncing the world, which they describe at the end of their Rules, the Master and Benedict bring together fear of God and humility, so that the former becomes the latter's basic element. Instead of leading from the world to the monastery, it emerges as the dominant and constantly fostered feeling which permeates the monk's entire life.

In the conclusion to the chapter, as we shall see, fear will be eliminated by love, which is the summit reached after climbing the twelve steps. When we follow John the Apostle in thus opposing fear and charity, we have in mind its least noble form, the fear of punishment, which impels a slave to obey, as it were, in spite of himself. Here the fear of God (and not of punishment) far transcends this baser feeling. As in the entire Old Testament and in almost all of the New, we are dealing with the religious attitude *par excellence*, consisting in unspeakable respect for the Lord whose word is listened to with veneration and whose law is lovingly observed. The high quality of this feeling is shown by the end to which it leads:

we are told that everlasting life is prepared for those who
fear God.

Here below, the person who fears God 'guards himself
at every moment from sins and vices'. We may remember
that the struggle against the vices of body and mind is the
monk's great task (1:5), and that the prospect of amending his vices is the great hope offered the abbot (2:40).
Guarding oneself against all manner of sin is evoked by
a list of the six parts of the human compound in which it
must be practised: thoughts, tongue, hands, feet, self-will,
and fleshly desires. The Master then goes over these six
areas in the light of Scripture. Benedict, aiming as always
at brevity, will include only the first and the last two in his
scriptural reflections.

Along with the struggle against these various sins and in
order that that struggle may be effective, our authors instil
the conviction that God, who is everywhere present, sees
us always. These two joint themes are characteristic of the
Rule of Saint Basil, from which the Master seems to draw
his inspiration throughout the first step and in the twelfth.
Basil however, is more reserved than our authors on the
role of fear in the search for God—seemingly at least, for,
as we have seen, the term 'fear' is an ambiguous one.

[14] This is what the Prophet indicates to us when he
shows that God is always present to our thoughts, saying: 'God searches hearts and minds'; [15] again: 'The Lord
knows the thoughts of men'. [16] And he says besides:
'From afar you understood my thoughts'. [17] And: 'For
the thought of man shall open up to you'. [18] Moreover,
that he may take care to avoid perverted thoughts, the
virtuous brother must always say in his heart: 'I shall
be blameless before him only if I guard myself from my
own iniquity'.

[19] As for our own will, we are forbidden to do it when
Scripture tells us: 'And turn away from your wishes'.
[20] And in the Prayer we also ask God that his will be done

in us. [21] We are thus rightly taught not to do our own will, when we beware of what Scripture says: 'There are ways which seem right to men and whose end plunges into the depths of hell', [22] and also when we dread what is said of the negligent: 'They are corrupt and have become depraved in their wishes'.

[23] In the desires of the flesh, we must believe that God is always present to us, since the Prophet says to the Lord: 'All my desires are before you'. [24] We must then be on guard against any evil desire, because 'death is stationed on the doorstep of pleasure'. [25] For this reason Scripture has given us this precept: 'Pursue not your lusts'.

Cut down to half its original size by Benedict, this scriptural anthology has a double purpose: to show both that God is present to all human action; and that man must guard himself from all sin. The second thesis obviously flows from the first, but the Master nonetheless strove to find distinct proof of it. He did not fully succeed in carrying out this twofold agenda. Granted that his first and last paragraph, devoted to thoughts and fleshly desires, offer biblical texts witnessing both to the presence of God and to the necessity of eliminating sin, his intermediate sections illustrate only one of the themes: that of the divine presence appears alone in the paragraphs on the tongue, hands, and feet (omitted by Benedict), and only the notion of mounting guard against sin is mentioned in connection with self-will.

The case concerning thoughts consists entirely of psalm quotations, arranged first in ascending and then in descending order (ascending: Ps 7:10; 93:11; 138:8; descending: Ps 75:11; 17:24). The passage regarding self-will begins with a saying from Ecclesiasticus (Si 18:30b) whose other half is to be found in the next paragraph; then, after the Lord's Prayer (Mt 6:10), the Rule quotes another wisdom book (Pr 16:25; cf. Mt 18:6), and finally the Psalter (Ps 13:1). As for fleshly desires, two phrases from the Old Testament

(Ps 37:10 and Si 18:30ª) frame another quotation, which remains anonymous and even implicit: 'Death is stationed on the doorstep of pleasure'. The phrase comes from one of those Passions of roman martyrs of which the Master was so fond, that of Saint Sebastian (*Pass. Seb.* 14).

At the end of the exposition on thoughts, one detail deserves to be noted. The virtuous brother (literally: 'useful', that is, good) must 'always say in his heart' a certain phrase from the psalms, but slightly rearranged. No doubt this precept is not to be taken strictly, as an invitation ceaselessly to repeat a prayer formula. The Master and Benedict do not have in mind here the exercise advocated by Cassian (repeating: 'God, come to my assistance . . .'), by oriental monasticism (the Jesus prayer) and by Hinduism (the mantra), still more since their psalm formula is addressed not to God but to the person who says it. Besides, by offering other words to be said constantly further on (7:65; cf. 7:50 and 52–54) our authors show clearly that they do not have in mind a contemporary practice of perpetual repetition, continued invariably throughout one's life. Yet, such recommendations do put us on the track of the methods of 'meditation' we mentioned. Whatever the formula used and the way it is used, the repetition of a sacred phrase is a device whose value has been tested by several great monastic traditions independently of one another, and can still be of great help to seekers of God today.

26 Accordingly, if 'the eyes of the Lord are watching the good and the wicked', 27 if 'the Lord looks down at all times from heaven on the sons of men to see whether there is one who understands and seeks God'; 28 and if every day the angels assigned to guard us report our deeds to the Lord day and night, 29 then, brothers, we must be vigilant every hour lest, as the Prophet says in the psalm, God observe us 'falling' at some time into evil and 'made worthless', 30 and lest, after sparing us in the present time because he is good and waits for us

to improve, he tell us in the future: 'This you did, and I said nothing'.

This long sentence, which concludes the first step, draws our attention back to the last things. But now we are dealing with an event which has not yet been mentioned—judgment. That is where we run the risk of hearing God say to us: 'This you did, and I said nothing' (Ps 49:21). Here below the Lord observes us in silence, with a continuous gaze which can already tell the good from the wicked (Pr 15:3), the God-seeking from the wayward (Ps 13:2–3). God's goodness, which leads him to await our conversion this way, has already been celebrated in the Prologue (Prol 35–38).

While simply copying what he read in the Master, Benedict has become so thoroughly convinced of it that he will repeat it in a section which is unique to him: the introduction to the chapter on psalmody (19:1–2). In his view, the Office is the time when faith in God's presence and sight reaches its point of incandescence.

> [31] The second step of humility is that we love not our own will nor take pleasure in the satisfaction of our desires, [32] but rather imitate in our actions those words of the Lord saying: 'I have come not to do my own will, but the will of him who sent me'. [33] Scripture also says: 'Will has its punishment and constraint wins a crown'.

This second step introduces us into the middle zone of the ladder, where the Master and Benedict draw their inspiration from Cassian's 'signs of humility'. While recasting these quite thoroughly, the Master has enriched them with scriptural illustrations which make them more attractive: in practising them we do not merely show that we are humble; we also answer God's calls.

This step, closely connected with the following one, presents the negative face of obedience before its positive

aspect. It corresponds to Cassian's first 'sign': the mortification of one's will, yet to this it adds desires. In the first
step, the two already formed a pair originating in the Bible
(Si 18:30; Gal 5:16–17).

As for the two quotations on which this detachment
from all personal will is grounded, they are very unequal
in weight. The first, which we have already come across
(5:13), is nothing less than words spoken by Christ of himself (Jn 6:38). The second, while also presenting itself as
'Scripture', is actually drawn from the legendary Passion of
Saint Anastasia, a martyr venerated in Rome (*Pass. Anast.*
17). In reproducing it, Benedict was most likely unaware
of its non-biblical origin. This saying, ascribed in the story
to a martyr called Irene, adds to the words and example
of Christ the witness of a disciple who followed him until
death.

> [34] The third step of humility is that, for the love of God,
> we submit to the superior in all obedience, imitating the
> Lord of whom the Apostle says: 'Having made himself
> obedient even to death'.

This third step contrasts by its conciseness with the Master's, from which it is drawn. Benedict has retained only
one of his forerunner's seven scriptural quotations, and it
is perfectly chosen. In fact, except for one expression, the
others have already appeared in both Rules in the chapter
on obedience and in the first step of humility. On the
contrary, the great pauline phrase which Benedict retains
(Ph 2:8) has not yet been quoted, and this evocation of
Christ on the cross is extremely valuable. Thanks to it, the
doctrine on obedience developed in Chapter 5 and here
condensed is enriched with a priceless touch. 'Imitating
Christ' was already suggested in the previous step, but it
is good to be reminded here that 'doing the will of the
Father', as Jesus said in the words of the Gospel quoted

there, entailed for him, in the last analysis, 'making himself obedient even to death'.

If we look to the Master's source-text, we find that he had in mind Cassian's third 'sign of humility': the humble monk follows not his own will, but that of the senior who watches over him. On the other hand, it had not occurred to the Master to motivate obedience by the words 'for the love of God'. This motivation is unique to Benedict. The addition is all the more significant because it muddles up the blueprint drawn by Cassian and the Master: only after humility, as we shall see, do we rise to charity. But the consistency of this doctrinal scheme matters less to Benedict than his own conviction, based on the first commandment of Scripture and on daily experience: all christian life, and *a fortiori* all monastic life, is rooted in divine love. Here as elsewhere (68:5; 71:4), he does not hesitate therefore to make divine love the motive behind obedience, even though he gets ahead of himself.

[35] The fourth step of humility is that in this very practice of obedience, when we are subjected to harsh treatment or contradiction or even to all sorts of injustices, our conscience silently embraces patience [36] and that, holding out, we neither become discouraged nor retreat, as Scripture has it: 'He who perseveres to the end will be saved'. [37] And also: 'Be firm of heart and bear with the Lord'.

[38] And wishing to show how the faithful must even endure any and every contradiction for the Lord's sake, it puts the following words in the mouth of those who suffer: 'For your sake we are put to death daily. We are regarded as sheep marked for slaughter.' [39] And sure of the divine reward which they expect, they continue, saying joyfully: 'But in all this we overcome because of him who loved us'.

[40] And elsewhere Scripture also says: 'You have tested us, o God, you have tried us as silver is tried by fire;

you have led us into a snare. You have placed affliction on our backs.' [41] And in order to show that we must be under a superior, it continues in these terms: 'You have placed men over our heads'.

[42] Moreover, they are fulfilling the Lord's command by patience in the midst of hardships and injustices: when struck on one cheek, they turn the other also; to whoever deprives them of their tunic, they also offer their cloak; when pressed into service for one mile, they go two; [43] with the Apostle Paul, they bear with false brothers, as well as with persecution, and when cursed, they answer with blessings.

Cassian's fourth sign consisted in remaining patient in obedience. Then, broadening the theme, the author of the *Institutes* advanced as a fifth sign the peaceful acceptance of wrongs of all kinds, things which can be caused not only by the superior who commands, but also by any member of the community.

These two signs are combined in the present step, the longest of the ten intermediate rungs in our Rule. By comparing it with two parallel passages from the Master, we can see that the latter regards such patience in obedience as an equivalent of martyrdom. In fact, scriptural illustration is drawn from the most heroic texts found in both Testaments.

These quotations go two by two. First the 'perseverance to the end' required by Jesus (Mt 10:22) and the courage to 'bear with the Lord' of which the psalmist spoke (Ps 26:14). Then 'daily death' for God's sake, another psalm image (Ps 43:22) taken up and elaborated on by Saint Paul, who turns it into a victory (Rm 8:36–37). The Psalter also provides the next two quotations, in which the evocation of the 'fire' and 'snare' of trial ends with a remarkably realistic figure of obedience: 'men are placed' by God 'over our heads' (Ps 65:10–11 and 12). We return at last to the Gospel, with several touches from the Sermon on the Mount (Mt 5:39–41), and to Saint Paul, that model of patience with false friends (2 Co 11:26), persecutors, and detractors (1 Co 4:12). In this last group of texts we can clearly make out troubles arising not from superiors, those accredited representatives of God, but from any brothers, as in Cassian's fifth sign.

The spiritual climax of the passage is surely to be found in two sentences from the Letter to the Romans. 'For your sake . . . because of him who loved us': without using the word—which he saves for the end of the chapter—the Master, followed by Benedict, here sketches an attitude very close to charity. The name he gives it—'hope'—marks a progression over the 'fear' of the first step. It is true that fear already included the thought of everlasting life, but now, in the fire of trial, faith in that reward turns into joyful confidence.

Combining the gospel themes of perseverance in persecution and not resisting evil, this fine passage is among those pages of the Rule to which we go back most often and most happpily in the course of our monastic life.

> 44 The fifth step of humility is that, by humble confession, we do not conceal from our abbot any evil thoughts entering our hearts or any evil deeds committed in secret. 45 Scripture exhorts us to do this by saying: 'Make known your way to the Lord and hope in him'. 46 It also says: 'Confess to the Lord, for he is good, for his mercy is forever'. 47 So too the Prophet: 'To you I have acknowledged my offense, and I have not concealed my injustice. 48 I have said: Against myself I will report my injustice before the Lord, and you have forgiven the wickedness of my heart.'

Cassian already required the humble monk to 'hide nothing from his senior, not only about his actions, but also about his thoughts' (second sign). In response, the senior gave a judgment concerning the actions and thoughts confessed, and the brother submitted to it fully (third sign). The confession of the one directed and the director's advice formed a pair which the *Institutes* placed in the first group of signs, the features of obedience.

By displacing this opening of the heart and by modifying its formulation, the Master and Benedict have changed its nature. In their texts it is no longer followed by its natural extension, direction given by the senior. Instead of an act of submission by which the monk prepared to receive his director's instructions, we are now dealing with an act of self-abasement in which he confesses his sins. For the object of the confession no longer consists in actions or thoughts of uncertain quality on which one expects a senior's verdict, but *evil* thoughts and actions already judged to be such by the one confessing them.

This fifth step thus no longer belongs like Cassian's corresponding sign, to the group of demonstrations of obedience, but rather to acts of self-abasement or humility proper, which will include the next three steps. Before putting up with all manner of treatment, acknowledging that we are the least of all people and withdrawing into the background by conforming entirely to accepted custom, we make ourselves known for what we are: sinners in thought and deed.

This 'humble confession' to a superior, who is not necessarily a priest, has no sacramental significance in the ecclesiastical meaning of the term. We are seeking not to obtain absolution but to acquire virtue. Yet, the scriptural illustration shows that the abbot to whom we make our confession holds the place of Christ, here as elsewhere. The three quotations, all drawn from the Psalter (Pss 36:5; 105:1; 31:5) speak unanimously of a confession made 'to the Lord' whose mercy and forgiveness we hope for. In the light of these texts, it appears that, besides the acquisition of humility, our authors have in view the remission of sin, which, for that matter, simply follows from the act of

humility performed (cf. Cassian, *Conf.* 20.8.3). Only midway through the Rule (46:5–6) will Benedict mention another fruit of secret confession: the healing of the soul's
wounds through the spiritual father's care.

> [49] The sixth step of humility is that a monk is content
> with the lowest and most menial treatment, and regards
> himself as a poor and worthless workman in whatever
> task he is ordered to do, [50] saying to himself with the
> Prophet: 'I have been reduced to nothing and I have
> known nothing. I have been as a brutish beast before
> you and I am with you always.'

Cassian's seventh sign, reproduced almost verbatim by
the Master, consisted in accepting the poorest objects (food,
clothing, shoes, etc.), without asking any other payment
for manual work worth much more. This glaring dispro-
portion between salary and work, which was the common
lot of egyptian cenobites, could be interpreted in terms
of humility: the monk regarded himself as a 'worthless
servant', according to the Gospel (Lk 17:10).

By changing one word, Benedict modifies the significance of the text. Instead of objects 'provided' (*praebentur*),
he speaks of things 'ordered' (*iniunguntur*). By this alter-
ation, the sixth step becomes an extension of steps 2–4:
we are dealing once more with obedience. As we already
knew, the latter must be total (step 3) and bear with any
and all injustice (step 4). Benedict now specifies that the
monk must accept the lowliest tasks and regard them as
too good for him.

The Master's scriptural quotation (Ps 72:22–23) lends itself to the new as well as to the former meaning. Beyond
giving the feeling of being reduced to nothing, it superbly
expresses the monk's sole desire: to be with God always.

> [51] The seventh step of humility is that, not content to
> state with our tongue that we are the last and lowliest

of all, we also believe it in the depths of our heart,
[52] humbling ourselves and saying with the Prophet: 'As
for me, I am a worm, not a man, scorned by men and
despised by the people. [53] I was exalted, humbled and
overwhelmed with confusion'. [54] And again: 'It was a
good thing for me that you humbled me, in order that I
might learn your commandments'.

This step, inseparable from the previous one, reproduces
Cassian's eighth sign. The most important change made by
the Master and Benedict consists in turning the contrast between the two kinds of behavior ('not . . . but rather') into a
progression ('not content . . . also'). In such a perspective,
statements of inferiority are acceptable and even useful,
although they are not enough. According to Cassian, on
the contrary, they are superfluous; the only useful attitude
consists in believing oneself to be the least of all. The apt
story told by abbot Serapion (*Conf.* 18:11) unmasks the
deception to which humble language too often amounts.
Instead of words by which we delude both ourselves and
others, we must cultivate real feelings, neither paralyzing
self-deprecation nor masochistic indulgence in abjection,
but an honest and peaceful acknowledgment of the actual
deficiencies of which we are presently conscious, as well
as all those which might reveal themselves under other
circumstances.

The conviction suggested by this step is so strange and
exaggerated that some have attempted to justify it by some
mystical illumination. Without ruling out such an interpretation, which can readily be illustrated by more than one
saint's life, we must note first of all that Cassian's target is
a kind of verbalism: one half-heartedly declares oneself the
least of all men. In reaction against such superficial words,
he suggests interiorizing them. When he talks of judging
oneself inferior to everyone else, it is the verbal formulas
he reproves: instead of saying this, try instead to believe it.

The monk is not being required to give a categorical verdict concerning his place in the human race—God is the sole judge of human worth—but asked to transfer his effort at humility from his mouth to his heart.

Our authors give us to understand that this step is one of 'humility' in a special way. This is implied in the phrase which introduces the quotations: the monk 'humbles himself and says. . . .' And the same verb 'to humble oneself' comes up twice in the quotations themselves. As for the content of the texts quoted, it is helpful to reflect that the first (Ps 21:7) applies naturally to Christ on the cross, even though our authors do not point this out. The second (Ps 87:16), which follows after it immediately, is likewise a lament of the Psalmist for himself. The third, (Ps 118:71–73), on the contrary, is addressed to God. Like the verse quoted in the previous step, it admirably expresses the undivided love of someone who has no other treasure than the divine will.

[55] The eighth step of humility is that a monk does only what is endorsed by the common rule of the monastery and the example set by his superiors.

Unlike the others, this step is not backed up by any scriptural text, since Benedict omits the two quoted by the Master.

While reproducing Cassian's sixth sign almost exactly, our authors modify it by adding a word: *monasterii*. According to Cassian, the 'common rule' to which the humble monk conforms is the universal custom of egyptian monasticism, deemed to have originated in the days of the apostles. By specifying that they have in mind the common rule *of the monastery*, the Master and Benedict particularize this general norm. Correlatively, those whose example is to be followed are no longer the 'seniors' of monastic tradition, but, according to another meaning of the same word (*maiores*), the 'superiors' of the monastery, as the Master's scriptural illustration clearly shows.

Although our authors thus specify the twofold norm to be followed by bringing it down to the setting of their own community, the spirit of the practice remains unchanged. The point is self-effacement pursued by conforming to the local customs, by making the common observance one's own, by unreservedly embracing a tradition.

> [56] The ninth step of humility is that a monk forbids his tongue to speak and, remaining silent, does not speak until asked a question, [57] for Scripture warns that 'in speaking a great deal you will not avoid sin', [58] and that 'a talkative man goes about aimlessly on earth'.

After the steps of humility (2–3), of patience (4) and of self-abasement (5–8), here are three which relate to speech and laughter. They correspond to Cassian's last two signs. Cassian's only sign concerning speech is split by our Rules into two steps: steps 9 and 11, which frame the one on laughter (10).

Cassian simply recommended 'restraining one's tongue'. The Master, followed by Benedict, turns 'restrain' (*cohibeat*) into 'forbid' (*prohibeat*). The mere restraint advocated by the *Institutes* thus becomes genuine mutism, the limit of which is, however, outlined further on in the sentence: we are to remain silent until asked a question. The Master thus refers to the complicated casuistry set out in his second chapter on stillness, a casuistry which he develops yet further in the rest of his Rule. Benedict neglects these subtle regulations, retaining only the principle set forth here. In so doing, does he still have in mind the specific discipline the Master was aiming at: in the presence of his superiors, abbot, or dean, the monk must wait to be questioned? He may instead be thinking of a general attitude, valid at all times and with regard to anyone; this is how we spontaneously understand the passage.

The first scriptural quotation (Pr 10:19) has already been called on in the treatise on silence (6:4). The second (Ps 139:12) is new. Both recommend that one speak sparingly, less in order to acquire humility than to avoid sin or missteps. We may recognize here one of the themes of the chapter on stillness. Whatever its motivations, silence has been a characteristic trait of monks, whether cenobites or hermits, from the beginning. In order to let the word of God reverberate in them and to answer it by constant prayer, they give up exchanging human words.

> [59] The tenth step of humility is that we are not given to ready laughter, for it is written: 'The fool raises his voice in laughter'.

This tenth step reproduces exactly Cassian's tenth and last sign. As for the scriptural motivation (Si 21:23), it was already found in Saint Basil (*Reg.* 8.29), who added the gospel cursing of those who laugh (Lk 6:21) and the example of Christ himself, whom Scripture depicts several times weeping but never laughing. Such reflections occur quite frequently in the writings of the Fathers. They surprise us and, however pertinent they may be, draw our attention to an aspect of monastic asceticism less prominent today than it was then. Perhaps we are too lenient when it comes to laughter; true joy lies elsewhere.

One of the tools of good works prescribed not speaking words that induce laughter, another not loving boisterous laughter (4:53–54). Here the scriptural quotation reminds us of the second, while the sentence borrowed from Cassian relates rather to the first tool: we must be inclined neither to laugh nor to induce laughter. For others as for ourselves, true joy consists in being mindful of God.

> [60] The eleventh step of humility is that, when a monk speaks, he does so gently and without laughter, humbly and seriously, saying only brief and reasonable words,

and avoids raising his voice, [61] as it is written: 'A wise man is known by the brevity of his speech'.

Cassian's ninth sign consisted not only in speaking sparingly, but also in speaking in a low voice. We find this last instruction, reproduced literally, at the end of the present step ('let him avoid raising his voice'). The Master availed himself of the opportunity to specify how monks should speak. The first of his three pairs of remarks renews the condemnation of laughter, the second advocates seriousness (*gravitas*), which goes hand in hand with stillness (cf. 6:3), and the third recommends brevity, as does the text quoted at the end.

Our two Rules couple different adjectives with 'brief' (*pauca*): 'holy' in the Master's, 'reasonable' in Benedict's. By 'holy', the Master meant spiritual and edifying words concerning Scripture and the things of God. Benedict is less ambitious; he requires only 'reasonable' talk. 'Reasonable' is a term he likes to use as an adjective (2:18) and especially as an adverb (31:7, etc.). Here his concern with the good use of speech in ordinary life filters through for the first time. Talking about the ordinary things of life is not simply a necessity, to be reduced to the unavoidable minimum. Such exchanges between brothers must have a certain quality, and they must above all bear the stamp of reason.

The final quotation is not drawn from Scripture, as our Rules seem to suggest, but from a collection of pythagorean maxims christianized in the third century: the *Enchiridion* or Manual of Sextus (*Ench.* 145). The author, a philosopher, has been confused with Saint Xystus or Sixtus, pope and martyr (+ 258), to whom the work is ascribed by the monk Rufinus, who translated it into Latin for the roman public around the year 400. Was Benedict aware of the origin of this maxim, which he inherited from the Master? Whether he was or not, he made it his own, as he had earlier the one drawn from the Passion of Anastasia, another roman writing. While sounding like an inspired proverb, this quotation from a philosopher reminds us that for some of its greatest founders, like Augustine, monastic life numbered among its roots the wondrous love of wisdom entertained by some currents of ancient thought.

> [62] The twelfth step of humility is that a monk always manifests in his bearing no less than in his heart his humility to those who see him, [63] in other words, that at the work of God, in the oratory, the monastery, or the garden, on a journey or in the fields, everywhere, whether he sits, walks or stands, his head is always bowed and his eyes cast towards the ground, [64] believing himself always guilty of his sins, he believes that he is already appearing at the fearful judgment, [65] constantly saying in his heart what the publican in the Gospel said with eyes cast down toward the ground: 'Lord, I am not worthy, sinner that I am, to lift my eyes to heaven'. [66] And also with the Prophet: 'I am bowed down and humbled to the utmost'.

As we may remember, this last step is not drawn from Cassian's 'signs of humility'. Like the first, which it resembles by so many of its details, it is a creation of the Master. In these two end-steps, the humble monk is turned towards God. Of course he is first required to 'manifest humility to those who see him', but afterwards there is talk only of gestures and feelings relating to God. It is in thinking of God, and of God alone, that the monk assumes the humble attitude which strikes peoples' eyes.

Heart and body: this couplet already appeared at the beginning of the Rule (Prol 40). It recalls those we found at the beginning of this chapter: heart and eyes, soul and body (7:3 and 9). In going from the first term to the second, the Master no doubt had in mind the seventh step, where he moved in the reverse direction, from tongue to heart. But the exteriorization of sorts which he now prescribes must not mislead us: here as elsewhere, what is essential takes place inside. This is evinced by the final words, which the monk must 'constantly repeat to himself in his heart'.

To manifest by all our movements and even by our facial expression that we are standing in the presence of God: Saint Basil regarded this as an excellent way of edifying our brothers when we are too old and tired to do anything else (*Reg.* 86.2). The Master required this same example of the fully active monk; the depiction of this activity goes from the center of the monastery—the divine office and the oratory—to its outskirts. Basil, however, did not indicate the precise attitude described by our Rules: bent head, downcast eyes. On this point, the Master drew only on his own principles, which he states several times in the Rule with various motivations. Here the reason for the bent head is the awareness of sin and the expectation of judgment, which is considered imminent.

This sense of already standing before the judge recalls the conclusion of the first step. There the Master and Benedict spoke of judgment as of a 'future' event. Here the future becomes present: the truth known to us by faith appears as an accomplished fact.

This anticipation results in a new relation to sin. In the first step, the point was to avoid it. At the twelfth, the monk considers no longer the misdeeds he might commit, but those he actually has committed. This time his glance goes backwards, as though life were virtually over and all that remains is to take stock of it.

The first of the two final quotations consists of words we must constantly say, as was already required at another phrase in the first step (7:8). Placed in the mouth of the publican in the Gospel (Lk 18:13), these words are not, however, those that Luke has him speak. The Master and Benedict replace the invocation 'Have mercy on me, a sinner'—used by Eastern Christians in their famous Jesus Prayer—with a phrase that begins with the centurion's

'Lord, I am not worthy' (Mt 8:8) but especially recalls the words of King Manasses: 'I am not worthy to look up to the heights of heaven, so many are my iniquities' (*Or. Man.* 10). Several verses of the *Prayer of Manasses*, a brief apocryphal work, are reproduced elsewhere by the Master (RM 14:34–40). Here the penitent king's confession (cf. 2 Ch 33:12 and 18–19) merges with Luke's description of the publican.

Immediately afterwards, the *Prayer* has Manasses say: 'I am bent under the weight of chains'. These words of the captive king probably suggested the second quotation found in our Rules (Ps 37:9), which begins similarly.

It may seem strange to end an ascent with a confession of sin which began with a resolve to avoid all manner of misdeeds. But Gregory the Great and many other saints observe that purification is accompanied by an ever sharper awareness of one's impurity. And Christ himself justified the publican, the model for those who humble themselves that they may be exalted.

> [67] Therefore, once the monk has climbed all these steps of humility, he will arrive at that love of God which is perfect and which casts out fear. [68] Through it, all that he once performed not without dread, he will now begin to observe effortlessly, as though naturally, from habit, [69] no longer out of fear of hell, but out of love for Christ and good habit and delight in the virtues. [70] May the Lord manifest this state by the Holy Spirit in his workman now purified of vices and sins!

After the final step, which is unique to them, the Master and Benedict revert to Cassian in this conclusion. They borrow nearly their whole first sentence from him, whereas the second is original.

The spiritual ascent which began in fear thus ends with love which casts out fear (1 Jn 4:18). Hinted at briefly in the text of the *Institutes* from which our Rules drew their inspiration, this passage from slavish fear to filial love is extensively analyzed in the eleventh *Conference*. It fits a pattern of ascent outlined by Clement of Alexandria and reproduced by many later authors, particularly by Saint Basil and by Evagrius Ponticus, Cassian's master.

Such perfect charity not only eliminates the fear of punishment, as the Letter of John already stated. According to Cassian, followed by our Rules, it does away with all toil: a person reverts to the state in which he was created and acts well effortlessly by virtue of the nature he has regained. Force of habit has a part to play in this recovery of our primeval sanctity, as the Master and Benedict note on their own part. Benedict sets himself off from his two forerunners by specifying that the object of love is 'Christ', not 'the Good', as we find in more abstract fashion in Cassian and the Master.

This picture of the marvelous effects of charity is less unreal than it appears. It doubtless represents no more than an ideal goal towards which we never cease tending here below. But granted that resistance to good and therefore the toil involved in performing it never disappear entirely before death, it is a fact of experience that love and its trail of virtues are a source of joy. Benedict had already observed this at the end of the Prologue. He now repeats it, following the Master and Cassian.

The last sentence, added by our authors to the text of the *Institutes*, is very important. It adds an important touch which was missing not only from Cassian, but also from all this long chapter of our Rules: the acknowledgment of the work of grace. If this has not yet been mentioned, even in the ample treatment of the first step, it is doubtless in order to give full force to the basic instructions regarding watchfulness without respite and ceaseless effort directed against sin, and to avoid letting the monk rely on a work of grace which, he might assume, can go on without his participation. But now a backward glance reveals this work of the Spirit. When did it begin? Our text does not say.

Nothing prevents us from thinking, as faith assures us, that the Lord acted long before this final stage of the ascent; in fact, from its very beginning.

The 'vices and sins' which we avoided at the first step (7:12) are thus eliminated now by the purifying action of the Spirit. For *he* performs the purification, if we refer to the Master's text (that of Benedict, which omits the preposition *ab*, is not quite so clear). And through the Holy Spirit, too, the Lord is the source of charity and of its effects. The Spirit's purifying role emerges from the Old Testament (Ps 50:11–13; Ez 36:25–27) as from the New (1 Co 6:11). His relation to the love poured out in the hearts of Christians appears likewise in Saint Paul (Rm 5:5; 2 Co 6:6).

Benedict ends his chapter and the entire spiritual portion of his Rule with this very fine sentence. The Master continues on at some length, describing the joys of paradise, for the ladder of humility is raised up to heaven and must lead to this eschatological goal. Benedict stops at the earthly summit of charity primarily because, here as elsewhere, he aims at brevity. He may also have been uncomfortable with the very down-to-earth description of the hereafter he found in the Master. Already, at the end of Chapter 4, he had cut a full and very colorful picture of the world to come down to a few words from Saint Paul. The present abridgment is still more radical, and does away completely with that horizon.

Benedict does not, therefore, lead his reader to the 'exaltation in heaven' announced in the preamble to the chapter. The unfolding of charity here below is the only goal he offers in his conclusion. In doing so he reverts to Cassian's presentation, which also stopped at perfect love without dealing with the hereafter. This is true at least of the passage from the *Institutes* which is the source of our Rules, for the first *Conference* deals admirably with the two ends of christian life, earthly and eschatological: purity of heart and the kingdom of heaven.

Cassian's tendency was to insist on the immediate and too often unrecognized goal through which we must pass in order to attain the ultimate end. The same emphasis can be found in Benedict's work. At the end of the Prologue, we may remember, he introduces into the Master's purely eschatological perspective, the hope of an 'inexpressible delight of love' experienced in this very life. Here the omission of the other Rule's depiction of heaven also has the effect, intentional or not, of bringing into sharper focus the wonders of perfect charity here below.

VIII
The Divine Offices at night

AFTER THE SPIRITUAL CHAPTERS we have just read, those we now come to carry us into another world. Instead of describing individual virtues, they regulate community observance. This new character, while marking almost everything that will follow up to the end of the Rule, is particularly visible in the liturgical section which begins here. True, it will end with two spiritual surveys on psalmody and personal prayer (19–20), but until then we will come across hardly anything besides dry rubrics.

This change in subject and style goes along with a new relation to the Rule of the Master. Until now, Benedict has been generally content to reproduce it, with many omissions and a few changes. From this point on he frees himself from his model; he no longer follows it literally, but in a much more flexible fashion retains only its sequence of themes—at least partially—and a certain number of prescriptions. As we may remember, this personal composition using the basic structure provided by his forerunner could already be observed in the chapter on counsel. There Benedict found himself faced with a practical subject for the first time. Confronted with subjects of the same kind, which he now repeatedly encounters in the Master's text, he permanently adopts the same editorial method.

Of all the sections of the Rule which we shall read, the present portion (8–20) is the one on which Benedict has gone to the greatest pains to create an original work. Its relative length is remarkable, as is the meticulous care with which it has been drawn up. Another sign of the importance attached to the topic is the new place granted it. In the Master's text, the description of the divine office comes up much further on and almost by chance. From this original place, which corresponds to Chapter 47 of our Rule, Benedict transfers the office to the beginning of the legislative part of his work, immediately after the spiritual section. It is as though he wished to apply ahead of schedule the principle he will lay down further on: 'Let nothing be preferred to the work of God' (43:3).

> [1] During the winter season, that is, from the first of November until Easter, it seems reasonable to arise at the eighth hour of the night, [2] so as to sleep until a little past the middle of the night and arise refreshed. [3] As for the time remaining after Vigils, the brothers who need to learn some of the psalter or readings should use it for that study.
>
> [4] Between Easter and the first of November mentioned above, the time should be adjusted so that the office of Vigils, after a very short interval during which the brothers may go out to care for nature's needs, will be followed immediately by Matins, which must be said at daybreak.

Like the Master, Benedict begins his liturgical regulations with the night office (8–11). He will go on from there to Matins (12–13), and after an appendix on the vigils of the saints (14) will deal with all the offices, both nocturnal and diurnal (15–16). Ending with the day offices (17–18), he will, however, add a few words on the psalms to be said at night (18:19–20).

The night schedule which occupies the present chapter requires first of all that we remember how time was reckoned in the ancient world. Both day and night were divided into twelve equal hours whose length varied according to the seasons. When some hour was referred to, the full hour was meant: the 'first hour' of the night fell an hour after sunset, and so on. In winter, the eighth hour, mentioned here, thus occurred around two-thirty according to our way of reckoning. We notice, for that matter, that winter according to Benedict begins on November 1st and continues until the feast of Easter, far beyond the symmetrical date in relation to the solstice.

The time set for rising, then, is much later than midnight, mentioned by the Master and, further on, by Benedict himself (16:4). It is thus a euphemism to say that the monks sleep 'until a little past the middle of the night'. In fact, Benedict significantly lengthens the time for rest allocated by the Master. It is true that the Master provided for some extra sleep between the nocturns and Matins,[1] at least for those who wanted it. Though he does not formally rule this out, Benedict certainly did not adopt this second period of sleep, which Cassian disapproved of (*Inst.* 2.13; 3.4).

The time after Vigils is devoted primarily, for those in need of it, to the memorization (*meditatio*) of the psalms and readings (cf. 48:13), a necessary prerequisite for active participation in the office at a time when it was almost entirely recited by heart. The occupations of the other brothers remain undefined, but in any case they do not seem to go back to bed. 'Night rising', that is, celebrating Vigils between two periods of sleep, does not therefore appear to be a benedictine practice in the strict sense, even though it had a long and fine history before Saint Benedict, in his immediate circle, and after him.

---

[1] The office usually referred to today as Lauds. See below, Chapter XII.

In summer, Vigils end just as dawn begins to break; in central Italy, this takes place about an hour before sunrise. Thus, at all seasons, the nocturns are celebrated entirely in the dark. No practice can be more meritorious and more beneficial than praising God at that unrewarding hour, at which monastic tradition has consistently placed the longest of its divine offices.

IX

How many psalms should be said during the night hours?

[1] During the winter season defined above, first of all the verse 'Lord, you shall open my lips, and my mouth shall proclaim your praise' will be said three times. [2] To this will be added Psalm III and the *gloria*. [3] After that, Psalm XCIV with an antiphon, or at least chanted straight through. [4] The ambrosian will follow; then six psalms with antiphons. [5] Once they have been said and likewise the versicle, the abbot will give a blessing, all will sit down on the benches, and the brothers in turn will read three lessons from a book on the lectern; between them, three responsories will be sung. [6] Two responsories will be said without a gloria, but after the third lesson, the one singing will say the gloria. [7] When the cantor will begin to say it, all will immediately rise from their seats in honor and reverence for the Holy Trinity. [8] The books endowed with divine authority of both the Old and New Testaments shall be read at vigils, as well as the commentaries of these written by reputable and orthodox catholic Fathers.

[9] These three lessons and their responsories will be followed by the six remaining psalms, which will be sung with an alleluia. [10] This ended, there follow the lesson from the Apostle recited by heart, the versicle and the

supplication of the litany, that is *Kyrie eleison*, [11] and thus the night vigils shall end.

THE MONKS of Lower Egypt, whether cenobites or hermits, were accustomed to reciting twelve psalms at the only two offices they celebrated: vespers and the nocturns. This twelve-psalm canon, observed in particular in the great centers of Nitria, the Kellia and Scete, was really consecrated by the *Institutes*. Drawing his inspiration from the legend that Pachomius' rule had been given him by an angel, Cassian ascribed the liturgical tradition of the monks of Egypt to an angelic apparition supposed to have occurred at the beginnings of cenobitism (*Inst.* 2.5). Stamped with a supernatural seal and linked to apostolic times, the twelve-psalm law then took on incomparable authority. Cassian forcefully sets it against the usages of the monks of Southern Gaul—who recited far more psalms—as the sole authentic tradition.

No man is a prophet in his own country. The monasteries of Southern Gaul went on celebrating their lengthy offices. But in Italy Cassian's message was heeded. Some basilical monasteries in Rome adopted the twelve-psalm canon, at least at the night office. The Master did not follow it entirely, but prescribed similar numbers, which vary according to the seasons. Benedict, for his part, unreservedly adopted the egyptian norm consecrated by Cassian. At all seasons, and even on Sundays, he sets the number of psalms at Vigils at twelve. This is the first essential point of his liturgical reform.

We have just mentioned the two main sources of that legislation: the Rule of the Master and the office of the roman monasteries. From the latter Benedict borrowed not only the twelve psalms, but also three lessons and the three responsories, with a versicle preceding them. But instead of being recited all in a row and then followed by the lessons, as was the case in Egypt and at Rome, the psalms are divided into two groups of six, before and after the lessons. Moreover, the psalmody is not uniform but differentiated: first with antiphons, then with an alleluia. This partition drew its inspiration from the Rule of the Master, which divided the psalms into two uneven groups, the first with no alleluia, the second with an alleluia. Benedict's introduction (opening verse and invitatory) and his conclusion (brief lesson, versicle, supplication) can already be found in the Master's text; it appears then that the Master provided benedictine Vigils with their overall structure, into which borrowings from the roman office have been introduced.

Besides these two major sources, Saint Caesarius' of Arles office may have suggested certain features, such as the hymn which Benedict inserts after the Master's invitatory (Ps 94). This 'ambrosian', as he calls it, has the same effect as the psalm of expectancy (Ps 3), also added by him. Both mention the nocturnal hour, which appears neither in the verse 'Lord, open my lips' nor in the invitatory. The triple 'opening verse', to use the Master's expression, simply marks the resumption of speech after the silence inaugurated, at the end of Compline, by the 'closing verse'.

The care with which Benedict speaks of lessons and responsories indicates that his readers were not familiar with these elements of the office. He no doubt places them in the middle of the psalmody so as to allow the monks to sit down between two bouts of antiphonal singing—which was performed standing. A refreshing of attention is added to physical rest. What Benedict says of the lessons, moreover, denotes his preoccupation with orthodoxy, and his remark concerning the *Gloria* signals his zeal for the worship of the Trinity, still threatened by contemporary arianism.

The 'supplication of the litany' is the *Kyrie eleison*. In the complete litany, this formula is inserted between variable invocations. But in Rome, as Saint Gregory was to note

later, it was sometimes simply repeated without any intermediate petitions. In Benedict's Rule, these come in only
in the 'litany' proper, which is reserved for the great hours
of Matins[2] and Vespers.

---

[2]Lauds

X

How nocturnal praise should be celebrated during the summer season

[1] From Easter until the first of November, on the other hand, the entire amount of psalmody indicated above shall be maintained in full, [2] except that because the nights are shorter no lesson shall be read from a book, but instead of these three lessons one drawn from the Old Testament shall be said from memory, followed by a short responsory. [3] Everything else will be accomplished as we have said, that is, the number said at Vigils will never be less than twelve psalms, not including psalms III and XCIV.

THE IMPORTANCE ATTACHED by Benedict to the twelve-psalm rule can be clearly seen here. Instead of shortening the psalmody in summer as the Master did, he maintains it at its full length and transfers the abridgment to the readings. The latter did not undergo any reduction in the roman office, which remained invariable throughout the year. By replacing them with a simple brief lesson, Benedict shows that he makes a distinction between the compulsory psalms and the more or less optional readings, along the lines of the egyptian cenobitism described by Cassian (*Inst.* 2.6). For, as in the chapter's title, the night office is primarily a form of 'praise' consisting essentially of psalmody. Alongside this main end, the teaching conveyed by the lessons, valuable though it is, appears accessory.

XI

How Vigils should be celebrated on Sundays

[1] On Sunday the monks shall arise earlier for Vigils. [2] At these Vigils the measure shall be adhered to, that is, after saying six psalms and the versicle, as indicated above, all will sit down on the benches in good order and according to their rank, and four readings with their responsories will be read in a book as said above. [3] Only at the fourth responsory will the one singing say the *gloria*. When he begins it, immediately all shall rise in reverence.

[4] After the lessons, there shall follow six more psalms chosen according to their sequence, with antiphons like the preceding ones, and the versicle. [5] After which four more lessons shall be read once more, according to the arrangement indicated above.

[6] After that three canticles from the Prophets chosen by the abbot shall be said; these canticles will be chanted with an alleluia. [7] A versicle will also be said, the abbot shall bless, and four more lessons from the New Testament will be read according to the arrangement indicated above, [8] but after the fourth responsory the abbot will begin the hymn *Te deum laudamus*. [9] Once it is ended, the abbot will read the lesson from the Gospel while all stand with respect and awe. [10] Once

that reading is finished, all will reply A*men* and the abbot will immediately intone the hymn *Te decet laus*, and once the blessing has been given they shall begin Matins.

[11] This arrangement for Vigils shall be followed equally on Sundays at all seasons, summer or winter, [12] unless—God forbid—the monks should arise too late: the lessons or responsories will be shortened. [13] But let special care be taken that this should not happen. If it does, let the monk responsible through his negligence make due satisfaction to God in the oratory.

BENEDICT OWES the Rule of the Master next to nothing here. He borrows nearly all his material from roman customs. For on Sunday the Master retained the ancient vigil which began the evening before and ended at the second cock crow. By contrast, like the roman monasteries, Benedict contents himself with an office at the end of the night, similar to that of weekdays, though longer. Again, as in Rome, this scaled-down and displaced 'vigil' includes three series of chants, as well as readings followed by responsories.

This time, therefore, the framework of the benedictine office is roman. On the other hand, the numbers are original. Instead of the eighteen or twenty-five psalms sung in Rome, unevenly distributed between the three nocturns, Benedict, faithful to his egyptian canon, stays with twelve as at the ferial office, divided, as there, into only two nocturns. At the third nocturn, three canticles from the Prophets replace the three psalms of Rome, which were chanted with an alleluia.

The reduction in the roman psalmody is accompanied by an expansion of the readings, from nine to twelve. Benedict thus matches the number of lessons to that of psalms, following the double tendency observed in the evolution of the roman office itself: less psalmody, more lessons and responsories.

The third nocturn stands out in this whole by the multiplicity of its components and the care with which they are listed. Compared to his roman models, Benedict is obviously innovating here. For, through unknown channels, another custom was exerting its influence over the end of his Sunday vigils: that of the Church of Jerusalem, as described a century and a half earlier by the spanish traveler Egeria. On Sundays, as the night came to an end, in the church of the Anastasis erected over Christ's tomb, three psalms were sung, each followed by a prayer. Then the bishop read the Gospel of the Resurrection. This simple structure, traces of which remain in many rites, can be discerned in particular in our Rule, with canticles replacing the psalms. In light of the Jerusalem custom, it seems likely that the Gospel prescribed by Benedict was also a Resurrection narrative, as was still the case in the contemporary office of Caesarius of Arles.

The community at Monte Cassino, gathered around its abbot, thus imitated the people of Jerusalem assembled around their bishop. In this weekly celebration of the paschal mystery, after the usual twelve psalms of the monastic office, the monks travelled in spirit to the Anastasis.

But Benedict was not content with the three canticles and the Gospel. Besides the four lessons which he inserts into this nocturn as into the other two, he introduces two new elements before and after the Gospel: the hymns *Te deum laudamus* and *Te decet laus*.

These two pieces in praise of the Trinity differ not only by their very unequal length but also by their origin and age. The long *Te deum* is western and was relatively recent (end of the fifth century?), the brief *Te decet* is eastern and much older. Perhaps unwittingly, Benedict here gathers the voices of East and West around the risen Christ, acclaiming the holy Trinity. We are reminded of the two seraphim in Isaiah who sing praise to the thrice-holy God. At this high point of the week, the monks join them in celebrating the central mystery of salvation and theology: the death and resurrection of Christ to the glory of God his Father, the salvation of humankind by Jesus to the praise of the three divine Persons.

The last paragraph of the chapter brings us back to more prosaic realities. Like Caesarius, Benedict foresaw that the monks might get up late and remedied the situation by shortening the lessons. We perceive once again his resolve not to transgress the sacred twelve-psalm canon, either by default or by excess.

XII

How the solemnity of Matins is to be celebrated[3]

[1] At Sunday Matins psalm LXVI shall be first be said straight through without an antiphon. [2] Then psalm L shall be said with an alleluia. [3] Then the CXVII[th] and LXIIth shall be said, [4] then the blessings and Lauds, a lesson from the Apocalypse recited by heart and the responsory, the ambrosian, the versicle, the gospel canticle, the litany, and that is all.

THIS LITTLE CHAPTER, to which the following one was originally joined, deals with Matins, beginning with Sunday so as to round off what has just been said about that day's Vigils. Unlike the night office, Matins has no opening verse, only a brief introductory psalm (Ps 66) analogous to that of Vigils and probably suggested, like the latter, by the customs of Arles. The office itself is distinctly roman in structure, with its five units of psalmody, the concluding one of which consists in a combination of the last three psalms (Ps 148–150, called 'Lauds') while the next to last is a canticle (Dan 3:57–88, called 'blessings').

In third position, the roman office put together two psalms (Ps 62 and 66). Benedict leaves only one of them there and, as we have seen, uses the other as an introduction. Psalm 62 is a morning psalm but is not specially

---

[3]Matins, for reasons that follow in the text, is often referred to as Lauds

related to Sunday, unlike Psalm 117, whose paschal character is obvious. As for Psalm 50, it is said every day at Matins in Benedict's schema as in the roman office, even though nothing in it strikes us as having to do with daybreak.

In the conclusion to Matins, the newest element is the hymn ('ambrosian'), which again recalls the office of Arles. On the other hand, the canticle of Zacharias (Lk 1:68–79) was to be found in the offices of Rome and the Master. We may note that at this major morning hour the complete 'litany' is used, that is, a series of invocations answered by *Kyrie eleison.*

According to tradition, which has often given the name 'lauds' to Matins as a whole, the most characteristic element of that office is the praise expressed by the last three pieces of the psalter. Human beings emerging from the throes of night and seeing once more the beauty of light and the wondrous world of creatures are in fact spontaneously moved to acclaim God the creator and saviour. Preceding Psalm 148, the canticle of the Three Young Men underlines this gratitude of the soul for creation thus recovered.

But light is more than joy to the eye and grounds for exultation of all one's being. According to Saint John, it represents God, and Christ called himself the light of the world. Called as we are to become children of light and light in the Lord, we too relive our baptismal sanctification— that passage from the night of sin to the broad daylight of divine holiness—at this hour of dawn, while waiting to pass over from the night of this world to the everlasting splendor of God. Hence we sing Psalm 50 at the beginning of the office in order to purify ourselves from sin, which night always symbolizes and too often occasions. And at the other end of the celebration, the canticle of Zacharias sings the coming of Christ the saviour shining from on high like the rising sun, in his descent here below as man, in his ascent from the underworld and his resurrection, and in the glorious return of his *parousia*.

XIII

Ordinary Days: How Matins are to be celebrated

[1] On ordinary days, on the other hand, the solemnity of Matins shall be celebrated as follows: [2] Psalm LXVI shall be said without an antiphon, somewhat protractedly, as on Sunday, so that all may be present for the Lth, which will be said with an antiphon. [3] Then two other psalms will be said according to custom, that is, [4] on the second feria, the Vth and the XXVth; [5] on the third feria, the XLII[d] and the LVIth; [6] on the fourth feria, the LXIII[d] and the LXIVth; [7] on the fifth feria, the LXXXVIIth and the LXXXIXth; [8] on the sixth feria, the LXXVth and the XCI[st]; [9] on Saturday, the CXLII[d] and the canticle from Deuteronomy, which shall be divided into two *glorias*. [10] On the other days a canticle from the Prophets shall be said, each on its day, as the roman Church chants them. [11] Then Lauds will follow; then a lesson from the Apostle recited from memory, the responsory, the ambrosian, the versicle, the gospel canticle, the litany, and that is all.

FROM MONDAY through Friday, the days of the week are called 'ferias' and are referred to simply by number. This austere system, which the Church did not succeed in imposing generally (it has survived only in Portuguese), aimed at replacing the pagan gods after whom the days were named by Christ alone, whose resurrection served as the starting point and reference of the entire series. In the romance languages, the name for Sunday, derived from the Latin *Dominica* ('the Lord's day'), remains as the sole relic of this unsuccessful attempt.

The variable psalms of the Rule, noted with meticulous care, correspond only partially to the roman 'customs' to which Benedict refers. In the monasteries of Rome, in fact, only the second psalm changed; the combination of psalms 62 and 66 was repeated daily in third place. Benedict's general tendency to diversify the psalmody can be perceived here for the first time. The variable element he adds is inserted either after the second roman psalm (Monday, Tuesday) or before it (Wednesday, Thursday, Friday) so as to form an advancing series with no going backwards. Psalm 75, however, upsets the numerical order. In order to preserve this as much as possible, Benedict has inverted Psalms 91 and 142, the first of which was reserved by roman custom for Saturday—the day mentioned in its title. All these psalms speak of light or of the Resurrection, although the latter is referred to less obviously in the case of Psalm 63.

The partition of the canticle of Moses, which goes against roman custom, is the first example of another tendency characteristic of Benedict: dividing up long psalms, as the monks of Egypt did (*Inst.* 2.11.1–2). Like diversifying psalms, dividing them up aimed at fostering attention. This canticle from Deuteronomy, like those from the 'prophets' assigned to the other days, is borrowed from the Church of Rome, as Benedict expressly notes—a valuable indication of our Rule's place on the map, both geographical and spiritual. These canticles are not all 'prophetic' in the strict sense of the term; while Monday and Tuesday have sections of Isaiah and Friday a passage from Habakkuk, the canticles of Hannah and Moses from *Exodus* (one of what we call the historical books) are allotted to the two intermediate days.

The end of the office is substantially the same as on Sundays. We can therefore give all our attention to the important final note on the recitation of the *Our Father*:

> [12] Assuredly, the morning and evening celebration shall never be concluded without the superior's reciting the entire Lord's Prayer at the end so as to be heard by all, because of the thorns of contention that are wont to spring up. [13] Thus the pledge they make by this prayer which has them say: 'Forgive us, as we ourselves forgive', shall enjoin them to purify themselves of this kind of vice. [14] At other celebrations the final part of that prayer shall be said, that all may reply: 'But deliver us from 'evil'.

At all the hours the Prayer *par excellence* seems to occupy the place of honor, perfecting and crowning the entire office, without the addition of a collect, as is the case today. The reason Benedict gives for the solemn manner in which he has it recited at Matins and Vespers, witnesses first and foremost to a concern we have seen him state in many key passages in the spiritual part of the Rule: purifying the monk of every sort of vice. But yet another preoccupation may be seen to emerge here, one which will manifest itself more and more clearly: fraternal relations. The purity to which the monk's soul aspires is not, as one might infer from the first step of humility, merely a matter of watching over oneself. It presupposes forgiveness asked of the Lord and granted to one's neighbor, the grace of God and love of others, in a current of divine and universal charity.

XIV

The Anniversaries of Saints: How Vigils are to be celebrated

[1] However on the feasts of saints and on all solemnities, the celebration shall take place as directed for Sundays, [2] except that the psalms or antiphons or lessons relating to that day shall be said. But the measure indicated above shall be adhered to.

IN ITALY, in Benedict's time, lists of holy martyrs from different parts of christendom were being assembled on a single calendar, which was to be called the martyrology. But in principle the only saints whose feasts were celebrated were those of the local Church, even granted the universal influence of the roman Church and the circulation of relics. The sanctoral cycle thus remained sparse. Even at Rome, where martyrs abounded, feasts of saints came up on average, according to the oldest sacramentaries and lectionaries, approximately only one day out of seven.

This little chapter, which no doubt originally followed the one dealing with Sunday vigils, confines itself to the night office, perhaps implicitly including Matins. The celebration of the saints does not seem to have gone any further. As always, Benedict takes care to recall the intangible 'measure' of twelve psalms. As for the 'lessons' proper to the day, he is probably referring to the passions of the martyrs, the writing of which was then in full swing. Although legendary and mediocre in quality, these works usefully extolled a form of sanctity for which monastic life was a substitute and continuation. Caesarius of Arles, Aurelian, and Ferreolus likewise have them read at the night office. Besides the martyrs, only some rare confessor-bishops, such as Saint Martin, were venerated at the time.

In addition to its practical significance, the conformation of the office of the saints to that of Sundays has the advantage of suggesting that Christ alone is holy and the sole source of all holiness. It is he whom we celebrate on these feasts of the sanctoral cycle, as well as on his weekly day and other solemnities.

XV

At what times the Alleluia is to be said

[1] From the holy feast of Easter until Pentecost 'alleluia' shall be said uninterruptedly with both the psalms and the responsories; [2] from Pentecost until the beginning of Lent, every night, it shall be said only at the nocturns, with the last six psalms. [3] But every Sunday, except during Lent, the canticles, Matins, Prime, Terce, Sext and None shall be said with 'alleluia', Vespers with an antiphon. [4] However the responsories shall never be said with 'alleluia', except from Easter until Pentecost.

ACCORDING TO CASSIAN, the egyptian cenobites answered 'alleluia' only to the last of their twelve evening and night psalms (*Inst.* 2.5.5). In the Rule of the Master, the use of the *alleluia* is extended: it accompanies the last third of the psalmody at all the offices. On weekdays, Benedict reserves the *alleluia* for Vigils, but there he uses it even more generously than the Master: his second group of psalms being equal in size to the first, he has the monks say the *alleluia* throughout this second half of the psalmody.

Modest though it may appear, the question dealt with in this chapter was the subject of much discussion in sixth-century roman circles. At Mass and in their offices, clerics reserved the *alleluia* for paschaltide, whereas monks readily extended it to other periods, with the exception of Lent. In the Master's view, this extension is a privilege attached to the 'special service of God' represented by monastic life. As God's house, the monastery resembles heaven. By way of anticipation, the *alleluia* is ceaselessly sung there, for, as in eternity, those who dwell there already live with the Lord.

Between the Master's liberality and the restraint of the basilical monasteries of Rome, where the ferial office was devoid of *alleluias* even at night, Benedict follows a middle way. While his ferial Vigils draw their inspiration from the Master, his Sunday practice is that of Rome: the *alleluia* is sung only from the second nocturn until None (the Master continued it at Vespers and Compline). The final rubric concerning responsories also marks a restriction in comparison with the Master.

Just as every Sunday recalls Easter, likewise every weekday retains an echo of the paschal and Sunday *alleluia*. This cry of praise, a foretaste of eternity, rings out at the darkest hour of the daily cycle. For Saint Paul 'Be always joyful' was inseparable from 'Pray without ceasing'. The joy of holy Easter is never long absent from the service of God even here below, as we expect the day when it will be 'without interruption' of any kind in a life without end.

XVI

How the Divine Offices are to be celebrated during the day

[1] As the Prophet says: 'Seven times a day I have sung your praise'. [2] We will fulfill this sacred number of seven by performing the duties of our service at the time of morning, Prime, Terce, Sext, None, Vespers and Compline, [3] for it was of these hours during the day that he said: 'Seven times a day have I praised you'. [4] As for night vigils, the same Prophet says regarding them: 'In the middle of the night I arose to give you thanks'. [5] It is at these times, therefore, that we shall send up our praises to our creator 'for the judgments of his justice': at Matins, Prime, Terce, Sext, None, Vespers and Compline; and 'at night we shall arise to give him thanks'.

THIS LIST of the seven day offices, presented as the fulfillment of a phrase from the Psalter (Ps 118:164), is no novelty: it was found already in the Rule of the Master. Neither does Benedict innovate in connecting Vigils with a verse from the same psalm (Ps 118:62): the Master did the same, at least as regards winter nocturns. This little chapter nonetheless has a note of originality. The two psalm texts, which were quoted separately in the other Rule, are brought together here to prove an argument: in the light of the second, the first must be understood as referring to the seven day offices, to the exclusion of the night office. For the Psalmist, 'day' does not mean the twenty-four hours of the legal day, but day proper as opposed to night.

By setting the total number of daily offices at eight, Benedict conflicts with some of his contemporaries, such as Eugippius and Cassiodorus, who had only seven, Vigils included. The day hour neglected by these authors was that of Prime, more recent than the others and not yet accepted by all. Here Benedict is campaigning in favor of that office. Further on he will even lay special emphasis on it, no doubt partly by way of reaction.

The use of the phrase from Psalm 118 as a basis for a cycle of daily prayer goes back at least as far as Eusebius of Caesarea, who was followed by Cassian. But this use of the scriptural 'Seven times a day' does not give a correct idea of the origin of the hours of the office. In actual fact, they were not originated from a desire to imitate the Psalmist, whose words merely contributed to the finalization of the list. As early as the year 200 or so—a century before Eusebius— writers such as Tertullian, Clement, and Hippolytus were culling Scripture for suggestions concerning the times at which we should pray. This search was motivated and dominated by a pauline maxim, the only command regarding the times for prayer to be found in the New Testament: 'Pray without ceasing' (1 Th 5:17; Lk 18:1).

'Pray without ceasing.' This imperative itself derives from the great commandment to love God. Time is being itself. Anyone who loves God with his whole heart turns to him at all times. The requirement is an infinite one, with no limitation other than human strength and the grace granted us. By nature, christian and monastic prayer tends to be continual.

In order to obey this command, therefore, fervent Christians set themselves hours for prayer long before the emergence of monasticism—hours suggested both by Scripture and by the natural or legal divisions of the day. This recurrence of prayer at more or less regular intervals did not prevent them from praying in between. On the contrary, their purpose was to remind the soul of the duty of praying ceaselessly and to bring it back to this by some sort of rule. Thanks to this minimum they imposed upon themselves, these early Christians were sure never to forget God for long. As a supportive structure for their prayer lives, the hours did not dispense them from striving to pray constantly, but revived that effort, when necessary, and sustained it.

While rooted in this ancient christian practice, the benedictine system of the hours is set off by its communitarian nature. Something begun as no more than private prayer, whose time and content each individual decided for himself, turned in cenobitic monasteries into collective prayer at times and in a form determined by rule. Accordingly, the cycle of the hours is no longer merely a framework intended to support a personal striving after constant prayer. Besides this bearing with respect to individuals, which remains fundamental, it has significance for the community, whose aim of sanctifying time both collectively and individually it demonstrates.

Some monastic bodies even attempted to pray without ceasing at the community level. The Acoemetae of Byzantium, followed by several great merovingian monasteries in the West, cultivated *laus perennis*, with squadrons of monks or nuns taking turns in choir uninterruptedly day and night. Without going as far, many communities, particularly in visigothic Spain and in cluniac monasticism, went in for multiple and protracted celebrations, so that the major part of the monks' time was taken up with these common prayers.

Halfway between the initial scantness of offices in Egypt (Matins and Vespers only) and this later exuberance, Benedict holds to a balanced measure which preserves the genuine role of community prayer: it must not replace the personal striving to pray without ceasing, but encourage and entertain it. Like the piles of a bridge, the hours of common prayer punctuate the course of time. It is up to each monk to connect them by the causeway of his unceasing prayer, so as to answer the Lord's call. Each hour is, for that matter, laden with multiple biblical reminiscences—the passion and resurrection of Christ, the outpouring of the Spirit, episodes from the acts of the Apostles—which add their particular harmonics to the essential role of all these sacred moments: reminding both community and individuals at regular intervals that 'the entire end of the monk is to tend towards uninterrupted prayer' (Cassian, *Conf.* 9.2).

XVII

How many psalms should be chanted at these same hours?

[1] We have already established the order for psalmody at Vigils and Lauds; now let us see to the remaining hours.

[2] At the hour of Prime, three psalms shall be said separately and not under one *gloria*, [3] the hymn for this same hour after the verse 'God, come to my assistance', before beginning the psalms. [4] After ending the three psalms, moreoever, a lesson, the versicle and the *Kyrie eleison* and the dismissal shall be recited.

[5] At Terce, Sext and None, on the other hand, prayer shall be celebrated likewise, according to this arrangement, that is, the verse, the hymns of these same hours, three psalms at each, the lesson and the versicle, *Kyrie eleison* and the dismissal. [6] If the community is larger they shall chant with antiphons, but straight through if it is smaller.

[7] At the evening synaxis, the number of psalms shall be limited to four, with antiphons. [8] After these psalms the lesson shall be recited, then the responsory, the ambrosian, the versicle, the gospel canticle, the litany, and the Lord's Prayer shall serve as dismissal.

[9] Compline shall be limited to three psalms. These psalms shall be said straight through, without antiphons.

10 After that, the hymn of this same hour, a lesson, the versicle, *Kyrie eleison*, and the blessing shall serve as dismissal.

AS WE HAVE SEEN, Benedict considered inviolable the egyptian canon calling for twelve psalms at night, handed down by Cassian. At Terce, Sext and None, which were not celebrated in Egypt, Cassian recommended saying only three psalms, as the cenobites of Palestine did (*Inst.* 3.1–3). In contrast to the six or twelve psalms of the gallic office, this very moderate norm aimed at allowing time for manual work, which filled the intervals between the hours. As at the night office, Benedict here adopts the rule suggested by the *Institutes* and already taken up before him by the monks of Rome as well as by the Master.

'Saying the three psalms separately and not under one *gloria*' contrasts with a practice permitted by the Master in an emergency. It went hand in hand with that of chanting 'straight through', that is, without antiphons (the *gloria* after each psalm was originally reserved for antiphonal singing). Benedict allows this form of chant at the little hours as well as antiphonal singing, but does not want it to entail the suppression of two out of three *glorias*. The psalmody of the little hours differs in this regard from the responsories at Vigils in winter, only the third of which, as we may remember, ended with the trinitarian doxology.

On many other counts, on the contrary, the little hours resemble Vigils. These four offices total twelve psalms, as do the nocturns. Although the initial verses (here Ps 69:2) differ, their existence is also a common feature, as is the place of the hymn at the beginning of the celebration and the versicle following the lesson at the end. Finally the *Kyrie eleison*, that is, the litany reduced to its 'supplication', unites night and day offices, in contrast to the full litany of Matins and Vespers. Just as these two solemn hours at the borderline between night and day visibly correspond, so likewise the brief celebrations spaced out at intervals throughout the day correspond to the long, continuous night prayer.

At the little hours, Benedict exempts small communities from antiphonal singing so as to simplify and shorten their offices, as is appropriate when there are fewer hands and more work. By thus allowing both forms of chant, with or without antiphons, according to the size of the monastery, the Rule adopts a position halfway between the old roman office, which never had any antiphons at those hours, and the new, which, like the Master's, always had them.

At Vespers, the four-psalm assignment—hardly more than at the little hours—seems remarkably light compared to the six psalms of the Master and to the five of the roman office, which Benedict maintains at the parallel morning hour. As we shall see, this cutback is connected with the weekly distribution of the psalter, in which only twenty-four psalms are set aside for Vespers. The importance of Vespers is measured not by the length of the psalmody, but by the fact that it changes daily. Moreover, they have the same solemn structure as Matins, with the canticle of Mary corresponding to that of Zacharias.

Compline, whose structure is original, ends with a blessing—something we have encountered only at Sunday vigils. The Lord, to whom we called for help at the beginning of Prime, thus blesses the day as it comes to an end. But we may think of something else. The coming of night, which is an image of death, invites us to place ourselves under God's protection. In Spain and Ireland in the sixth and seventh centuries, the monks explicitly made ready to breathe their last at the final office of the day, as if to give liturgical expression to Benedict's recommendation: 'Keep death before your eyes every day as an imminent event'.

XVIII

In what order are these psalms to be said?

¹ First of all, the verse 'God, come to my assistance; Lord, make haste to help me' shall be said; then the hymn of each hour.

² Then at the hour of Prime, on Sunday, four sections of psalm cxviii shall be said. ³ At the other hours, that is Terce, Sext and None, three sections of this same psalm cxvii shall be said each time. ⁴ At Prime of the second feria three psalms shall be said, that is the ᵢˢᵗ, the ᵢᵢᵈ and the vᵢᵗʰ. ⁵ And thus, each day at Prime until Sunday, three psalms in a row shall be said each time as far as psalm xix; psalms ix and xvii shall each be divided into two sections. ⁶ In this way, Sunday Vigils will always begin with the xxᵗʰ.

THIS LONG CHAPTER, which regulates the distribution of the psalms over the week, is singularly precise and detailed. Benedict has gone to remarkable pains to leave nothing to chance and to eliminate all uncertainty. This very elaborate description has made it possible to observe his *ordo* throughout the centuries with very few hesitations; those there are only over the division of the longer psalms at Vigils.

Unlike the Master, who always had the psalms said in sequence so that the monks began at each office where they had left off at the previous hour, the roman monasteries already practised the weekly recitation of the Psalter. They divided it into two main series, one for the night office (Ps 1–108), the other for Vespers (Ps 109–147). This roman system forms the basis for Benedict's, whose reshuffling tends to cut down on repetition and therefore diminish the length of the offices.

Thus at Prime the roman scheme had the first four sections of Psalm 118 recited daily, preceded by Psalm 53. Benedict reserves this beginning of Psalm 118 for Sunday and replaces it by constantly varying psalms from Monday through Saturday. These new psalms at Prime (Ps 1–19) are drawn from the roman series for vigils. Changing as they do each day, they lend this celebration a prominence comparable to that of the ancient vigils and Vespers, with which it also shares the privilege of dividing up the longer psalms.

The verse 'God, come to my assistance' (Ps 69:2), already mentioned in the previous chapter, is reproduced in full here. Along with the hymn that follows, it seems to have been added to a primitive *ordo* which did not mention it. Benedict's insertion of it not only into the office but also into the ritual (35:17) is probably due to the famous passage where Cassian extols this verse as a prayer formula appropriate for all needs and all circumstances (*Conf.* 10.10).

The author of the *Conferences* saw the repetition of the *Deus in adiutorium* as the best way of attaining unceasing prayer. In the Rule of Saint Benedict we are no longer dealing with a formula used continually by all and sundry in their personal prayer lives, but with a liturgical introduction to the hours of the office and to the cooks' week of duty. Similar uses can be found in Cassiodorus, who reports that the italian monks repeated the verse three times at the beginning of every action, and in Saint Columban, whose Rule prescribes saying it three times during the period of silent prayer which follows each psalm of the office.

Such limited and regulated use differs profoundly from the spontaneous and unceasing one advocated by Cassian. The latter did not succeed in convincing latin monks to use the 'God, come to my assistance' in order to pray without ceasing. His praise of that formula simply led to its adoption for much more limited purposes.

The recitation of the verse at the beginning of each office is nonetheless a valuable suggestion. It reminds us that our very prayer is God's work in us. To pray is to address the Father whom the Son reveals to whom he wills, through this same Son known to the Father alone, in the Holy Spirit who makes us cry out 'Abba' and 'Jesus, Lord'. Without the Spirit we do not know how to pray. By asking God's help, we enter the single gateway to prayer: the humble acknowledgment of the mysterious gift upon which everything depends.

> [7] At Terce, Sext and None of the second feria the nine remaining sections of psalm cxviii shall be said, three at each of these same hours. [8] Having thus completed Psalm cxviii in two days, that is on Sunday and the second feria, [9] on the third feria they shall chant three psalms each at terce, sext and none, from the cxix[th] to the cxxvii[th], that is, nine psalms. [10] These psalms shall always be repeated in identical fashion until Sunday at these same hours; a uniform arrangement shall also be maintained every day as regards the hymns, lessons and versicles. [11] And thus on Sunday they will always begin with psalm cxviii.

Like the psalms of Prime, those of the next three hours switch from daily repetition to variety. In the roman office, Psalm 118 was begun at Prime, continued each day at Terce and Sext and concluded at None. Instead of having it recited in one day, Benedict distributes it over two. More-over, on the following days he assigns other psalms (Ps 119–127) drawn from the roman series for Vespers. Though not as varied as that of Prime, the psalmody at Terce, Sext and None is thus much more diverse than in the roman office.

Like the previous paragraph, this one ends by prescrib-ing that on Sunday the cycle must begin again at a definite place in the psalter. Not that Psalm 20 and those which follow are particularly appropriate for Sunday vigils, nor that Psalm 118 is especially suited to that day. These rubrics aim rather at preventing the psalter from being recited over more than a week, as Benedict will state positively at the end of the chapter. It must be begun again every Sunday. Such is the limitation imposed upon variety.

The new psalms of the little hours are the first nine of a series of fifteen (Ps 119–133) uniformly entitled 'Songs of Ascent' (*canticum graduum*). This collection was dear to the Christians of ancient times; they were fond of examining its arrangement, comparing it to the heavenward 'ascent' of our lives. In Rome in particular it played an important role in the liturgical organization and spirituality of Lent. Although Benedict does not seem to pay special attention to this—the nine psalms of Terce, Sext and None are cho-sen because they follow immediately on Psalm 118 and are suited to the little hours because of their brevity—we would do well to remember that these 'gradual psalms', so meaningful in themselves, were laden with the wondrous significance which the old commentators of the psalter discovered in them.

[12] Vespers shall be sung every day by modulating four psalms. [13] These psalms shall begin with the cxi[th] and end with the cxlvii[th], [14] except for those that are set aside for other hours, that is, from the cxvii[th] to the cxxvii[th], as well as the cxxxiii[d] and the cxlii[d]; [15] all the remaining

ones are to be said at Vespers. [16] And since three psalms are missing, those of the above-mentioned series that are longer shall be subdivided, that is, the cxxxviii[th], the cxliii[d] and the cxliv[th]. [17] As for the cxvi[th], since it it short, it will be combined with the cxv[th]. [18] The arrangement of the psalms being thus ordered, everything else, that is, the lesson, the responsory, the hymn, the versicle and the canticle, shall be performed as we have prescribed above.

[19] At compline the same psalms shall be repeated each day, that is, the iv[th], the xc[th] and the cxxxiii[d].

The brevity of Vespers—four psalms—, already noted in the previous chapter, can now be explained: having cut down the roman series (Ps 109–147) by nine units assigned to the little hours, Benedict must reduce the vesperal psalmody. With meticulous care, he very precisely adjusts the available psalms to the offices to be provided for, dividing and combining some of them. We have already come across the division of longer psalms at Prime. As for combining several psalms, the end of Matins provides an example of this and the roman office offered another one at the same hour (Ps 62 and 66).

At Compline, Benedict prescribes the same three psalms as the roman office. Each of them brings out a different aspect of night. These hours of darkness are a time for sleep and rest, but also for 'compunction' and hope (Ps 4); they are also those during which the enemy is most threatening and thus the time when we must take refuge in God (Ps 90). Finally, the last 'song of ascent' (Ps 133) invites us to bless the Lord during the night, to bless the Lord at all times as we shall bless him throughout eternity.

[20] The arrangement of the psalmody during the day being thus organized, all the remaining psalms shall be distributed evenly over the Vigils of the seven nights; [21] the longer psalms shall be divided, and twelve of them assigned to each night.

22 Above all else we give the following warning: if someone does not like this distribution of the psalms, let
him adopt another arrangement, if he deems it better,
23 provided that he maintains by all means the complete
recitation of the hundred and fifty psalms of the Psalter,
always beginning again on Sunday at Vigils, 24 for monks
betray too much laziness in their service of devotion
when they say less than the psalter, together with the
customary canticles, in a week's time, 25 since we read
that our holy Fathers once valiantly performed this in a
single day. Lukewarm as we are, may we at least achieve
it in a whole week!

The roman vigils series included the first one hundred-
eight psalms, except for a dozen assigned to Matins, Prime
and Compline. Notably diminished by new withdrawals in
favor of Matins and Prime, the benedictine series (Ps 20–
108) suffices only thanks to the partitioning of the longer
psalms, since Benedict is absolutely set on maintaining the
sacred number of twelve units of psalmody each night,
as he reminds us one last time in this very section. In
practice, nine psalms must be divided in two in order to
reach the desired total. In contrast to what he did in the
case of Prime and Vespers, when it comes to Vigils Benedict
leaves the choice of the psalms involved up to his reader.
In actual fact, monasteries did not always divide the same
psalms, nor consequently recite exactly the same psalms on
the same days, until the system we know through printed
breviaries was arrived at.

But this small liberty left to the users is a trifle compared
to what Benedict grants them at the conclusion by allowing
the distribution of the psalter which he has so carefully
established to be completely modified. Such breadth of
outlook and such humility have always struck his readers.
They can be explained partly by Benedict's awareness that
he himself had retailored the roman distribution of the
psalms, which, for that matter, was not very old. As yet

devoid in those days of the patina of time, the arrangement of the weekly Psalter seemed fully open to reshaping.

The firmness with which Benedict goes on to demand the recitation of the hundred and fifty psalms in one week becomes then more striking. Because he had himself shortened the roman office, he knew that this same tendency can lead to even greater brevity, and he is intent on imposing an absolute limitation on this sort of development. Here we touch on one of the three inviolable principles of his liturgical legislation, the other two being the celebration of eight daily offices and the recitation of twelve psalms at the night office.

To justify his injunction, Benedict calls on a apophthegm of the desert fathers known as well to his monks as to himself ('we read'). The text involved is a brief story from the systematic greek collection which had just been translated by a roman deacon, the future pope Pelagius I:

> A senior went to see one of the Fathers. The latter cooked a small dish of lentils and said: 'Let us perform the work of God before we eat'. One of them said the whole Psalter, the other recited the two major prophets from memory by way of readings. When morning came, the senior who had come on a visit went off. They had forgotten to take food. (*Vitae Patrum* V.4.57)

This story, as humorous as it is edifying, recounts an uncommon happening which took place once. The daily recitation of the Psalter was not, therefore, a liturgical custom which Benedict deliberately brought down to weekly recitation, as is too often stated. We are dealing here with an occasional feat, legendary at that, which Benedict mentions simply in order to stigmatize the lukewarmness of the monks of his day. Further on, we will see him return to the admirable if inimitable examples of the holy Fathers.

Appealing to a one-time event as a basis for daily observance is not quite convincing. We may also be surprised at seeing lukewarmness and fervor evaluated according to a somewhat material criterion: the number of psalms recited in a given time. But our surprise gives us food for thought about the very down-to-earth nature of the monastic way. As an incarnate form of wisdom, it involves the acceptance of specific norms and clearly defined practices. The total gift of self to God called 'devotion' by ancient writers, which holds the promise of holiness and everlasting life, begins with faithfulness to this humble 'service'.

XIX

Behavior during psalmody

¹ We believe that the divine presence is everywhere and that 'in every place the eyes of the Lord are watching the good and the wicked'. ² However, beyond the least doubt we should believe this to be especially true when we attend the divine office.

³ We must always remember, therefore, what the Prophet says: 'Serve the Lord with fear', ⁴ and again: 'Sing psalms wisely'; ⁵ and: 'In the presence of angels I will sing to you'. ⁶ Let us consider, then, how we ought to behave in the presence of God and his angels, ⁷ and when we stand to sing the psalms, let us see to it that our minds are in harmony with our voices.

THIS BRIEF CHAPTER and the next correspond very exactly to two chapters of the Master's Rule which bear the same titles and are similarly placed at the end of the section on the office (RM 47–48). In the Rule of the Master, both 'psalmody' and 'prayer' are clearly liturgical realities which form a pair: 'prayer' is the silent prayer which follows each psalm in the office. Before concluding his *ordo*, the Master therefore gives spiritual and practical advice on how to perform the two activities which are continuously alternated in the course of the divine office.

In Benedict's text the object of the two chapters is less distinct. With the initial sentence of the first one it is clear that under the word psalmody, which appears alone in the title, the entire divine office is intended. The two terms seem to be synonymous for Benedict: psalmody forms the office, as will be the case in the following centuries up to our own day. Had the prayer after each psalm already disappeared?

This introductory sentence in Benedict has no equivalent in the Master's text. Like the first step of humility in both Rules, one of whose biblical quotations it reproduces (Pr 15:3), it states that God is present everywhere and watches human beings, good or wicked. Faith in this presence and sight, constantly held by monks, reaches its maximum intensity at the time of the office. The work of God thus appears to be the high point of an attention which strives to be constant: 'Pray without ceasing'.

One of the three psalm texts quoted next (Ps 2:11[a]) has its equivalent in the Rule of the Master (Ps 2:11[b]), and the other two (Ps 46:8; 137:1) are found verbatim there. 'Fear' once more recalls the first step of humility. 'Wisdom' or intelligence consists primarily in paying attention to the words of the psalm, and will be expressly recommended at the conclusion. The 'presence (or 'sight') of the angels joins that of God and gives it a kind of metaphorical expression—another echo of the first step.

The conclusion sums up the long exposition found in the other Rule in one succinct sentence. 'Let us be mindful that we are in God's presence', as Cyprian had already remarked at the beginning of his treatise on prayer (*Or. dom.* 4). As for harmony between mind and voice, many christian authors require it in nearly identical terms. This is an arduous ideal which, while demanding mental effort, can only be attained through trusting abandonment to the Holy Spirit, the divine author of the psalms.

XX

Reverence in prayer

[1] If, when we want to present some request to powerful men, we do not dare do so except with humility and reverence, [2] how much the more must we lay our petitions before the Lord God of the universe with utmost humility and very pure devotion! [3] And we must know that we shall be heard because of our purity of heart and tears of compunction, not our many words. [4] Prayer should therefore be short and pure, unless perhaps it happens to be prolonged through the effect of a feeling inspired by grace. [5] In community, however, the time of prayer shall always be very brief, and as soon as the superior has given the signal, all shall rise together.

IN THE RULE of the Master, we recall, the 'prayer' discussed in this chapter is the silent prayer which followed each psalm in the office. Is this also the case in Benedict? A reading of his faithful summary of the Master's text (verses 1–4a) could give that impression. But the two remarks he adds (4b–5) show that he has in mind more broadly all prayer, whether it takes place during the office or outside of it, in community or in private.

Moreover, it is uncertain whether the community prayer which Benedict mentions in closing is, as in the other Rule, prayer after each psalm. He may instead have in mind a prayer which concludes the office, like one mentioned in an episode of his life (*Dial.* II.4). No decisive indications of the existence of prayers after the psalms can be found in his Rule. It can be neither positively asserted nor ruled out.

Whether or not it was present in the benedictine office, prayer following each psalm was in any case an important element of the *opus Dei* as it was understood and experienced everywhere by the first generations of monks. For the ancients, psalmody was less a prayer than an invitation to pray. After hearing God speak in the psalm, they answered him in prayer. Psalmody and prayer were the two stages of a dialogue which continued outside the offices in other forms—reading and prayer, 'meditation' on Scripture and prayer—so that the monk's entire life is unified in this unceasing rhythm of listening and answering, of hearing the divine word and praying.

Benedict's first sentence, an exact copy of the Master's, develops a line of reasoning which can also be found in Basil, Cassian, and many others. In this classic analogy, God appears as the 'Lord God of the universe' (Est 13:11) who can be addressed only with unspeakable respect. To the 'humility' mentioned by the Master, Benedict adds 'purity' and 'devotion'; here as before (18:24), this second term refers not to the sentimental piety it calls to mind today, but to the gift of one's whole self to God.

Contrasted with the profusion of words frowned on by the Gospel (Mt 6:7), 'purity' appears in the following sentence. This 'purity of heart' (Mt 5:8), like the 'tears of compunction' which accompany it, is another expression unique to Benedict. No such expressions are to be found in the Rule of the Master; they remind us of Cassian, whose teaching on prayer Benedict has assimilated. Under this same influence, in the next sentence he again adds 'pure' to 'brief'—the only word he found in the Master. This triple call for purity is impressive. It indicates a firm belief and a deep conviction: what God asks of us is pure prayer springing from a pure heart. We see how where the conclusion of the great chapter on humility was aiming, when the Master and Benedict wanted to see the monk 'purified of vices and sins'.

Along with purity of heart, Benedict requires tears of compunction. Tears recur in all his descriptions of prayer, whether in the tools for good works (4:57) or in the chapters on Lent and the oratory (49:4; 52:4). There again we sense a well-defined teaching derived as much from experience as from reading: Benedict, according to his biographer, usually wept when he prayed (*Dial.* II.17.1). Tears are in fact the sign that the heart is touched, and that is precisely the meaning of the word 'compunction' used here and in the chapter on Lent. Prayer with tears reaches God because it springs from a heart touched by the word of God.

This compunction experienced by the one praying has as its prime motive the consciousness of being a sinner, the pain caused by the loss of salvation. We entreat primarily 'for our sins': this is explicit in the Rule of the Master and implicit in Benedict's. But there is another, higher compunction, which springs from the desire for everlasting realities. It also leads to tears, not of pain owing to the loss of salvation, but of joy because of salvation regained. Cassian had described it before Benedict (*Conf.* 9.29.2). After him, Gregory was to speak of it magnificently (*Dial.* III.34).

In conclusion, Benedict adds two remarks concerning the brevity of prayer. The evangelical condemnation of long-windedness does not prevent us from praying more at length, without many words, if we are so impelled by divine grace. On this point Benedict follows Saint Augustine (*Ep.* 130.20), whose justification of prolonged prayer did not, however, mention the action of grace.

As for community prayer, the end-signal given by the superior is an old cenobitic custom, which the Rule of Pachomius (*Praec.* 6) and Cassian (*Inst.* 2.7) speak of in nearly identical terms. Like his two forerunners, Benedict asks that 'all rise together'. In Pachomius' text the prayer which ends this way is connected with the recitation of scriptural passages drawn from the psalter or from other books. In Cassian's it follows each psalm of the office. Might this also be the case in the Rule of Saint Benedict?

XXI

The deans of the monastery

HAVING REGULATED the divine office as a matter of priority, Benedict here reverts to the Master's subject order. The earlier Rule dealt with the deans, called 'provosts', immediately after the chapter on humility. In his view, spiritual teaching is the abbot's business, and the implementation of that doctrine falls to the deans, whose job it is to repeat what the Rule says to their subordinates and to see to their compliance.

'Dean' is a translation of *decanus*, which means the leader of ten men. The term is both military and biblical. The roman legions were divided into centuries and decuries, commanded respectively by centurions and by decurions, or deans. On their departure from Egypt Moses divided the people of Israel into groups of a thousand, a hundred, fifty, and ten (Ex 18:21–25; Dt 1:13–15), with leaders to whom the latin Vulgate naturally gave the names of the corresponding roman officers. This organization of Israel in the desert served as a model for the egyptian cenobites described by Jerome and Cassian. Those large communities had had their 'deans' and groups of ten. The Master in turn divided his small communities into groups of ten. This decimal organization is a characteristic feature of egyptian cenobitism and of the forms of monasticism deriving from it. It is found neither in Cappadocia (Saint Basil) nor in Africa (Saint Augustine).

> [1] If the community is rather large, some brothers of good repute and holy life shall be chosen among them and appointed deans, [2] so that they may watch over their groups of ten in all affairs according to the command-ments of God and the orders of their abbot. [3] These deans are to be chosen in such a way that the abbot may securely share his burden with them. [4] And they are not to be chosen according to seniority, but according to the merit of their life and the wisdom of their teaching.
>
> [5] As for these deans, if perhaps one of them, coming to be puffed up with any pride, showed himself deserving of censure, and if, after having been reproved one, two, three times, he refused to amend, he shall be removed from office [6] and someone who is worthy shall take his place. [7] We prescribe the same course of action with regard to the provost as well.

The Master set forth at length the reasons for instituting 'provosts', the criteria for choosing them, the ritual of their taking office, and especially the manner in which they were to perform their role as tutors and supervisors. The brief benedictine chapter—it is fifteen times shorter—deals almost solely with one of these points: the choice of the deans; and adds a possibility not considered by the other Rule: the removal of an unworthy dean.

Benedict's expressions show that he has biblical mod-els in mind. 'Good repute' was one of the criteria set by the apostles for the choice of the first deacons (Ac 6:3). The criterion regarding their 'life' recalls the nomination of Moses' helpers. The phrase 'appointed deans' comes from the same passage of Deuteronomy, as does the men-tion of the 'wisdom' required of them for 'teaching' pur-poses, while the parallel passage of Exodus speaks of their 'choice', which allows the supreme leader to 'share his burden'.

The monastic community is thus analogous to the people of God of both Covenants. It is headed by the abbot, who as a new Moses is responsible for leading his brothers out of the Egypt of sin towards the Promised Land. Abbots also carry on the office of the apostles. Along with their helpers, the deans and cellarers, they form a hierarchy parallel to that of the shepherds and ministers of the Church, bishops, priests and deacons.

Benedict rejects the criterion of seniority and indicates two others: a worthy life, and teaching which bears the stamp of wisdom. The same guidelines will be given for the choice of the abbot (64:2). First of all, the candidate's life must be 'meritorious' or 'holy'. Just as Jesus 'acted' before 'teaching' (Ac 1:1), so the behavior of monastic officers comes before their words. The expression 'teaching of wisdom' which characterizes the latter had already been used four times by Saint Augustine in his fine commentary on the loves of Jacob, in connection with the contemplative life. The contemplative, who is responsible for instructing his brothers, must put at their service the wisdom he loves above all (*C. Faust.* 22.52–58).

The Master did not foresee that his 'provosts' might lapse. Benedict, who was less of a theoretician and more experienced, considered the possibility and so anticipates the penal code he will soon map out. The 'provost', to whom he applies the same sanctions as he does to the deans, is no longer the mere head of a group as in the Rule of the Master, but the abbot's second-in-command for the entire community, the person we call 'prior'.

'To become puffed up with pride' (1 Tm 3:6): there is the risk run by a brother who is set above others. For a monk dedicated to humility, this is a mortal danger. While in the body of Christ the greatest must be the humblest, nowhere is this law more imperative than in the monastery.

XXII

How the monks are to sleep

IN THE RULE of the Master the matter of the brothers' sleep was connected with the question of the group leaders, who were responsible for supervising their men by night as by day. Beds, night hours, and rising were dealt with in a long appendix to the chapter on 'provosts'. Like his forerunner, Benedict legislates concerning the dormitory immediately after discussing deans, but he separates the two matters more clearly. As already in the case of the council of the brothers, which he separated from that of the abbot, he makes the Master's appendix into a distinct chapter.

[1] Each shall have a bed to sleep in. [2] The abbot shall see to it that they receive bedding suited to their personal asceticism.

[3] If possible, all are to sleep in one room. Should their number preclude this, they will sleep in groups of ten or twenty with their seniors, who shall watch over them. [4] A lamp must burn constantly in the room until morning.

[5] They shall sleep clothed and girded with belts or cords, so as not to have knives at their sides while sleeping, lest the sleeper be hurt in his sleep, [6] and so that the monks will always be ready and that when the signal

is given they will rise without delay, each hastening to arrive at the work of God before the others, yet with all seriousness and decorum. [7] The adolescent brothers shall not have their beds next to each other, but interspersed among those of the seniors. [8] On arising for the work of God they will quietly exhort each other, on account of the excuses of the sleepy.

Individual beds were not self-evident in the ancient world, not even in monastic circles, as is evidenced by the gallic rules of Ferreolus and Walbertus. As for sleeping fully clothed, this was something peculiar to monks. In reproducing what the Master prescribes on both these matters, Benedict does not omit his recommendation concerning belts, but abridges it to the point of rendering it somewhat unclear. Both authors had in mind heavy belts equipped with sheaths containing knives. Worn during the day, such articles of clothing must not be used by night for fear of accidents.

Nor was sleeping in a dormitory a universal custom in monasteries. This new arrangement had been adopted by certain communities in Gaul, Italy, and Constantinople in the Master's day, shortly before Saint Benedict. Originally, cenobites slept in individual cells. This solitary housing, sometimes mitigated by the presence of one or two companions, was a remnant of primitive anchoritism. Though gathered in communities, the monks preserved a dimension of solitude which could go as far as a ban on leaving their cells during most of the day, as in the case of the egyptian cenobites described by Saint Jerome.

The grouping of monks into dormitories, which began in the early sixth century, was intended to remedy certain disadvantages of the cell, particularly in the area of poverty and morals. The reform was useful, not to say necessary, but it did sacrifice the values of recollection, watchfulness over one's own behavior, and prayer attached to the cell.

Hierarchical and mutual supervision was to replace God's sight.

A constantly burning lamp, sleepers who keep their belts on, always ready to spring from their beds: this picture calls to mind the parables of Christ's return (Lk 12:35–40; cf. Mt 25:1–13). Each signal heralding the nocturnal office is like the sound of the master knocking at the door, like the cry ringing out in the middle of the night: 'The bridegroom is coming, go out to meet him'. Each awakening is an encounter with the Lord, a sign of the Parousia.

Framing this central scene reminiscent of the Gospel, a few touches shed light on the meaning of community life. At the beginning, Benedict speaks of bedding that varies according to the way of life (*conuersatio*) of each individual. Thus the common life does not prevent each monk from practising personal asceticism with his abbot's assistance, according to the grace he has received, his needs, his capacity. Augustine's Rule had already provided for differences between the brothers, not only in food and clothing but also in bedding and blankets (*Praec.* III.4).

At the other end of the chapter, on the contrary, Benedict emphasizes community relations. On rising, each monk tries to outstrip the others by arriving more quickly at the office. What is more, in spite of the night silence which a later chapter will impose, the brothers encourage one another to get up without delay. This eagerness must, however, avoid unruliness. To rule out the latter, the younger brethren have their beds not next to each other, but interspersed with those of the seniors. All these details come under one and the same educational method, careful to make the most of the resources of fraternal life. The Master thought only in terms of supervision on the part of superiors. To this, Benedict adds mutual relations among brothers.

XXIII

Excommunication for faults

BENEDICT NOW goes into a series of eight chapters devoted to the repression of offences. Like the paragraph on the dormitory, the penal code is related to the chapter on deans, here called 'seniors'. Strongly marked in the Master, this connection is slightly blurred by Benedict, but it remains apparent: it is the group leaders who take note of the offences of their men and level the first warnings at them.

> [1] If a brother is found to be stubborn or disobedient or proud, if he grumbles or in any way goes against the holy rule or the orders of his seniors, with a show of contempt, [2] his seniors shall warn him privately, first once and then a second time, according to our Lord's command. [3] If he does not amend, he must be rebuked publicly in the presence of everyone. [4] If even then he does not reform, let him be excommunicated, provided that he understands the nature of this punishment. [5] But if he is a nasty sort, let him be subjected to corporal punishment.

Benedict's text closely follows a brief chapter of the Master's which is hardly longer (RM 12), and likewise refers to the Gospel. When a Christian is injured by one of his brothers, he first remonstrates with him face to face, then before one or two witnesses, then before the Church community. If the culprit refuses to listen to the community, he is rejected from its midst like a public sinner and a pagan (Mt 18:15–17).

This procedure is applied to the monastery with a few adjustments. The initiative is no longer taken by an individual but by the seniors who are responsible for the offender (like the Master, Benedict probably has in mind two deans for every group of ten). That being the case, no witnesses are needed: the second warning does no more than repeat the first. Moreover, rejection from the community is not the only penalty contemplated: excommunication may be replaced by corporal punishment.

Compared to the Master, who implemented the Gospel in a slightly different way, Benedict is set off first in that he reduces the deans' role and brings in the Rule. After three warnings, the Master's 'provosts' were to denounce the culprit to the abbot. This step is omitted by Benedict. On the contrary, he adds a mention of the Rule. Offences, therefore, no longer consist only in disobeying one's superiors, but also and primarily in violating this 'holy Rule'. Thus we encounter once more, with a change as to the identity of the superiors, the pair found in the definition of cenobites (1:2): 'rule and abbot', law and leader.

Another innovation on Benedict's part is the final distinction between those who understand and those who do not. Like the Gospel, the Master here inflicted no penalty other than excommunication. Prompted by a concern we have already encountered in the treatise on the abbot (2:27–29), Benedict shows solicitude for the less intelligent and provides appropriate punishments for them. Throughout this section, he shows a keen educational and pastoral sense, multiplying his efforts to amend offenders. In the case at hand, he goes beyond the letter of the Gospel; love of the lost sheep, which is its soul, motivates this search for treatments capable of procuring the salvation of sinners. The Church and the monastery itself are full of the sinners. We all belong to their number, and Church and monastery must make the mercy of God available to all, according to each one's frame of mind.

XXIV

What the degree of excommunication is to be

[1] The degree of excommunication or punishment must be measured according to the seriousness of the fault. [2] This seriousness of faults is left up to the abbot's judgment.

[3] However, if a brother is found guilty of lesser faults, he will be deprived of participating in the common table. [4] Anyone deprived of the common table shall be treated as follows: in the oratory he will not lead a psalm or antiphon, nor will he recite a lesson until he has made satisfaction. [5] As for the food which makes up his meal, he will take it alone, after the brothers' meal: [6] for instance, if the brothers have their meal at the sixth hour, this brother shall have his at None; if the brothers have it at None, he shall have it at Vespers, [7] until he gains pardon by proper satisfaction.

MONASTIC PENANCE is closely modeled on the canonical penance of the Church during the early centuries, and its roots can be found in the New Testament. This system of public penance was already in a state of crisis in Benedict's time; it was replaced shortly afterwards by private confession, which had originated in Ireland and has survived in the Church up to our day. Just as by the ancient penitential discipline the Christian guilty of a serious offence was excluded from the assembly of the faithful and had to gain readmittance by submitting to practices imposed on him by the bishop, likewise the monk at fault, after being sentenced by the abbot, was excluded from the community until he had 'made satisfaction'. But in the monastery everything is reduced to a very small scale: the offences are much less serious, and the penalties are accordingly less stringent and, especially, of much shorter duration.

According to Cassian, the egyptian cenobites knew only one form of excommunication: exclusion from common prayer. When he began to legislate, the Master no doubt had in mind only this excommunication properly so called, which in his Rule implied the total isolation of the transgressor. Experience led him, however, to allow mitigations on account of the differences between offences. In his groping and somewhat confused legislation, we see, in addition to total separation, the gradual emergence of a minor form of excommunication in which the guilty brother is only deprived of the common meal and barred from all active participation in the office.

Benedict, who benefitted from the Master's searching, establishes at the outset a clear and consistent system based on the distinction between the two forms of excommunication. Here we see him begin with the lighter form. The excommunicated monk is not absent from common prayer, but he may not let his voice be heard there: in those days the psalms, whether they were accompanied by antiphons or not, were said by soloists, and he may not 'lead' (sing) any, or recite any lessons. As for his meal, he takes it alone, three hours after the community.

Offence and forgiveness. These two words with which the chapter begins and ends are like a summary of the spiritual adventure of humankind, from Adam's transgression to the remission of sins in Christ. After baptism, even after profession, the excommunicated monk retravels this path of pain and grace. His penance in the eyes of all is an image of the fate of all and of God's inexhaustible goodness.

XXV

Serious faults

[1] As for the brother guilty of a serious fault, he is to be excluded both from the table and the oratory. [2] No brother shall associate or converse with him at all. [3] He will work alone at the tasks assigned to him, persisting in the sorrow of penance, aware of that fearful judgment of the Apostle: [4] 'Such a man has been handed over for the destruction of his flesh, that his spirit may be saved on the day of the Lord'. [5] As for the food making up his meal, he is to take it alone, in an amount and at a time the abbot considers appropriate for him. [6] No one passing by shall bless him, nor the food that is given him.

IN DEALING with major excommunication, Benedict seems to remember not only the Master but also Cassian, who was acquainted only with this form of exclusion, which he calls 'suspension from prayer' (*Inst.* 2.16). The *Institutes* had quoted the words of the Apostle in this connection: 'Let such a man be handed over to Satan' (1 Co 5:5). While reproducing the quotation more fully, Benedict omits 'to Satan', either in order to mitigate the horror of this 'fearful judgment' or, more probably, because like other latin authors he did not find those words in the version of the New Testament available to him.

This reference to the pauline corpus is neither the first nor the last to be observed in the penal code of the Rule. Earlier, in prescribing that the transgressor be 'rebuked in the presence of everyone' (23:3), Benedict had already echoed a sentence from the Apostle (1 Tm 5:20) which he will quote explicitly in other sections of his work, as we shall see. In the chapters following this one, we will find other pauline reminiscences. These borrowings from Saint Paul, particularly from the passages concerning the excommunicated Corinthian, are among the personal touches with which Benedict enriches his summary of the Master in the course of this section. The Gospel, which is the starting point of both Rules, is thus completed in ours by the Apostle.

Another scriptural reminiscence surfaces in the last sentence of this chapter, but this time it comes from the Master and refers us back to the Old Testament. Both our authors obviously have in mind the Psalmist's curse: 'And those passing by did not say: "The Lord's blessing be upon you! We bless you in the name of the Lord"' (Ps 128:8). Asking and giving a blessing is a rite which the brothers are instructed to perform when they meet (63:15): the junior asks it (*Benedic*, 'bless me'), the senior gives it (*Deus*, 'May God bless us!'). Made trite by use, these sacred words take on their full weight and value when banned by excommunication. We perceive then what a blessing words exchanged between servants of God truly are.

More broadly, the entire treatment inflicted on the excommunicated monk brings out the grace of common life. In the eyes of Saint Paul and of his correspondents, the believer who was excluded from the christian community fell back into a world ruled by Satan. The torments which the devil would not fail to inflict on the wayward sheep would, it was hoped, be a lesson that would bring him back into the fold and ensure his salvation on judgment day. So it is for the monk who is made an outlaw in his monastery. Like the Church community of which it is a part, the monastic community defends its members against the devil. To separate oneself from it is to fall into Satan's clutches.

XXVI

Those who associate with the excommunicated without permission

[1] If a brother, without the abbot's permission, presumes
to associate with an excommunicated brother in any way
or to speak to him or to send him a message, [2] he shall
undergo a like penalty of excommunication.

BENEDICT HAS ALREADY carved two chapters from the
one which the Master devoted to the fate of the excommunicated. Here is a third, remarkably brief, which merely
sums up a paragraph three times its length in the other
Rule (RM 13:54–59). Benedict's only innovation is the clause
'without the abbot's permission', which excepts the case of
brothers sent to the excommunicated monk to urge him to
repent (27:2).

Like anathema in the Old Testament, excommunication
spreads by contagion: coming into contact with the person
under it entails shrouding oneself in it. But we are not
dealing with a blind law. Obvious reasons demand such
strictness. As Cassian had already explained (*Inst.* 2.16),
breaking the excommunicated monk's isolation robs his
punishment of effectiveness and causes the effort undertaken with a view to his salvation to fail. Love must be

enlightened by discernment. True charity consists not in rescuing the unfortunate brother from his solitude, but in leaving him to it.

XXVII

How the abbot must show concern for the excommunicated

[1] The abbot shall take care of wayward brothers with the utmost concern, for 'it is not the healthy who need a physician, but the sick'. [2] Therefore he must use every skill like a wise physician: send *senpectas*, that is, wise senior brothers, [3] who, as though under the cloak of secrecy, shall console the wavering brother and urge him to make satisfaction humbly and 'console him lest he be overwhelmed by excessive sorrow', [4] but as the Apostle also says: 'Let love for him be reaffirmed', and let all pray for him.

[5] Indeed, the abbot must have the utmost concern and act with all speed, wisdom and diligence in order not to lose any of the sheep entrusted to him. [6] For he must know that he has received the care of sick souls, not tyrannical power over healthy ones. [7] And let him fear the threat of the Prophet in which God says: 'What you saw to be fat you claimed for yourselves, and what was weak you cast aside'. [8] And let him imitate the loving example of the good shepherd who, leaving ninety-nine sheep in the mountains, went off in search of the one who had strayed; [9] so great was his compassion for its weakness that he deigned to put it on his sacred shoulders and thus carry it back to the flock.

THE EXCOMMUNICATED monk had to beg forgiveness in the Rule of the Master by reminding the abbot of the example of Christ, the physician who had come not for the healthy but for the sick (Mt 9:12), the good shepherd (Jn 10:11) who left his flock on the mountain to search for the lost sheep (Mt 18:12; cf. Lk 15:4). Like Christ, moreover, the penitent was to say: the shepherd of the monastery must carry the wayward on his shoulders (Lk 15:5).

The Master had the excommunicated monk issue this appeal to the abbot (RM 14:1–19); Benedict addresses it to him in the name of the Rule itself. The objective is no longer, as in the other legislation, to bring the superior to forgive the culprit and reintegrate him into the community by means of a touching ceremony of reconciliation. Benedict asks the abbot to imitate Christ by devoting all his efforts to the conversion of the sinner. The Master's text presupposed the transgressor's repentance. Benedict has the opposite case in mind: a brother who does not want to give in, or at least 'hesitates' to do so.

Thus a new situation and a new kind of pastoral care appear in this chapter, one of the most remarkable in the Rule. It reflects Benedict's realism and his love for sinners. Experience had taught him that many of those excommunicated take a long time to repent. Instead of driving them away after three days as incorrigible, as the Master prescribes (RM 13:68–73), he sets his heart on curing them.

So now the abbot turns physician. The treatment he is told to apply could already be glimpsed at in the previous chapter: sending the recalcitrant monk some brothers able to bend him by good advice. These wise senior brothers are called *senpectas*; the meaning of the word is uncertain. Some believe it was a medical term ('mustard plasters, poultices'). We are more likely dealing with a greek word meaning 'playmate' (*sympaictes*): without stating the mission they have received from the superior, these accomplices come 'as though under the cloak of secrecy', after the fashion of consolers, and, without seeming to do so, deftly advise him to submit. By playing the abbot's game in this way, they bring the obstinate monk to humble himself and make satisfaction. The *Lives* of Saint Pachomius report that his disciple Theodore played this role of mediator between the superior and an oft-rebuked brother who wanted to leave (*SBo* 62; G¹ 66).

These helpful brothers are called 'senior' and 'wise' (*seniores sapientes*) because of the assonance between these words and *senpectas*. As for their task as 'consolers', it was suggested to Benedict by Saint Paul, who did not want the sinner of Corinth to be overcome by sorrow and asked that charity towards him be redoubled (2 Co 2:7–8). The 'prayer of all for him' which Benedict adds here heralds what will be prescribed in the following chapter.

Two images overlap in the last paragraph: the sick soul and the lost sheep. But the first, which recalls the beginning of the chapter, is much less elaborated than the second. In connection with the latter, the pastoral figures of the Gospels are introduced by a passage from the Old Testament, quoted, to be sure, with exceeding freedom (Ez 34:3–4). The Good Shepherd of the New Covenant whose coming Ezechiel had predicted contrasts with the wicked herders of Israel blamed by that same prophet: in the person of Christ, God himself has come to shepherd his people.

The abbot must make himself an instrument of this continuing mystery of salvation. For him as for Christ, placing the sheep on his shoulders is no more than an image, but very genuine 'compassion for its weakness' is required of him, that he may imitate Christ (Heb 4:15). This fine exhortation recalls and rounds off the abbot's directory, in which Benedict has already insisted so much on the care of souls, especially of those lacking in flexibility and intelligence. The monastery is not a select circle for the elite, but an infirmary where God lovingly looks after the wounded.

XXVIII

Those who refuse to amend after frequent reproofs

[1] If a brother has been reproved frequently for any fault, if even after being excommunicated he does not amend, let him receive a sharper punishment, that is, let him be subjected to the penalty of the rod. [2] If he does not reform by this means or even, which God forbid, he is carried away by pride and would defend his conduct, then the abbot shall act as a wise physician: [3] if he has in turn applied poultices, the ointment of encouragement, the medicine of divine Scripture, and finally the cauterizing iron of excommunication and strokes of the rod, [4] and if he perceives that his efforts can no longer be of any avail, he shall yet resort to an even better remedy: his prayer for him and that of all the brothers, [5] so that the Lord, who can do all things, may bring health to this sick brother. [6] If even thus he is not healed, then the abbot shall take the knife so as to amputate, as the Apostle says: 'Banish the evil one from your midst'; [7] and again: 'If the unbeliever departs, let him depart', [8] lest one diseased sheep infect the whole flock.

THE SINNER'S STORY goes on. The case considered here is that of subsequent offence: after being excommunicated, the culprit lapses back into his misdeed. In his stubborn

166

desire to save him, Benedict arranges for him two new means of salvation: the rod and common prayer. After that nothing remains but to expel him.

This hypothesis of recurrent offence, for which the Master made no provision, affords Benedict a new opportunity of showing his love for souls. In the other Rule, the rod was a vindictive penalty inflicted before eviction. In his, it becomes a medicinal penalty by means of which the abbot hopes still to save the culprit. The same is true of eviction. The Master presents it as a punishment for pride. Benedict makes it into a remedy, if not for the scabious sheep, at least for the flock which runs the risk of infection (cf. Mt 5:30).

The previous chapter contained two metaphors: the sick man and the wayward sheep. The second appeared only at the end of the chapter, merged with the first in the image of the 'diseased sheep'. The rest of the chapter is entirely medical. This identification of the care of souls with medical science is common practice, but Benedict seems to be remembering especially a page from Origen (*Hom. on Joshua* 7.6). As for the scriptural substratum, it is not limited to the two final quotations (1 Co 5:13 and 7:15). Earlier, 'carried away by pride' is also a pauline expression (1 Tm 3:6), and the hope of 'salvation' placed in 'God who can do all things' brings Christ's words to mind (Mk 10:26–27; cf. Lk 1:36).

Trust in God's omnipotence, belief that prayer, individual and collective, is a means 'better' than all others: these traits spring from a spirit of faith which Benedict also evinces elsewhere. The 'prayer of all' has already been asked on behalf of the unrepentant brother. It now comes to the aid of the relapsed offender. The Master was not unacquainted with this way of helping brothers in difficulty, but he prescribed it on occasions of a different sort: the reconciliation of a penitent and efforts at relieving a brother assailed by temptation.

Although the two scriptural maxims at the end are drawn from the same pauline letter and from nearby chapters, they relate to distinct matters. 'Banish the evil one from your midst' is quoted by Saint Paul from the Old Testament (Dt 13:5) in order to justify, as in the Rule of Saint Benedict, the exclusion of an unrepentant major sinner. The Rule has already made use several times of passages from the Letters to the Corinthians concerning this matter. Benedict applies these texts now to excommunication, now—as here—to eviction. The Church community has only the first of these two sanctions at its disposal. The monastery, on account of the more intense community life led within it, can inflict both.

'If the unbeliever departs, let him depart'. This second maxim of the Apostle has nothing to do with the excommunicated Corinthian. It deals with the non-believer, man or woman, who separates from his christian spouse. The term 'unbeliever', originally aimed at absence of faith in Christ, refers in its monastic application to lack of faithfulness to the call of Christ. Faith and faithfulness: two forms of the same love for one and the same person.

XXIX

Whether brothers who leave the monastery are to be readmitted

[1] If a brother who has left the monastery through his own fault wishes to return, he must first promise to make full amends for the failing which caused his departure, [2] and he shall then be received in the last place, as a test of his humility. [3] If he leaves again, he shall be received likewise up to three times, knowing that after this he will be denied all permission to return.

THE PROBLEM of the readmission of monks who had left was not part of the penal code in the Rule of the Master. The case of renegades was considered in passing in another section of the Rule, in connection with going out and with travelling (RM 64). The question that worried the Master was: how many times should the brother who has left be readmitted? Referring to the Gospel (Mt 18:15–17), he answered: as many as three times. The principle calling for three warnings—face to face, before witnesses, in the presence of the Church—thus was given a new application: there are as many chances of reinstatement offered a renegade before final eviction as there are chances of amendment offered a transgressor prior to excommunication.

Benedict places this little chapter—which is almost as long in his Rule as in the Master's—at the end of his penal code because he is set on dealing fully with the fate of sinful monks who matter so much to him. In his text, the renegade (the monk who abandons religious life) appears to be the expelled brother of whom he has just spoken. Everything possible and impossible seems to have been done to save this obstinate sinner. But after leaving, he can return. Benedict thus resumes his pastoral efforts. The question of the number of readmissions shifts to the background. In closing, he will settle it with a single word, omitting all the Master's justifications. His foremost concern is with re-educating the culprit, and with a view to this he takes two steps which are missing from the other Rule: a promise of amendment will be demanded of the man, and he will be assigned the last place.

This chapter thus provides new and remarkable evidence of the pastoral concern which runs through the entire benedictine code. The case of the renegade monk, which the Master had settled in a legal way with a view to good order, is dealt with here in an educational perspective with a view to the salvation of souls. The amendment of vice which the readmitted brother must promise is the constant purpose of the penal code, indeed of the whole Rule. Humility, which is tested by assigning the man the last place, is the decisive point in this pastoral care of sinners as well as in the Rule's entire educational method: earlier, Benedict had already seen savation in 'humble satisfaction', and the height of evil in being 'carried away by pride'. Even setting the number of returns takes on educational significance in Benedict's text: *knowing* that he will not be readmitted again, the brother will be more careful.

In prescribing that the returning monk not be given the rank of his profession, Benedict may be remembering an article from the pachomian Rule (*Praec.* 136). But most of all he is being faithful to his habit of using community rank for spiritual purposes. The Master's community entailed no fixed rank. Benedict's, on the contrary, is ordered according to seniority. The legislator is quite set on this and sometimes takes advantage of it for the good of souls, as we see here.

In restricting the number of returns to three, is the Rule not forgetting that one must forgive one's brother seventy times seven times, that is, indefinitely? Benedict provides no explanation, but we know from the Master that his limitation is no mere rule of human prudence designed to protect the community from being chronically troubled. Suggested as it is by the words of the Gospel, this measure attempts to solve the problem according to Christ's will. Explicitly in most cases, or implicitly as here, the Rule is always set on taking as its foundation the word of God.

XXX

Young children: How they are to be reproved

[1] Every age and level of understanding must receive appropriate treatment. [2] Therefore, as often as children and adolescents in age, or adults who cannot understand what the penalty of excommunication is, [3] whenever they are guilty of a misdeed, they shall be subjected to severe fasts or sharply punished with the rod, so that they may be healed.

COMING BACK to the Master's penal code, Benedict ends with the correction of children. With his usual exactitude, the Master set the age limit at fifteen: the rod was to be resorted to before and after excommunication, since the significance of that spiritual penalty became understandable at that age (RM 14:79–87). Benedict, on the other hand, is careful not to be too exact. He ranks adolescents with children and adds unintelligent adults to these two age groups. From the very beginning of the penal code (23:4–5), we have seen his concern with adapting the penalty to the person's understanding, reserving excommunication to those able to grasp its significance.

Ranking less gifted adults with children like this is something new. At the end of his paragraph on those under fifteen the Master had also contemplated thrashing older culprits, but for another reason: the enormity of such misdeeds as stealing. The practice of punishing very serious offences with corporal chastisement, regarded as harsher than excommunication, was already in force in the monasteries of Egypt, according to Cassian (*Inst.* 4.16.3). Benedict replaces this objective reason—the seriousness of the misdeed—with a subjective criterion: the inability to understand spiritual penalties. Adults are thrashed no longer for scandalous offences, but on account of their lack of intelligence. The point is no longer to suit the punishment to the crime, but to adjust it to the person. We recognize here the educator, mindful of the nature of his charges and concerned with the effectiveness of correction, who had already emerged in the preceding chapter.

The mention of fasts is also a novelty, compared either with the Master or with what Benedict himself had said at the beginning of the penal code (23:5). But fasting has already been combined with thrashing under the term 'corporal punishment' in the parallel passage of the treatise on the abbot (2:28). Besides, these practical details matter less than the intention so clearly stated in the last words: 'so that they may be healed'—a superb conclusion to a series of chapters which truly exhibits no other aim than to heal.

XXXI

The monastery cellarer: What he must be

FOLLOWING THE DISCIPLINARY section, which is linked to the chapter on deans, Benedict, like his forerunner, places directories for the monks responsible for the cellar and tools. In the eyes of the Master, these officers in charge of material affairs were far from being endowed with the same dignity as the leaders of groups of ten, who were the abbot's assistants in the educational task around which community life was polarized. Conversely, in Benedict's view the deans seem much less important than the cellarer. The brief, perfunctory chapter on the deans is here followed by the remarkably long, insistent and substantial chapter regulating the conduct of the cellarer.

This reversal of proportion is due primarily to Benedict's novel interest in fraternal relationships. Absorbed as he was by his educational concerns, the Master was interested solely, on the spiritual plane, in the hierarchical action of the abbot, the teacher in the school of the Lord, and of his tutor-supervisors, the leaders of groups of ten. In contrast to these, the cellarer was no more in his view than a brother among others, in charge of a purely material job—fraught though it was with religious responsibility on account of the divine origin of the food entrusted to him—, a job whose practical details he contented himself with minutely regulating.

For Benedict, on the contrary, this officer has a key role in an area barely considered by the Master, but essential in his eyes: fraternal relationships. The cellarer's importance derives from the fact that he controls the monks' food, that is, their prime need as living creatures. Benedict has thus made him the prototype of what all the members of the community entrusted with some duty must be—their brothers' servants. The directory he outlines here for the cellarer is neither shorter nor less pressing than the one he will draw up at the end of his Rule (64:17–22) for the abbot himself. For that matter, these two passages have many common traits.

[1] As cellarer of the monastery a member of the community shall be chosen who is wise, mature in conduct, temperate, not an excessive eater, not arrogant, excitable, offensive, dilatory or wasteful, [2] but God-fearing; he shall be like a father to the whole community. [3] He will take care of everyone, [4] he will do nothing without an order from the abbot; [5] he will keep what he has been ordered; [6] he shall not give the brothers cause for sadness. [7] If a brother should present him with an unreasonable request, he shall not give him cause for sadness by rejecting him with contempt, but he shall humbly answer the improper request with a reasonable refusal. [8] Let him keep watch over his own soul, ever mindful of that saying of the Apostle: 'He who serves well secures a good standing for himself'. [9] He must show every care and concern for the sick, children, guests and the poor, knowing for certain that he will be held accountable for all of them on the day of judgment. [10] He will regard all vessels and goods of the monastery as sacred vessels of the altar; [11] he shall not consider anything to be negligible. [12] He shall not give in to avarice, nor be extravagant or wasteful with the goods of the

monastery, but he shall do everything with moderation and according to the abbot's orders.

The portrait of the cellarer begins with a long list of qualities which recalls the descriptions of the bishop and deacon in the Pastoral Letters. The Master, who dealt with the choice of the cellarer and the necessary qualities at the other end of the chapter (RM 16:62–66), contented himself with requiring that he be able to overcome his appetites, to avoid his taking advantage of his position to allot himself extra food and drink. The same concern filters through in two of Benedict's epithets ('temperate, not an excessive eater'), but the rest of the list has different overtones.

Two traits, which we will come across again in the portrait of the abbot (64:9 and 16), call to mind biblical models: 'not excitable' reminds us of the Servant of the Lord in Isaiah (Is 42:4), and 'temperance' was required of the bishop by Saint Paul (Tt 1:8). Similar to the porter by his 'wisdom' and 'maturity', the cellarer must possess several virtues essential in a life of relationships where arrogance, excitability, and insults are intolerable. Moderation will lead him to avoid the opposite excesses of delay and wastefulness in handing out goods. But the importance of this list of three positive and six negative qualities lies especially in its conclusion, which sums up the essentials of Benedict's requirements in an expression dear to him: the fear of God.

By putting the cellarer in a class with the abbot, 'to be like a father to the whole community', likens him to a character from the Old Testament in whom the Advent liturgy sees a figure of Christ: Eliakim, the provost of the Temple (Is 22:21). According to the Master, and Benedict for that matter, the abbot is given the title father because he is Christ's representative. Just as Christ is present in each of our destitute brothers, he is also represented by each of those who mercifully provide for the needs of others.

Together with obedience to the abbot, which opens and closes the next series of instructions, we must first and foremost note among them the religious significance which Benedict acknowledges in all of the cellarer's activity. By applying Saint Paul's phrase concerning deacons to him (1 Tm 3:13), he already insinuates the sacred nature of his task. This is asserted with full clarity when, following a comparison already present in Scripture (Zch 14:20) and dear to monastic tradition (Basil, Cassian, the Four Fathers), the modest objects for which he is responsible are put on a par with the sacred vessels of the altar. The Master also regarded the food entrusted to the cellarer as 'divine' because it was given by God, who is Providence, to his servants, but he did not extend this consecration to all the objects used in discharging his duties as Benedict does.

The cellarer's office is also and especially religious, indeed sacred, because he must see to the livelihood of those 'little ones'—the sick, the guests and the poor, to whom the Rule adds the children—of whom Christ will say on the day of judgment that whatever concerns them concerns him (Mt 25:31–46; cf. Mt 12:36). The Master already appealed to the day of judgment to instil into the cellarer a sense of his responsibility, but the latter's only object was the distribution of food, which was not to be tainted by any dishonesty. Benedict replaces this responsibility for things with responsibility for people, through whom the cellarer is in constant relation with Christ.

We will encounter these 'little ones' again further on. For the time being, Benedict concerns himself with another underpriviledged category: those who lack understanding. The cellarer must not heap scorn on them, but turn down their requests reasonably and humbly. This care not to give them cause for sadness heralds the superb conclusion to this chapter.

Like the list of qualities at the beginning, these recommendations end with a warning against extravagance and its opposite, now called avarice. A sense of moderation whose result is abiding by a happy medium will also be recommended to the abbot, as we shall see. In managing material things, the cellarer must act as the abbot does in caring for souls, since material goods are at the service of souls and condition their progress towards God.

> [13] Above all, let him be humble, and when he has nothing to give someone, let him offer a kind word in reply, [14] as it is written: 'A kind word surpasses the most valuable gift'. [15] He shall have the responsibility of all that the abbot enjoins on him; he shall not presume to do what he has forbidden. [16] He will provide the brothers with the allotted ration without arrogance or delay, lest they be irritated, remembering what that person deserves who 'shall irritate one of these little ones', according to the divine word.
>
> [17] If the community is large, he shall be given helpers, that with their assistance he too may perform the duties entrusted to him without losing his peace of soul. [18] What must be given shall be given and what must be requested shall be requested at the proper times, [19] so that no one may be disquieted or saddened in God's household.

'Before all else, a monk must be humble', a desert father, John the Theban, had already said (*Vitae Patrum* V.15.23). Benedict, who explicitly quotes the apophthegms of the Fathers twice, may have remembered this maxim. According to John, it was grounded on the beatitude of the 'poor in spirit' (Mt 5:3), regarded as Christ's first commandment. In actual fact, according to the common interpretation of the ancient Church, the poverty in spirit called blessed by Jesus is no different from humility, and his teaching begins with it.

The cellarer must therefore answer humbly and kindly that he has nothing to give. This 'kind word' which is equal in value to all gifts is commended by a wisdom text (Si 18:17) which Saint Gregory will likewise quote in exhorting those who give alms to be humble (*Moralia* 21.29). Besides these words from Scripture, Benedict probably recalls what Saint Augustine said in his Explanation of Psalm 103 (I.19): 'When you cannot give someone what he asks for, avoid showing him contempt. If you can give, do so. If you cannot, show affability.' These words of the great teacher already underlay the advice given the cellarer not to 'show contempt' when faced with troublesome petitioners. The two passages complete one another: both concern refusals which are necessary, either because the request is unreasonable or because the thing requested is lacking. The influence of Augustine, which we can guess at here and there, will likewise contribute, in the abbot's directory, to enriching the Rule with touches on the manner of dealing with one's neighbor.

Just as in this sentence he has gone back over a point already dealt with in the first part of the chapter, Benedict also repeats that the cellarer must act in total subordination to the abbot. And the warning against arrogant and irritating manners also comes close to being a repetition. Earlier the Rule forbade the cellarer to 'give the brothers cause for sadness'; it now forbids him to 'irritate' them, literally to 'scandalize' them, according to the gospel term which is recalled here (Mt 18:6). The expression 'without arrogance or delay' recalls a sentence from Augustine on the way in which clerics must treat the faithful who request offerings for the dead (*Ep.* 22.6).

The final invitation to comply with schedules also brings to mind a guideline given by Augustine, this time in his Rule for the monks of Hippo (*Praec.* V.10). Making requests at the right time was recommended by Augustine only in connection with books, which were placed in the care of a librarian. By reiterating this principle in the cellarer's directory, Benedict gives it a formulation so general that it appears to apply to community life as a whole.

This broader perspective is even more tangible in the superb maxim which concludes the chapter: 'That no one may be disquieted or saddened in the house of God.' An echo of the first part can be heard here: there the cellarer was required not to cause the brothers disquiet (by being 'excitable') or 'sadness'. The legislator now complements the concern he showed there for their peace by adding a reciprocal proposition: the cellarer too must preserve his peace of soul, and the community must help him do so, either by providing him with assistants (the Master did not give him any) or by sparing his time. Here we touch on one of Benedict's firmest designs: to bind the members of the community together by mutual consideration inspired by charity. Thus the household of God—that name concludes the chapter, as it ended the list of qualities at the beginning—shall be, in the image of its mysterious master, naught but peace and joy.

XXXII

The tools and goods of the monastery

¹ As regards the goods of the monastery—tools, clothing and belongings of all kinds—the abbot shall appoint brothers whose life and conduct he can rely on, ² and he shall issue to them these various articles as he sees fit, so that they may keep them and collect them after use. ³ The abbot shall keep an inventory of these articles. Thus, when the brothers succeed one another in the job, he shall be aware of what he hands out and receives back.

⁴ If someone should treat the belongings of the monastery without cleanliness or care, he shall be reproved. ⁵ If he does not amend, let him be subjected to the punishment prescribed by the rule.

COMPARED TO THE PASSAGE from the Master which it summarizes (RM 17), this little chapter evinces two correlative aims: broadening the horizon, and emphasizing the abbot's role. The Master's text was down-to-earth, detailed, and picturesque; it dealt first with tools—more specifically still, with garden tools—and then went over all the equipment entrusted to one caretaker. Six different chests were listed and labeled, to which were added, all jumbled together, shoemaking and wardrobe equipment, the finished or unfinished products turned out by artisans, the tools used for different crafts, and last but not least the monastery cash: the caretaker also acted as bursar and paymaster.

Instead of this meticulous list, Benedict sums up all the equipment in three general terms and entrusts it not to a single caretaker, but to as many brothers as the abbot sees fit to appoint. Besides marking the switch from the Master's small monasteries to Benedict's doubtless by larger communities in which charges are multiplied, these changes appear motivated by a resolve to take a broader view of things. The Rule avoids going into too much detail, and aims at general principles. This shift to a higher plane results in increasing the role of the abbot, who is now free to define the various jobs as well as to appoint those who discharge them. A detail in wording emphasizes this broader perspective: 'to hand out' (*consignare*) and 'to receive back' no longer refers, as in the Rule of the Master, to the daily movement of tools between the hands of the caretaker and brothers, but to the far less frequent transfer of equipment under the abbot's control when a monk in charge is replaced by his successor.

Taking care of the monastery's goods is a task loftier than it appears. Like the cellarer's job, it shares in the sacred character of God's household. The qualities required of the caretakers are the same as those of the deans: the abbot must be able to 'rely' on the 'life and conduct' of both.

The final sanction follows the general line of what comes before it. The Master penalized only returning a garden tool to the caretaker without first cleaning it. Benedict replaces this specific misdeed with any sort of carelessness or disregard for cleanliness. As for punishing the offence, the Master's specific sanction—the culprit was denounced by the caretaker in the refectory and his bread ration was cut by one slice—is also replaced by a general procedure formulated in abstract terms. We will frequently come across this intentionally vague 'punishment prescribed by the rule' (*disciplina regularis*)—often, as here, at the end of a chapter. Unpleasant as this language may be, it reminds us that community organization cannot do without a rule nor the rule do without sanctions, whatever the form taken by both in the course of time.

XXXIII

Whether the monks are to have anything of their own

¹ Above all, this vice must be uprooted and removed from the monastery: ² let no one presume to give or receive anything without permission from the abbot, ³ nor to retain anything as his own, not one single thing—neither book, tablet nor stylus—in short, absolutely nothing, ⁴ since they are not even entitled to have their bodies or their wills at their own disposal. ⁵ They are to ask the father of the monastery for all they need, and no one is entitled to have anything which the abbot has not given or allowed him. ⁶ 'Let all things be common to all', as it is written, so that 'no one presumes to call anything his own' nor deems it to be such.

⁷ If anyone is caught indulging in this extremely evil vice, he shall be warned a first and a second time; ⁸ if he does not amend, let him be subjected to punishment.

IN LINE WITH the preceding chapters which introduced the monks in charge of the monastery's goods, in the present and the next chapter Benedict will deal with all the brothers as users of those same goods. He has just punished anyone who treats things carelessly. Now he takes a position against a related misdeed: making any one of these things one's own.

Although an analogous chapter does not occur in the Master's text until much farther on (RM 82), what Benedict says here is to some degree rooted in the corresponding section of the other Rule. Towards the end of his treatise on the cellarer (RM 16:58–61), the Master had inserted a note, in connection with kitchen equipment, specifying that these things—and more generally everything found in the monastery on any account—'belongs to everyone and to no one'. Benedict here transforms this brief passage of his forerunner into a separate chapter twice as long. Given his customary abridgment, this unusual treatment hints at the importance he attaches to dispossession.

He considers dispossession from a well-defined angle: as a consequence of the monk's subjection to a superior. Having given his body and his will to God, he cannot dispose of exterior objects any more than he can his own being. By this logic, which proceeds from the person to things, poverty follows from obedience. We will come across it again in the chapter on profession, in which Benedict reiterates his present reasoning (58:24–25). Basil and the Master had offered him examples of this.

From such a perspective, the monk's relationship to the abbot is the determining factor. Poverty consists essentially in having nothing at one's disposal without his permission. Twice called by the usual name of abbot, he is also referred to once by the less common expression 'father of the monastery'. In reading that we must 'ask' this 'father' for 'everything', we are reminded of Jesus' exhortations and promises (Lk 11:11; cf. 12:30). As our heavenly father's representative, shall the abbot be less prompt in answering sons who ask him for what they need? Be that as it may, the monk's voluntary deprivation spells abandonment in God's hands. Asking is an act of hope, as the latin verb *sperare* suggests.

The cenobitic tradition had not always allowed monks to ask. In the oldest picture we have of a community, Jerome noted that egyptian cenobites might not request anything for themselves (*Ep.* 22.35), and an abbot contemporary with Benedict, the African Fulgentius of Ruspe, still forbade the monks of his monastery in Sardinia to do so. By allowing this and even prescribing it, Benedict does not relieve his monks of the blessed necessity of being dependent.

By quoting the Acts of the Apostles in conclusion (Ac 4:32), Benedict deviates from the Master and draws closer to Augustine, whose influence will be obvious in the next chapter. This scriptural phrase replaces the Master's final 'maxim': 'The monastery's property belongs to everyone and to no one'. Equivalent in meaning, it adds a most valuable reference to the early Church of Jerusalem, where common ownership of goods spelled oneness of heart.

XXXIV

Whether all are to receive essentials equally

[1] As it is written: 'Distribution was made to every one according to his needs'. [2] Here we are not implying that there should be partiality toward persons—God forbid!—but rather consideration for weaknesses. [3] Whoever has fewer needs shall thank God and not give in to sadness; [4] as for whoever needs more, let him humble himself because of his weakness and not become self-important because of the mercy shown him, [5] and thus all the members will be at peace. [6] First and foremost, the evil of grumbling must not show itself for any reason, by any word or sign. [7] If someone is caught at it, let him undergo very severe punishment.

THIS CHAPTER completes the preceding one and again evinces Benedict's interest in the way in which the brothers are provided with material things, for nothing in the Rule of the Master can have suggested these lines to him. He has added them on his own impulse, or rather under another influence, that of Augustine.

The augustinian Rule begins with a dissertation whose substance Benedict offers us here. Straightaway, the bishop of Hippo confronts the brothers with the model of the early Church: one heart and one soul, no private ownership, everything owned in common (Ac 4:32); food and clothing are not distributed equally to all, but to each according to his need (Ac 4:35). This uneven distribution copied from the Acts of the Apostles occasions a series of reflections in which Augustine, taking the brothers' social background into consideration, gives his psychological keenness and his sense of people free rein: the formerly rich and the formerly poor are exhorted in turn to practise detachment and humility. While accepting differences in treatment—not out of regard for their past standing but because of the differences in strength and needs created by the latter—, they must live in harmony and honor one another (*Praec.* 1.2–8).

Further on, in connection with meals, Augustine goes back to this analysis of the differences between monks. The brothers of higher birth, who are better treated on account of their weakness, must not be envied by the brothers of modest rank, who are given less because they are hardier. Moreover, illness, convalescence, and return to health create many distinct situations which overlap with the effects of social background. In concluding these finely shaded reflections, Augustine coins an apt formula, inspired by Seneca, in which the best of pagan wisdom is enlisted in the service of christian monasticism: true wealth consists in being content with little, for 'it is better to have few needs than many possessions' (*Praec.* III.3–5).

As we can see, Saint Benedict follows in the wake of Augustine. Like him, he quotes the two phrases from Acts, one at the end of his previous chapter (Ac 4:32), the other at the beginning of this one (Ac 4:35). Without mentioning the brothers' secular past, barely hinted at by the rejection of 'partiality towards persons' (cf. 2:20), he distinguishes, as does his forerunner, between weak and strong, those who have more needs and those who have less. The latter are invited to give thanks and cautioned against feelings of sadness—a vice to which Benedict is highly inimical, as we already know from the chapter on the cellarer. The weak, who are better treated, are urged in turn—more explicitly than in the other Rule—to be humble. The conclusion, which exhorts all the 'members' to remain in peace, recalls that of Augustine's first development.

The final note is analogous to the punishment with which the preceding chapter ended—Benedict detests grumbling no less than he does private ownership—and brings us back to the hardier monks. These less favored brothers are obviously the ones who might grumble. Besides condemning this 'evil'—a condemnation which shall be renewed many times—the present chapter contains a wealth of teaching: the thanksgiving to which it invites us is, along with joy and prayer (1 Th 4:18), among the constant traits of the christian soul; humility, cherished by the Rule as well as by the Gospel, guarantees peace; like the body of Christ which is the Church, the monastic community is made up of organically connected 'members'; finally, this summary of Augustine's reflections refers us back to the bishop's closing maxim, which is the exact opposite of the agenda of our consumer society and a true digest of the philosophy of monasticism: happy are they who cut back their needs!

XXXV

The kitchen servers of the week

AFTER HIS TWO novel little chapters on dispossession
and the distribution of essentials, Benedict here returns to
the Master's sequence of topics. In the latter's Rule the
cellarer and the keeper of tools were followed immediately
by the servers of the week, who formed the subject matter
of eight chapters which Benedict condensed into only one.
He replaces the many details gone into by his forerunner
with a presentation much poorer in concrete guidelines,
but one which brings out the significance of service in a
completely new fashion.

[1] The brothers shall serve one another, and no one shall
be excused from kitchen service except in case of illness,
or if he is engaged in business of major importance, [2] for
this increases reward and charity. [3] The weak shall be
given helpers so that they may serve without sadness,
[4] but all shall have helpers according to the size of the
community and local conditions. [5] If the community is
large, the cellarer shall be excused from kitchen service,
as well as those who, as we have said, are occupied
with tasks of major importance. [6] The rest shall serve
one another in charity.

7 On Saturday the brother who is completing his week shall do the cleaning. 8 They shall wash the towels which the brothers use to wipe their hands and feet. 9 They shall also wash the feet of all, not only the one who is finishing, but also the one who is about to begin. 10 He shall return the utensils used for his service to the cellarer, clean and in good condition. 11 The cellarer in turn shall issue them to the one beginning, so as to know what he hands out and what he receives back.

The principle of taking turns at serving one another goes back to the origins of cenobitism. Weekly rotations appear as early as the Rule of Pachomius, and in his famous description of the monks of Egypt, Jerome (*Ep.* 22.35.4) notes that each in turn served at table for a week's time. Through Cassian and the Master, Benedict is thus heir to a traditional custom which had spread from Egypt to both East and West.

The purpose of the institution is brought out straightaway here: to endow everyone with the incomparable merit of charity. Love places us at the service of those we love. 'Serve one another out of love', said Saint Paul (Gal 5:13). To serve is the Christian's greatness because it is the hallmark of Christ (Mt 20:26–28; Lk 22:26–27). In speaking of the 'reward' thus acquired, Benedict also brings to mind the 'glass of fresh water given to one of these little ones' (Mt 10:42) and the judgment scene which concludes Jesus' teaching (Mt 25:40).

In the orbit of this great principle drawn from Scripture, two practical questions are settled in the first paragraph: dispensations and helpers. In speaking of the grounds for dispensation—illness, necessity, occupations which contribute to the common good—Benedict speaks as does Caesarius in his Sermons. But whereas the bishop of Arles mentioned such exceptions in connection with attendance at lenten and Holy Week services (*Serm.* 196.2; 202.5), in our Rule for monks we are dealing with serving in the kitchen—a humble daily task which is no less beneficial and sacred than the most venerable liturgical actions.

As for the help to be given the servers, Benedict comes back to what he prescribed regarding the cellarer. The reason given—to banish sadness—also calls that chapter to mind.

The operations carried out at the end of the week—cleaning and washing, handing over the utensils to the cellarer and to the next team—center around the washing of feet, performed by those beginning their week as well as by those completing theirs. In the Rule of the Master this was a daily ritual; in Benedict's it regains the solemnity attached to a weekly ceremony such as that performed, according to Cassian, by eastern cenobites. Cassian took care to indicate its gospel model: the act of Jesus at the Last Supper (Jn 13:1–17). As a sign of Christ's supreme love for his own, it worthily concludes a service wholly inspired by charity.

> [12] When there is only one meal, the kitchen workers of the week shall each receive a drink and some bread over and above the regular portion beforehand, [13] so that at mealtime they may serve their brothers without grumbling or hardship. [14] But on non-fast days they shall wait until grace. [15] On Sunday immediately after Lauds, those beginning as well as those completing their week shall bow at the knees of all in the oratory and ask for their prayers. [16] Let the server completing his week recite this verse: 'Blessed are you, Lord God, who have helped me and comforted me'. Having said it three times, the one completing his week shall receive a blessing. Then the one beginning will continue, saying: 'God, come to my assistance; Lord, make haste to help me'. [18] All shall repeat these same words three times, and having received the blessing, he shall begin.

Between two paragraphs concerning the passage from one week to the next, Benedict inserts a note allotting the

servers extra food. This concession is a novelty with regard to the Rule of the Master; we encounter it again in
Caesarius', although the bishop allowed the sisters of Arles
only a drink of unwatered wine. As for the motive, in
which the expression 'to serve one's brothers' echoes once
more, it is derived from the augustinian Rule (*Praec.* V.9).
Benedict adds 'hardship' to the 'grumbling' mentioned by
Augustine. Augustine, moreover, contented himself with
exhorting those in charge to serve without grumbling. In
the benedictine Rule, a practical measure is taken to make
that service less difficult and help the brothers perform it
willingly.

'Only one meal . . . non-fast days'. These expressions,
which herald the timetable for meals (ch. 41), confront us
for the first time with an important reality which sharply
differentiates conventual life of old from our own: the existence of genuine community fasts consisting in eating
only once a day, in the afternoon or evening. A revival
of this basic observance, as feasible and beneficial today as
it was then, is one of the pressing needs of contemporary
monasticism.

Going back to the changeover ritual, Benedict describes
the blessings given those completing and beginning their
week much more succinctly than did the Master. Instead
of separating them as his forerunner does—one in the refectory on Saturday evening, the other in the oratory on
Sunday after Prime—he combines them into a single ceremony placed at an intermediate time, that is, on Sunday
after Matins. The threefold repetition of the verses and their
content are also new. Both psalm texts chosen by the Master exuded fear of the devil. Benedict has kept only the first
formula's final mention of divine 'help' and 'consolation'
(Ps 85:17) and replaced its beginning ('Let those who hate
us see and be confounded . . .') with a blessing addressed
to God (Dan 3:52).

As for the Master's second formula (Ps 16:8: 'Keep us, o
Lord, as the apple of your eye; protect us in the shadow of

your wings'), Benedict replaces it with Cassian's famous
invocation (Ps 69:2) which he has already placed at the
beginning of each day office (18:1). Italian monks were in
the habit of saying this verse three times when beginning
any action. By inaugurating their week of service this way,
the kitchen workers remind themselves that no work is
pleasing to the Lord without the help of his grace and
without prayer for his assistance.

XXXVI

The sick brothers

THIS CHAPTER and the following one again interrupt the
sequence of topics found in the Rule of the Master. After
kitchen duty, the Master dealt with meals, although the last
of these three chapters contained provisions relating to the
sick and to children (RM 28:13–18 and 19–26). That is no
doubt what gave Benedict the idea of legislating here on
these two categories of monks. As regards children, he remains within the Master's perspective, which is limited to
food. But as for those who are ill he goes further—he does
not expressly discuss the matter of food except in closing—
and considers the full extent of the sick brothers' needs.
The whole idea of 'service' of the sick is involved—an all-
enveloping notion which closely connects this chapter to
the preceding one.

¹ The sick must be cared for above and before all else
and they must truly be served as Christ, ² for he said:
'I was sick and you visited me', and ³ 'What you did
for one of these least brothers you did for me'. ⁴ But
the sick on their part shall bear in mind that they are
served out of honor for God, and shall not give the
brothers who serve them cause for sadness by their
superfluous demands. ⁵ Still, they must be borne with

patiently, for such people are the source of a greater reward. [6] The abbot shall therefore be extremely careful that they suffer no neglect.

[7] These sick brothers shall have separate premises assigned for their use, and an attendant who is God-fearing, attentive and concerned. [8] The sick shall be offered the possibility of taking baths whenever this is helpful, but the healthy, and especially the young, should be permitted to do so less often. [9] Moreover, the sick who are very weak shall be allowed to eat meat; but once they are better they shall all abstain from meat as usual. [10] The abbot must take the greatest care that the sick not be neglected by the cellarers or attendants; for he is also responsible for any failing in his disciples.

One refrain punctuates this chapter. At the beginning, in the middle, and at the end, Benedict forcefully states that care of the sick comes before all else. The principle is first set forth very generally; then, the second time, it is specially impressed on the abbot. To the latter's responsibility, which is recalled the third time, the text adds that of the cellarers and infirmarians.

These three sentences, in which the refrain is expanded and made more specific, frame two paragraphs, the first of which deals with the spirit of this service and the second with the concrete forms it takes. Benedict's special love for the sick has made him come up with a remarkably neat and polished literary arrangement in speaking of them.

The priority given the care of the sick is grounded first and foremost on the words of Christ stating that in them we visit him (Mt 25:36). Like the one following it (Mt 25:40), this quotation is drawn from the last judgment scene. The chapter on the servers of the week barely afforded us a glimpse of this great page from the Gospel. Here it is set in full light. Summed up as it was by the washing of feet, weekly kitchen duty especially called to mind the Last Supper, that is, the example of Jesus serving his disciples.

Now the other face of the mystery is revealed: Jesus being served in each of his brothers. For Christ is both Servant and Lord, a model of service and a master whom we serve.

The sick must therefore be served as Christ. Conversely, they must behave as members of Christ. These mutual duties of infirmarians and their patients were already indicated in the light of the Gospel by Saint Basil (*Reg.* 36–37). The recommendation not to give the attendants 'cause for sadness', which is unique to Benedict, is reminiscent of the chapter on the cellarer and the one on the servers of the week. As for the final recommendation on patience, it recalls a story which Benedict doubtless does not have in mind but which aptly illustrates what he is talking about: the episode of Eulogius and the cripple in the *Lausiac History* (ch. 21). When both were on the point of death, that cantankerous invalid and his volunteer attendant were so tired of one another that they were tempted to part; Anthony prevented them from doing so to avoid their losing their crowns. Benedict evokes these under the evangelical name 'reward', which he had already used in connection with the charity of the servers of the week.

Infirmary and infirmarian, baths and meat: all these details are missing from the Rule of the Master. Special premises and staff assigned to the sick are an old tradition of egyptian cenobitism, but in speaking of the infirmarian Benedict may also remember the augustinian Rule (*Praec.* V.8). In any case, he draws his inspiration from its feminine version (V.5) in next discussing baths. Restrictive though he may appear to us in that area, his provisions are broad compared to the usual hostility of the monks of old. Saint Anthony never washed, and monasticism generally followed him in taking a negative attitude towards whole-body ablutions. Jerome forbids them several times, and especially, like Benedict, in the case of younger ascetics whose flesh they might 'stir up'.

Baths and meat. The drawbacks of these things have largely disappeared today in the eyes of those who seek God. While firmly maintaining that no kind of food is bad in itself, ancient monasticism was convinced that an ascetic who wanted to master his passions must give up both meat and baths. And a monk is essentially an ascetic. Whether or not we are able to justify it on grounds provided by a differing science, our Fathers' lesson is still worth listening to attentively.

But these are no more than occasional remarks on the fringe of the subject. Coming back to it, Benedict charges the abbot one last time to watch over the sick, together with the cellarers and infirmarians, also mentioned in this connection by Caesarius of Arles (*Reg. uirg.* 42.5). And they are saluted once more by their glorious title: servants.

XXXVII

The elderly and children

[1] Although human nature itself inclines us to compassion toward these ages, that of the elderly and of children, the authority of the Rule must nevertheless provide for them. [2] Their weakness shall always be taken into account, and they shall in no way be required to follow the strictness of the rule with regard to food, [3] but they are to be treated with kindly consideration, and they shall anticipate the regular hours.

THE MASTER listed the dispensations allowed children in the middle of a long chapter on fasts. He did so with his customary exactitude, omitting neither the hours for meals, nor the differences between seasons, nor the age limit for children. The young alone were directly envisaged; the elderly were merely mentioned in closing.

The present chapter, which is twice as short as that set of rules, contains none of its concrete norms, which are left to the superiors' discretion. But it insists on the mercy and kindness which inspire such dispensations. In this regard, man-made law does no more than sanction the natural law in which such sentiments are rooted. By dealing with the question even before setting the timetable for meals, the legislator shows his concern: he too 'anticipates' the treatise on fasting, which would be the usual place for the exceptions from it.

Instead of being simply mentioned in conclusion, the elderly appear here on the same footing as children, indeed before them. In writing this, Benedict may have been re-membering the egyptian monks described by Saint Jerome, who aptly described the weakness common to these two stages of life (*Ep.* 22.35.4).

In closing, let us note the final words of the chapter. The 'regular hours' (or 'canonical hours', as the Latin says) remind us of the mobility of meals among the ancient monks as well as of the material and spiritual importance of this variation in the time for eating, which is the pivot around which the day is structured.

XXXVIII

The reader for the week

BEFORE ENDING his description of kitchen duty, the Master inserts a chapter on the refectory reader (RM 24). Benedict here summarizes this long passage from his forerunner. Yet he omits his remarks on the book to be read during meals: the Rule itself, constantly repeated to the community so that no one might be ignorant of it. Benedict replaces what he omits from the Master's text with a note on silence at table, inspired from egyptian monasticism.

[1] The brothers' table shall never be without reading. Nor should the reading be performed haphazardly by the first one who just happens to pick up a book; rather, a reader for the whole week will take up his duties on Sunday. [2] Upon beginning, after Mass and communion, he will ask all to pray for him so that God may shield him from the spirit of pride. [3] And let all in the oratory say this verse three times, but after he has begun it: 'Lord, you shall open my lips, and my mouth shall proclaim your praise.' [4] And then, having received the blessing, he shall take up his duties as reader.

[5] And there shall be complete silence, so that no one in the room shall be heard whispering or raising his voice except the reader alone. [6] As for what is necessary

for eating and drinking, the brothers shall serve one another in turn so that no one need ask for anything. [7] If, however, anything is required, it should be requested by an audible signal of some kind rather than by speech. [8] Neither shall anyone in the room presume to ask a question about the reading or about anything else, lest occasion be given, [9] unless the superior should wish to say a brief edifying word.

[10] The brother who is reader for the week shall be given mixt before he begins to read, because of holy Communion and lest the fast be hard for him to bear. [11] But he shall take his meal later with the weekly kitchen servers and the attendants.

[12] Not all the brothers shall read and sing all in sequence, but only those who edify their hearers.

The custom of reading at table comes, not from Egypt, but rather from Cappadocia. Egyptian cenobites ate in silence. This blessed practice appears for the first time in Basil's Great Asceticon. The legislator saw in it an opportunity for preferring spirit to flesh: the monks are to listen more avidly than they eat (*SR* 180). A little later, Augustine reiterates this parallel between food for the body and food for the soul (*Praec.* III.2). In the same line, Caesarius of Arles and the Master were to quote the words of Moses and the Gospel: 'Man does not live by bread alone, but by every word of God' (Lk 4:4). The figure of Christ in the desert thus looms over every monastic refectory.

Like the Master, Benedict entrusts the task of reading to the same brother for a week's time, starting on Sunday. Like him also, he marks the beginning of his duties by a blessing ceremony during which the reader and the community say the verse 'Lord, you shall open my lips . . .' (Ps 50:19), already used in the office at the beginning of vigils. On the contrary, the aim here assigned to the prayer is a novel one. It expresses Benedict's special loathing for every kind of pride.

Two other details are new. Both of them call to mind the blessing of the kitchen servers: first, the ritual takes place in the oratory, rather than in the refectory as in the Rule of the Master; next, the verse is recited not once but three times. The change of premises occasions one of the Rule's very rare references to Eucharist and communion. The latter will be mentioned again later on in connection with mixt.

The words read must ring out against a background of religious silence analogous to that in the church. But it might be objected that speech is necessary for the progress of the meal. To avoid this, Benedict first recommends 'serving one another' perfectly. This first means of preserving silence, which he alone indicates, appeals to the key notion so often used in previous chapters. Secondly, Benedict advocates the use of audible signals in place of speech. This time we are dealing with a traditional method already prescribed by Pachomius and transmitted by Cassian (*Inst.* 4.17).

Questions about the reading are another potential source of interruption. Wishing to promote perfect understanding of the text to be read—his own Rule—the Master allowed and even encouraged them. In forbidding them, Benedict corrects his predecessor. The reason he gives— 'lest occasion be given'—refers to Saint Paul's warnings against moral failures which are so many victories for the devil (Eph 4:27) or enemies of the faith (1 Tm 5:14). When read publicly, Scripture sometimes aroused negative reactions, as we know from Saint Augustine (*Praec.* III.2). These complaints were aimed sometimes at its obscurity, sometimes on the contrary at its overly clear demands, judged too harsh for human weakness. Benedict doubtless wishes to prevent such complaints, heard even in monastic refectories.

While prohibiting questions on the part of the brothers, the Rule allows the superior to speak briefly. When he felt tension mounting among the hearers, he could add a

pacifying explanation to the irksome text. With one reservation—the superior's comments must remain 'brief'—
Benedict here agrees with the Master, who encouraged the
abbot to explain the obscure points of the Rule in the course
of the reading and to question the brothers to make sure
they had listened.

Granting mixt (watered wine) to the reader also has two
motives; the first comes from the Master, while the second
bears Benedict's personal stamp. Communion was received
at the end of Mass on Sundays and feast days and outside
Mass on ordinary days; it was given immediately before
the meal. Thus it was fitting to rinse out one's mouth before
beginning to read. But Benedict adds a concern of his own
to this direction of his forerunner: to spare the brothers
hardship. What he says of the reader here is modeled on
what he said earlier in connection with the cooks.

The last question raised in the benedictine chapter is the
one with which the Master began: who should read? We
will come across it again further on (47:3). In answering
it, Benedict, for the second time in this chapter, utters an
important word: 'to edify'. Like the comments made in
connection with them by the superior, the words that are
read must build up the body of Christ by strengthening
the faith of each of its members (Eph 4:12 and 29). In order
to achieve this, the reading must be fully intelligible and
intelligent, as well performed outwardly as it is devoid of
conceit in the person performing it.

XXXIX

The measure of food

THIS CHAPTER and the next two complete the section on food which began with the rules for the servers (35). Like the Master (RM 26–28), Benedict deals successively with food, drink, and the hours for meals.

[1] It is enough, we believe, to provide all tables at the daily meal—whether it takes place at sext or at none—with two cooked dishes on account of the various weaknesses, [2] so that the person who may not be able to eat one kind of food may partake of the other. [3] Therefore two cooked dishes shall suffice for all the brothers, and if fruit or new vegetables are available, a third shall be added. [4] A generous pound of bread shall be enough for a day, whether there is only one meal or both dinner and supper. [5] If there is to be supper, the cellarer shall set aside a third of this pound and hand it out at supper.

[6] Should it happen that the work becomes heavier, the abbot shall have all authority to add something, if this is useful, [7] and provided that above all overindulgence is avoided and that a monk never experiences indigestion, [8] for nothing is so inconsistent with the life of a Christian as overindulgence, [9] as our Lord says: 'Take care that your hearts are not weighed down with overindulgence'.

[10] As for young children, they shall not receive the same amount, but less than their elders; frugality shall be the rule in everything. [11] As for the flesh of four-footed animals, all shall abstain entirely from eating it, except the sick who are very weak.

From the title to the next to last sentence, the benedictine text closely follows the Master's, omitting only a few details and adding motivations. Only the final directive on abstinence was lacking from the source text. In inserting it, Benedict repeats what he has already said in connection with the sick (36:9).

Compared with his forerunner, Benedict constantly evidences a spirit of restriction and austerity. The only exception concerns the bread ration: here he is a little more generous. His program of two cooked dishes and one raw, together with a pound of bread, must be compared with the oldest community menu known to us, that of the egyptian cenobites described by Jerome (*Ep.* 22.35). They were entitled to bread, green vegetables, peas and beans, seasoned with salt and oil, in contrast to the stricter diet of the anchorites, who were restricted to bread and salt. We are also reminded of the daily sustenance of egyptian hermits according to Cassian: a pound of bread, no more and no less (*Conf.* 2.19–26). This 'pound' of ancient times was, for that matter, much lighter than ours (about 327 grams). Just as Benedict and the Master set a third of it aside for supper, likewise—but for other reasons—Cassian advised eating only half of it at None and keeping the rest for evening.

The Rule indicates only the ingredients of the main meal, without specifying anything as to supper. According to the Master, that secondary meal included simply an uncooked dish, along with the bread taken from the pound at noon, unless there were leftovers of the cooked dishes served at dinner.

Both Rules allow the abbot to add extras, but under opposite circumstances. For the Master, an extra is a sign of celebration and joy. For Benedict, it is justified by work and toil. This difference no doubt stems from the difference in period. Legislating as he did during the reign of Theodoric, a time of peace and relative prosperity in Italy, the Master exempted his monks from heavy agricultural work. Benedict, who writes during the troubled era of the gothic wars, is confronted with a more difficult situation, which forces him to accept work in the fields and the ensuing fatigue.

The extra must not entail overindulgence (*crapula*). This thrice-reiterated word is drawn from the Gospel (Lk 21:34). In the refectory as in the dormitory, the brothers must think of the master's return and always remain ready and in good form. Thus keeping one's heart nimble simply means acting as a disciple of Christ: the monk is nothing else. There is no difference between him and 'any Christian' other than renewed, intensified, and exclusive attention to the present and imminent Lord. The 'all the more so' with which Benedict shifts from one to the other calls to mind a remark made by Saint Severinus as he lay dying: 'It is a great abomination when even a secular gives in to sin; how much more so in the case of monks' (Eugippius, *V. Seu.* 43.6).

In the beginning, according to Genesis, human beings were vegetarians. They were not allowed to eat the flesh of animals until after the flood. Though christian ascetics did not reject meat as evil in itself, as the gnostics did, they gave it up out of nostalgia for that early bliss as much as in an attempt to rule the passions. They were preceded and accompanied on this blessed path by the elite of the pagan world. Benedict, like many others, also based himself on the creation narrative in distinguishing four-footed animals from other living beings: birds and fish emerge from the waters on the fifth day, whereas land animals and man appear on the sixth. Poultry and fish are also less 'exciting' than the flesh of four-footed creatures.

While making these distinctions, monasticism has always sought to eliminate animal products as much as possible. As it stands, the program laid down by the Rule in the area of food remains easy for normally healthy people today to practice. Taking it seriously is up to us. Happy are they who adhere as closely as they can to the norm suggested by a verb Benedict uses three times at the beginning of the chapter, and who limit themselves to what 'suffices'.

XL

The measure of drink

[1] 'Everyone has his own gift from God, one this and another that'. [2] It is, therefore, with some uneasiness that we specify the amount of food and drink for others. [3] However, with due regard for the infirmities of the sick, we believe that a pitcher of wine per head and per day is enough. [4] But those to whom God gives the strength to abstain must know that they will have their own reward.

[5] If local conditions and work and the summer heat call for more, this is left to the superior's judgment, always seeing to it that the excess of drunkenness should not creep in. [6] We read, it is true, that 'wine is absolutely not for monks', but since the monks of our day cannot be convinced of this, let us at least agree to drink moderately, and not to the point of excess, [7] for 'wine leads even wise men to apostasy'.

[8] When local conditions make it impossible to obtain the amount indicated above, but rather much less or even nothing at all, those who live there shall bless God and not grumble. [9] For above all else we admonish them to refrain from grumbling.

THIS CHAPTER relies much less on the Master than did the preceding one. The only elements of the other Rule retained by Benedict are the words of the title, then mention of the 'pitcher' (*hemina*) and finally permission to exceed the ordinary norm, with a warning against the drunkenness that might ensue. Everything else is new, although a possible echo of the earlier text can be perceived here and there.

Besides, as in the chapter on food, Benedict consistently proves more restrictive and austere than his forerunner. For the Master, the use of wine appears to have involved no problems. With no reservations or hesitations, he allotted a rather generous ration. Benedict, on the contrary, states his 'uneasiness' straightaway, and seems reluctantly to concede what he does grant.

This reservation about wine goes back to the first monastic generations. Like meat, wine appeared only after the flood, after the fall. In line with this observation, christian asceticism gave a strict interpretation of Saint Paul's words to his disciple: 'Drink a little wine on account of your stomach and of your frequent illnesses (*infirmitates*)' (1 Tm 5:23). To the Apostle, it seemed, drinking wine was legitimate only in the case of sickness.

Benedict may have had this in mind when he speaks of the 'weakness of the sick' (*infirmorum*), in connection with which he determines the wine ration. But the expression may also be aimed at the moral weakness which he then stigmatizes: that of today's healthy monks, who are unable to do without a drink they do not need. In any case, he is aware of both primitive ideal and present reality. While accepting the latter as the Master did, he confronts it with ancient discipline—as the Master did not—and judges it in the light of those beginnings.

To Benedict's mind, happy are they who have received the gift of abstinence. A general norm for the monks of old, abstinence has now become a special 'gift'. Another axiom from Saint Paul serves as a reference here (1 Co 7:7). In formulating it for the faithful of Corinth, the Apostle had in mind abstaining from sexual activity. Benedict applies it to abstaining from wine. The early monks had drawn from the pauline corpus a sentence concerning wine which appeared to be reserved for the sick. Now Benedict extracts from it a saying aimed at the charism of virginity and extends it to another form of renunciation.

A final text from the same Letter probably underlies what comes next. When Benedict says that the abstinent monk 'shall have his own reward', he is echoing a sentence in which Paul, comparing himself to Apollo and other helpers of God, appeals to divine judgment which will determine their remuneration (1 Co 3:8). A reward will then be given 'to each according to his work'. Each servant of God no doubt receives his own gift, but each can also gain merit through his own efforts, with the help of divine grace.

After the normal measure of one 'pitcher' (*hemina*: at least a quarter of a liter), Benedict considers upward and downward variations. The former, like extra food, are to be allotted on account of tiring work or heat, and not on grounds of rejoicing as provided for by the Master. Also as in the previous chapter, the granting of extras is accompanied by a warning against excess. It is formulated after the manner of Basil, who asked that eating not be pushed 'to the point of excess' (*Reg.* 9.7). As for the scriptural motivation that follows (Si 19:2), it replaces the Master's common-sense reflections on the unfortunate consequences of excessive drinking.

The more or less complete shortage of wine led Benedict to repeat what he had said regarding the distribution of essentials (34:3–6): the disadvantaged monk must not grumble, but rather bless God. For a call to detachment is a grace; happiest are they who are content with less.

Regarding extras, Benedict has quoted a saying by abba Pastor (Poemen) which he had read in the systematic collection recently translated by two roman clerics, Pelagius and John: 'Wine is absolutely not intended for monks' (*Vitae Patrum* V.4.31). A succinct expression of the most ancient monastic wisdom, this apophthegm must be paralleled with the one quoted by Benedict at the end of his section on the office (18:25). Both are drawn from the same *Libellus* 4, entitled 'On Continence'. In the anecdote on psalmody, two seniors, absorbed by the celebration of an endless office, forget to sleep and take their meal. In the one now mentioned by Benedict, another great monk bans wine. In both cases, the same generosity lifts human beings above their bodily appetites.

In both cases also, Benedict argues from the example of the Fathers in order to suggest a mere minimum of decency to his contemporaries. Beyond this limited inference, the great model of old remains attractive. Drunk in moderation, wine which brings rejoicing to the heart is good, very good, but nothing equals the jubilation and freedom of those who can do without it.

XLI

At what times shall the brothers take their meals?

[1] From holy Easter to Pentecost, the brothers shall take their meal at noon and sup in the evening.

[2] Beginning with Pentecost, all summer long, if the monks are not working in the fields and are not oppressed by extreme summer heat, they shall fast until none on Wednesdays and Fridays. [3] On the other days, they shall eat dinner at noon. [4] If they are working in the fields and if the summer heat is extreme, dinner shall remain at sext, and it is up to the abbot to provide for this. [5] He shall regulate and arrange all matters so that souls may be saved and the brothers may go about their activities without well-founded grumbling.

[6] From the Ides of september until the beginning of Lent, the meal shall always be at none.

[7] In Lent, until Easter, the meal shall be at vespers. [8] However, vespers shall be celebrated so that there is no need for lamplight while eating, and that everything can be finished by daylight. [9] Indeed, at all times, let the hour of supper or of the meal be early enough so that everything can be done by light.

THE EGYPTIAN CENOBITES described by Saint Jerome (*Ep.* 22.35) took only one meal a day, after None, all year

round. This austerity was accentuated or tempered only by
Lent and Paschaltide. The primitive discipline, still maintained on the whole by the Master, undergoes an important
mitigation in Benedict's Rule, as in that of his contemporary Caesarius: the summer dispensation from fasting,
which is restricted during that season to Wednesdays and
Fridays. Such flagging is explained by the length of the
days, the heat, and the fatigue ensuing from work in the
fields. The basic schedule remains that of winter, with its
sole meal in midafternoon.

Paschaltide, summer, winter, Lent: these four periods
span a march from broadest to strictest, from the two daily
meals to the sole evening meal, from the apparitions of the
risen Christ to his fast in the desert and his Passion. The
two sacred days of summer, Wednesday and Friday, also
commemorate his sufferings. More generally, fasting is a
sign of his absence, dispensation from fasting symbolizes
his presence (Mt 9:15).

As in the case of restrictions regarding food and drink,
Benedict relaxes the rigor of the schedule on grounds of
fatigue, not in order to celebrate with visiting guests as
the Master does. The purpose of fasting is the salvation
of souls and when they grumble, they are not saved, but
perish. The abbot, who is responsible for this discernment,
is told that the monks' grumbling may be 'well-founded'.
This is certainly the only passage of the Rule where this
loathsome thing appears justified.

As the boundary between summer and winter, the date
of September 13 (the 'Ides') seems to have been chosen on
account of its approximate symmetry with that of Easter.
The 'beginning of Lent' is the first Sunday of that period,
the sixth Sunday before Easter—not yet our Ash Wednesday. We would also like to know why 'everything must be
done by light' of day. Is this because night is the time and
the symbol of sin (Rm 13:12–13, etc.)? The Master, for his
part, absolutely forbade eating or drinking after Compline
(RM 30:23).

But these details matter less than the great human and religious reality at stake here. Fasting is an act that shapes a person, an irreplaceable experience. Setting the daily meal at noon, with supper in the evening and breakfast in the morning, was a disaster for monastic life, which was thus deprived of one of its constituent elements. Nothing prevents us from recovering it. It has been argued too often that the general weakening of health prevented this. In fact, we are just as capable as our fathers of eating once a day, toward the end of the day. All that is needed is the personal and collective will to do it. Those who do revert to this practice learn to 'love fasting', as a tool for good works. Human beings are never so much themselves as at those times when, with empty stomachs and nimble souls, they experience in their hearts the surge of joy, prayer, and thanksgiving placed in them by the Spirit.

XLII

Let no one speak after Compline

AFTER HIS SECTION on food, the Master spoke of the siesta—which sometimes followed the meal—and of sleep at night. He thus went from refectory to dormitory, there to regulate going to bed and rising (RM 29–32). This, immediately followed by night prayer, introduced the section on the office. Benedict, who has anticipated the description of the office, retains only one element of the Master's transition: the present chapter on going to bed and on night silence. It forms a good sequel to the preceding chapter, which closed with recommendations concerning the end of the day.

> [1] Monks must diligently cultivate silence at all times, but especially during the night hours. [2] Accordingly, at all times, whether on a fast day or a noon-meal day— [3] if there is a noon meal, as soon as they have risen from supper, all shall sit down together and someone shall read from the Conferences or the Lives of the Fathers or something else that will edify the readers, [4] but not the Heptateuch or the Books of Kings, because it would not be good for those of weak understanding to hear those writings at that time; they shall be read at other times.

⁵ On a fast day, once Vespers have been said, after a short interval they shall go on to the reading of the Conferences, as we have said; ⁶ four or five leaves shall be read, or as many as time permits, ⁷ once all have assembled, thanks to this reading period, in case any were engaged in assigned duties—, ⁸ they shall celebrate Compline, and on leaving Compline no one will be permitted to say anything further to anyone—, ⁹ if anyone is caught transgressing this rule of silence, he shall be subjected to severe punishment—, ¹⁰ unless some necessity arises on account of guests or the abbot gives someone a command. ¹¹ However, even this is to be done with the utmost seriousness and proper restraint.

The subject announced by the title—silence after compline—is referred to only in the first sentence and the final lines. Between this beginning and ending, two thirds of the chapter deals with an original institution which Benedict added to those of the Master: reading before Compline. It was not actually new. He found it in the augustinian Rule. But Augustine indicated it by only a word: 'After vespers, at the appropriate time, all shall sit down and there will be reading; after this, they shall say the psalms customary before sleeping' (*Ordo monasterii* 2). To this laconic prescription Benedict adds many details: differences in schedule according to the day, books to be read or not read, the length of the reading and its preparatory role in getting everyone assembled for Compline.

The first sentence makes night the privileged time for silence. At the beginning of the chapter on psalmody, we already encountered this habit of contrasting an ongoing custom with periods of greater intensity when it reaches a climax: just as silence deepens during the night hours, so faith in the divine presence becomes livelier at the time of the office (19:1–2). We will soon come across the same process in connection with purity of life, in another introductory sentence, that in the chapter on Lent (49:1–2). Attention to God, silence, integrity of one's whole being: these are various aspects of the one mystery of the monastic soul intent on God. In this triad night takes its place, next to the office and Lent, among those sacred moments when the monk is more himself because he is more atturned to God.

'Edifying' reading is to be chosen in preparation for this time of grace. It may seem strange that some parts of Scripture are eliminated, but the Rule explains the purely subjective grounds for this quite clearly: some hearers would go no further than the literal and carnal meaning, and the sacred time of night is also that of temptation.

Instead of these 'historical' books—the Pentateuch, Joshua and Judges, Samuel and Kings—spiritual works such as Cassian's *Conferences* and the *Lives of the Fathers* are to be read. Under the latter heading, Benedict no doubt had in mind primarily the collection of apophthegms recently translated in Rome, which he has already fervently quoted twice (18:25; 40:6). We may note that *Conferences* and apophthegms came mainly from anchoritic circles. The special esteem which they enjoy in Benedict's coenobium is an obvious sign of the unity of monasticism in its two forms, communal and solitary.

Night silence is an observance as old as cenobitism. Pachomius had already prescribed it (*Praec.* 94) and through Cassian or directly, this ban on 'speaking in the darkness' caught on. But pachomian monks slept in cells, and the silence imposed on them aimed mainly at safeguarding chastity. In the Rules of the Master and Benedict, with the monks grouped in dormitories, the point is rather to protect everyone's sleep. This community dimension is accentuated by the benedictine text, which insists three times that 'all assemble' before Compline.

In recommending the utmost restraint when speaking at night, as he does in closing, Benedict seems to remember a passage from Saint Basil (*Reg.* 137). He was concerned with words exchanged in the monastery during the offices, while Benedict has in mind those said after Compline. Once more the analogy between office and night appears. Both must be wrapped in silence, seriousness, and sacred reverence, for just as the office places us in the presence of God, night uncovers the immensity of his works. While veiling the things of this earth, it reveals the depths of the cosmos.

XLIII

Those who arrive late at the work of God or at table

THIS CHAPTER and the next three have a repressive character which makes them a sort of appendix to the penal code (23–30). The penalization of tardiness, with which this little section begins, was regulated in a different place by the Master, that is, much further on (RM 73). Benedict deals with it here no doubt because the other Rule, in connection with rising, instructed the brothers to assemble promptly in the oratory so as not to miss the beginning of the night office (RM 32:7–15).

¹ At the hour of the divine office, as soon as a monk has heard the signal, he shall immediately set aside whatever he has in hand and go with utmost speed, ² yet with gravity, so as not to give occasion for unruliness. ³ Thus nothing is to be preferred to the work of God.

⁴ Whoever arrives at night vigils after the gloria of Psalm xciv—which we wish, therefore, to be said at quite a slow and leisurely pace—is not to stand in his place in choir, ⁵ but shall stand in the last place or in one apart from the others assigned by the abbot to such negligent brothers, that they may be seen by all and by him, ⁶ until they do penance by public satisfaction once the work of God is over. ⁷ Now we have decided that they should stand in

the last place or apart, so that they may be seen by all and thus amend at least out of shame. [8] Besides, should they remain outside the oratory, there may be those who would return to bed and sleep, or sit down outside and engage in idle talk and give occasion to the evil one. [9] Better that they come inside so that they will not lose everything and may amend in the future.

[10] At the day hours those who do not arrive at the work of God until after the verse and the gloria of the first psalm said after the verse shall, according to the rule laid down above, stand in the last place, [11] and they shall not presume to join the choir of those chanting the psalms until they have made satisfaction, unless the abbot allows them to do so by granting his pardon, [12] but not, however, without the culprit making satisfaction.

Before proceeding to discourage tardiness, Benedict invites the monks to hasten to the work of God. He prescribes this immediate response to the signal of the office under the joint influence of the Master and the Second Rule of the Fathers. Cassian had already given a lively description of how promptly egyptian cenobites, busy at their individual tasks in their cells, obeyed any signal calling them to a common exercise, whether an office or group work (*Inst.* 4.12). In making this description his own, the Master had to modify it. His monks are no longer in cells—these have been replaced by a dormitory—but rather toiling away in workshops or in the garden, and the signal which rings out no longer summons them to any exercise, but solely to the divine office (RM 54). The same is true in Benedict's text. In both Rules the nub is less obedience than religion: the brothers are no longer setting aside a personal occupation in favor of a common endeavor, but work for prayer, the things of this world for God.

A fine maxim borrowed from the Second Rule of the Fathers of Lérins (2RF 31) thus asks that the work of God be preferred to all things. 'Prefer nothing to the love of

Christ' was a tool for good works (4:21). By way of Saint
Cyprian and other ancient authors, the maxim was derived
from the Gospel. On that model the monks of Lérins coined
their formula, in which 'love of Christ' is replaced by 'work
of God'. For the monk, in fact, love of the Lord is expressed
first and foremost by continuous prayer, the main act and
the strongest support of which is the office. The expression
'work of God', which in the New Testament referred to the
full scope of the life of faith (Jn 6:29) and the Christian's
way of acting (1 Co 15:58), has thus taken on the more
limited meaning of common prayer—which appears as the
opus Dei par excellence in a life wholly dedicated to God.

At the very beginnings of cenobitism, Saint Pachomius
had provided a way for atoning for tardiness at the offices.
He made a distinction between the day hours, for which he
was stricter, and the night, at which the grace period was
longer (*Praec.* 9–10). Following him, Cassian and the Master made the same distinction. Along the lines of his two
forerunners, Benedict in turn formulates a rule regarding
tardiness; in the process he simplifies the Master's discipline and makes it more flexible. His most original feature
consists in having the latecomers come into the oratory
instead of leaving them outside. Like Compline reading
in the previous chapter, this novelty is carefully explained.
Three motives are adduced: correcting the transgressors by
shaming them; keeping them from misbehaving outside;
and providing them with the benefits of the office. The
second goes back to the pauline notion of 'occasion given
to the evil one' (cf. Eph 4:27; 1 Tm 5:14) already used by
Benedict in connection with refectory reading (38:8).

[13] At table, whoever has not arrived in time for the verse,
so that all may say the verse and pray together and sit
down at table at the same time, [14] whoever has not
arrived on account of his negligence or of some fault,
shall be reproved up to the second time. [15] If he still

does not amend, he shall not be permitted to share the common table, [16] but shall be separated from the company of all, and he shall take his meals alone and be deprived of his portion of wine until there is satisfaction and amendment. [17] The penalty shall be the same for whoever is not present for the verse said after eating.

[18] And let no one presume to eat or drink anything before or after the time appointed. [19] Moreover, if the superior offers something to anyone and the latter refuses to take it, when he comes to want what he first refused or something else, he shall receive absolutely nothing until he has made appropriate amends.

Like the Master, Benedict combines two categories of latecomers—those late to the oratory and those late to the refectory—but he considers the latter's offence from a different standpoint. The Master taxed them with not having 'spoken to God' in prayer. Benedict is concerned instead with the breach of community discipline: here as in the preceding chapter, he wants everyone to 'pray together' and, he now adds, 'all are to sit down at table at the same time'.

The penalty also occasions some differences. The Master meted out immediate punishment for all tardiness. In accordance with the general principle (23:2, etc.), Benedict has two warnings precede punishment. Thus delayed, the penalty is, on the other hand, increased: loss of wine ration is added to the sequestration called for by the Master.

Eating outside mealtime is both an offence against common life and an act of gluttony. This second aspect is the one Benedict hints at by referring to the meal as the 'appointed time'. Compliance is vital not only for cenobites (Cassian, *Inst.* 4.18) but for all monks, even hermits (*Inst.* 5.20). It was even costlier on fast days when there was only one meal, at a late hour. Even if a brother cannot fast, he must, according to Augustine, take nothing outside of 'the dinner hour' (noon), except in case of illness (*Praec.* III.1).

The little scene outlined in closing—a brother refusing extra food or drink offered by the superior, who in turn refuses when the brother later asks for it—calls to mind similar retaliations prescribed by Basil and the Master. The former aimed the measure at the irritable refusal of a religious who does not find what is offered good enough (*Reg.* 96). The second challenged the refusal to receive communion or to come to meals on grounds of special fasting (RM 22:5–8). We may add to these cases those foreseen by Caesarius of Arles: some nuns whose health is poor cannot bring themselves to accept the surplus nourishment they need. Caesarius kindly exhorts them to overcome their scruples (*Reg. uirg.* 42.4). Benedict is stricter: he punishes such a lack of simplicity. Gregory the Great was to state similarly that eating out of obedience was more meritorious than any deprivation (*In I Reg.* II.127).

XLIV

Those who are excommunicated: How they make satisfaction

AFTER DEALING with the satisfaction owed by latecomers, Benedict quite naturally went on to that demanded of the excommunicated. But whereas he found the first in a later chapter of the other Rule, he borrowed the second from an earlier section which he had long since left behind. The Master placed the return to favor of those excluded immediately after the chapters on excommunication (RM 14). Benedict had skipped over his forerunner's exposition on reconciliation because at the end of his penal code he was concerned with another question: how can the impenitent sinner be saved? In going off in search of the lost sheep, he had neglected the normal case of the excommunicated monk who agrees to make satisfaction. He will now make up for this omission.

[1] Anyone excommunicated for serious faults from the oratory and from the table, at the end of the celebration of the work of God, is to prostrate himself at the oratory entrance and remain there in silence, [2] but only lie face down at the feet of all as they leave the oratory. [3] And let him do this until the abbot judges he has made satisfaction. [4] When he comes, at the bidding of the abbot, he is to prostrate himself at the abbot's feet, then

at the feet of all that they may pray for him. [5] Then, if the
abbot orders, he shall be admitted to the choir in the
rank the abbot assigns, [6] but he shall not presume to
lead a psalm or a reading or anything else in the oratory
unless the abbot again orders him to do so. [7] And at all
the hours, as the work of God is being completed, he
shall fling himself on the ground in the place where he
stands, [8] and he shall make satisfaction thus until the
abbot again bids him cease this satisfaction.

[9] As for those excommunicated from the table only for
less serious faults, they shall make satisfaction in the oratory until there comes an order from the abbot. [10] They
shall do so until he gives his blessing and says: 'Enough'.

Already among egyptian cenobites, the excommunicated
made satisfaction by prostrating before the community and
abbot (Cassian, *Inst.* 2.16; 4.16.1). The Master added a grand
and pathetic ceremony: during the prayers following the
office psalms, the culprit begged the superiors and brothers
for readmission; at the end of the hour, the provosts and
the community joined their entreaties to his, all prayed
together, and the penitent made another pathetic speech of
supplication to the Lord. Admonitions on the part of the
abbot and verses by which everyone answered completed
this touching ritual, inspired by the customs governing
ecclesiastical penance.

Benedict mentions only the central element of the whole
operation: community prayer, which the brother asks for
by prostrating. Everything else is omitted. By specifying
that the culprit prostrates 'in silence', Benedict even seems
to rule out the words put in his mouth by the Master.
Compared with that of the other Rule, the benedictine
ritual is cold and severe. The legislator is not interested
in ceremonies and speeches, but in healing the sick monk.
So to be more certain of securing it, Benedict prolongs
the process of satisfaction: the prayer of reconciliation is
followed by another period of penance during which the

partly reinstated brother remains in a state of minor ex-communication, forbidden to take any active part in the offices (cf. 24:4) and still bound to prostrate himself at the end of them.

Like everything that came before, the duration of this period is at the discretion of the abbot, whose interventions Benedict notes at every juncture. The abbot, mentioned seven times in just a few lines, emerges as the main agent of the transgressor's rehabilitation and as the one fully responsible for it. There is nothing automatic about reconciliation; in his hands, it becomes a pastoral undertaking aimed at better ensuring conversion. We re-encounter here the educational skill and the concern for sinners which ran through the last chapters of the penal code. By moving the absolution procedure here, Benedict gave it a pastoral orientation.

Two details, in addition to this general inspiration, should be noted. First, the 'rank' assigned to the reconciled monk by the abbot: here as in the preceding chapter, Benedict implicitly refers to the system of community rank which he will later determine with such great care (63:1–9). Then the verb 'to lead' (*imponere*). This involved not simply intoning a psalm, in the modern fashion, but reciting all of it: lessons as well as psalms were 'led', the latter usually being chanted solo.

The satisfaction due for less serious faults, with which the chapter ends, was touched on very briefly by the Master. It consisted merely in bending before the superior's knees (RM 13:61 and 67). For Benedict, it involves prostrating on the ground (cf. 44:7). In this it resembles satisfaction for serious faults. It does so, moreover, by its indefinite duration; both hang on the abbot's judgment. Once more there is nothing mechanical about penance; it is entrusted to the superior as a tool with which to educate the sinner.

XLV

Those who make mistakes in the oratory

THIS LITTLE CHAPTER and the next are very similar. They are obviously connected by the theme of satisfaction to what has just been said about latecomers and the excommunicated. Moreover, the misdeeds which they punish—making a mistake in the oratory, breaking something—were mentioned along with tardiness at the beginning of the list of offences drawn up by Cassian in connection with the penitential discipline in force among egyptian cenobites (*Inst.* 4.16.1). Cassian's enumeration may have given Benedict the idea of adding these two chapters on mistakes in psalmody and broken objects to the one on tardiness.

> [1] Should anyone make a mistake in reciting a psalm, responsory, antiphon or lesson, and should he not humble himself right there before all by making satisfaction, he shall be subjected to more severe punishment, [2] for refusing to correct by humility the failing committed through negligence. [3] As for children, they are to be beaten for such a fault.

In Cassian's list, breaking was mentioned before mistakes in psalmody. In Benedict's Rule the order is reversed, for the work of God comes before all else.

As in olden times in Egypt (*Inst.* 3.7.1), humility atones for negligence. We are tempted to say: happy the fault which invites us to practise the Rule's major virtue.

Children who do not spontaneouly atone for their failing are subjected to corporal punishment, according to the principle laid down at the end of the penal code (30:2–3). There the beating administered to brothers who were too young or too unintelligent replaced the spiritual penalty of excommunication. Benedict no doubt has them in mind when he speaks of the 'more severe punishment' inflicted on adults. It is ordinarily preceded by warnings. Here it seems to strike the transgressor immediately. To fail in humility is always a serious misdeed on the part of a monk, but when it is committed in the oratory, where everything recalls the presence of God, it more gravely offends the humble-hearted Christ.

XLVI

Those who commit faults or anything else

¹ If someone, while at any work—while working in the kitchen, in the storeroom, in the bakery, in the garden, in any craft or anywhere else—commits a fault, ² or breaks or loses something or fails in any other way in any place, ³ and does not of his own accord immediately come before the abbot and community in order to make satisfaction spontaneously and admit his fault, ⁴ if it is made known through another, he is to be subjected to a more severe penance.

⁵ But in the case of a sin of the soul whose cause lies hidden, he shall reveal it only to the abbot or to spiritual seniors, ⁶ who know how to care for their own wounds and those of others without exposing them and making them public.

SATISFACTION FOR BREAKING something was prescribed by Cassian, as we have mentioned. Benedict extends it to losing things, and generally to every kind of material failing. Moreover, he adds the spontaneous admission of the misdeed, in contrast to discovery by someone else. In this connection, he visibly remembers the augustinian Rule, according to which the brother guilty of receiving a letter on the sly was forgiven if he spontaneously admitted his misdeed, and severely punished if he did not (*Praec.* IV.11). Once more Benedict generalizes, shifting from the particular offence of 'hidden reception' which, like Augustine, he will discuss later (54:1–5) to all manner of exterior failings.

The secret confession of interior faults brings us back to Cassian (*Conf.* 2.12–13; cf. 20.8.8). He had already stressed the duty of secrecy incumbent on the person receiving the admission, and noted that advanced age was not enough to qualify someone for this delicate role. This is probably what Benedict has in mind when he speaks of 'seniors' who are 'spiritual'. Already, in the tools for good works, he had inserted the recommendation to 'disclose to a *senior spiritalis*' all evil thoughts (4:50).

There as here, it seems that such confessions are not reserved to that greatest spiritual father, the abbot, as the fifth step of humility would lead us to believe (7:44). That step derives from the Rule of the Master, who also assigns a role to his 'provosts' (deans) in this area, but subordinates it to that of the first-ranking superior: the provosts merely receive the tempted brother's confession and convey it to the abbot, who then sees to the spiritual care to be imparted (RM 15). Nothing in Benedict's text indicates such sharing of responsibility. The 'spiritual seniors' appear to have the same powers as the abbot, whom they purely and simply replace when someone approaches them.

Those powers are not, moreover, priestly ones. The person who confesses does not ask for sacramental absolution but for a remedy, that is, an appropriate satisfaction. This ministry of direction, ensured by monks who are not necessarily priests, aims simply—and this requirement remains at the heart of the sacrament of reconciliation—at discovering the 'worthy fruit of penance' whereby the sinner, thanks to Christ, will make his peace with God and dwell in it.

XLVII

Announcing the hours for the Work of God

BRIEF THOUGH IT is, this chapter deals with two different questions: announcing the office and reciting it. In the Rule of the Master, these were the subjects of distinct chapters which respectively opened and concluded the liturgical section (RM 31 and 46, cf. 47). Having already dealt with the latter, Benedict here brings together the remains of its beginning and end.

> [1] Announcing the hour for the work of God, day and night, shall be entrusted to the abbot, whether he does so personally or delegates the responsibility to a brother who is careful enough so that everything may be done at the proper time.
> [2] As for the psalms and antiphons, they are to be led, after the abbot, by those bidden to do so, whatever their rank. [3] As for reading and singing, no one shall presume to do so if he cannot perform this task so as to edify the hearers. [4] This shall be done with humility, seriousness and trembling, and at the abbot's bidding.

In the Rule of the Master, announcing the office was simultaneously up to two hebdomadarians—provosts or especially conscientious brothers—and to the abbot who, informed by them that the time had come, sounded the signal himself in the oratory. In Benedict's text a single person is in charge, but this person can be either the abbot or a brother chosen by him. In both Rules, resorting to the abbot himself and requiring care and attention on the part of those responsible underlines the importance attached to the work of God.

The greatness of the divine service also emerges from the directions given in the second part. The abbot himself, followed by the brothers according to rank, leads, that is, intones psalms and antiphons. The order of seniority does not operate automatically, however. A special injunction from the abbot is required each time, to exclude those who might not discharge this duty in a worthy fashion.

Here we reencounter almost literally the final note on the refectory readers (38:12). But whereas Benedict ruled out the readers' succeeding one another in order of seniority, he now accepts it, provided a choice entrusted to the superior intervenes. This system based on community rank (63:1–9) differs from the Master's, who did not establish any set order among the brothers within their groups of ten.

We already know that humility is particularly fitting in the oratory (45:1–2). Safeguarding it requires an effort, for reading or singing can easily be a source of pride (38:2). As for seriousness and trembling, the Master already required this frame of mind in those who chant the psalms (RM 47:1 and 4). Together, all three attitudes radiate that sense of the divine majesty which permeates the first step of humility and the chapter on behavior during psalmody (19:1–7).

XLVIII

Daily manual labor

UNDER AN ELLIPTICAL title which does not mention reading, Benedict now indicates the daily schedule according to seasons, as the Master had done in a dissertation three times longer (RM 50). There it was placed immediately after the section on the office (RM 33–49), whose beginning and end left traces in Benedict's chapter 47, as we have seen. The Master thus went from community prayer gatherings to the intervals between them: that time, he asserted, must not remain vacant. This explains the place of the present treatise on daily occupations, designed to fill in the framework formed by the hours of the work of God.

[1] Idleness is the enemy of the soul. Therefore the brothers must be busy with manual labor at specified times, and also with divine reading at specified hours.

[2] We thus believe that both occupations will be well distributed in time according to the following schedule: [3] from Easter to the first of October, starting in the morning after Prime they shall do whatever work needs to be done till about the fourth hour. [4] From the fourth hour until the hour when they celebrate Sext, they shall devote themselves to reading. [5] After Sext, upon leaving the table, they shall rest on their beds in

complete silence, or if someone wishes to read privately, he shall read so as not to disturb anyone. [6] None shall be celebrated a little early, midway through the eighth hour, and they shall return to whatever work is necessary until vespers. [7] If local conditions or poverty require them to do the harvesting themselves, they shall not give in to sadness, [8] for they are really monks when they live by the labor of their hands, as our fathers and the Apostles did. [9] Yet, all things are to be done with moderation on account of the faint-hearted.

Evagrius and Cassian had forcefully asserted that idleness was dangerous for monks, particularly in their reflections on the fearsome vice of *acedia*. There is only one remedy for it: work. Yet work is not only a condition of mental balance and spiritual health. It is also a duty toward one's neighbor: a Christian must earn his living and give alms (Eph 4:28; 1 Th 4:11; 2 Th 3:6–12). A social aim thus complements the ascetic purpose, which is the only one mentioned by Benedict in the initial maxim; that social dimension was clearly noted by the Master at the end of his corresponding passage (RM 50:6–7).

The distribution of time between two occupations, manual work and reading, goes back to the first western rules. Whereas Pachomius and Cassian spoke only of work and did not provide any specific time for reading, the augustinian *Ordo monasterii* had set aside three out of the twelve hours of the day for the reading. So did the Four Fathers, and following them the series of Lérins rules, with a tendency to cut the three hours down to two.

This step, which assigns a quarter of the time available to spiritual occupations, signals a reaction against the primitive gallic monasticism of Saint Martin, in which the whole day was available for prayer. This 'messalian' (that is, purely 'prayerful') notion of monastic life, also imported from the East to Carthage, was vigorously opposed by

Basil, Augustine, Cassian, and others. Certainly, the faithful must 'pray without ceasing' (1 Th 5:17), but not to the detriment of the obligation of work, also instilled by the Apostle. So it is that the brothers work most of the day, combining prayer with manual activity.

Human prayer, however, is a response to the word of God. In order to speak to God without ceasing, we must first of all listen to him without ceasing. Hence the necessity of reading and learning Scripture by heart. The continual prayer which accompanies work implies times when the monk does not work, but reads and memorizes the Bible. Knowledge of the sacred text acquired during the three daily hours of reading allows the worker to repeat it throughout the day, and thus to listen constantly to God, answering him with brief prayers.

Not unlike the twentieth-century workman who listens to his transistor on the job, the fourth- to sixth-century monk who recites the word of God is compared by ancient writers to an animal chewing its cud. Like an ox, he chews his cud after eating: he repeats the word of God after reading it. According to the Law of Moses, ruminants alone are ritually pure animals. Repeating the word of God does in fact sustain the soul in a state of purity as well as of prayer.

Throughout the year, the augustinian *Ordo* placed reading between Sext and None, just before the one and only meal: this is a privileged moment, for on an empty stomach humans are at the height of their strength and ability to concentrate on God. During the summer Benedict also has his monks read in the middle of the day, but earlier. Since the meal is usually at noon during that season, the two hours before Sext are similar in quality to the three hours provided by the *Ordo*. This more limited time can be rounded off during the siesta, as shown by Benedict's recommendations on the subject. In the Rule of the Master the brothers read after the meal, between None and Vespers—a less propitious time.

[10] From the first of October to the beginning of Lent, they shall devote themselves to reading until the end of the second hour. [11] At the second hour terce is celebrated, and all shall work at their assigned tasks until none. [12] At the first signal for the ninth hour all are to put aside their work, and they shall ready themselves for the moment when the second signal is sounded. [13] After the meal, they shall devote themselves to their reading or to the psalms.

[14] During the days of Lent, from morning until the end of the third hour they shall devote themselves to their reading, and until the end of the tenth hour they shall perform the tasks assigned to them. [15] During these days of Lent each one is to receive a book from the library, and is to read the whole of it straight through. [16] These books shall be distributed at the beginning of Lent.

[17] Above all, of course, one or two seniors must be deputed to make the rounds of the monastery while the brothers are reading. [18] They shall see to it that no brother suffering from acedia wastes time or engages in idle talk instead of reading, and not only harms himself but also distracts others. [19] If one is found—God forbid—he shall be reproved a first time, a second time; [20] if he does not amend, he shall be subjected to the punishment of the rule, so as to inspire fear in the others. [21] A brother is not to associate with another brother at inappropriate times.

In this new schedule as in the preceding one, Benedict moves the office of Terce. Instead of being celebrated at the exact hour, it is delayed in summer (to the fourth hour) and advanced in winter (to the second). Other shifts may be observed in winter regarding Sext and None, and this very passage provides that during Lent work is to stop in the middle of the interval between None and Vespers. In the Master's horarium, the offices are kept at their usual hours and the beginning and end of the various occupations are made to coincide with them. In comparison, there is something complicated about the benedictine schedule. We can sense that Benedict is moved by a new concern: adjusting the horarium for the greater benefit of its users. The search for the optimum time of reading is doubtless the source of this experimentation; the schedule is thus freed from the strict framework of the hours of prayer which tradition as a whole had almost always rigorously observed.

Given the shortness of the winter hours, the time assigned to reading is about the same as in summer. In both cases Benedict provides for a continuous period of two hours, with an addition (optional or compulsory) after the meal. But the place of the two hours is not the same: instead of coming before noon, they occupy the beginning of the day. This initial place is the most traditional one. Around the year 400, we find it almost simultaneously in the writings of Evagrius and Pelagius, in Athanasius' *De uirginitate* and in the Rule of the Four Fathers. Following the last, it becomes a constant norm in the Rules of Lérins until Caesarius of Arles and even later. The Master also had his monks read between Prime and Terce in winter. While usually cutting this time down by an hour, Benedict maintains it in its entirety during Lent.

This place allotted reading—at the beginning of the day —is a tribute paid to its spiritual dignity. According to Pelagius, the best part of the monk's time is thus consecrated to God. Before engaging in any other occupation, he listens to the word of God. Hippolytus' *Apostolic Tradition* already asked Christians to begin their day in this fashion. Around 380, the spanish traveler Egeria noted that in Jerusalem, during Lent, the bishop catechized the candidates for baptism at this time. Every day, from Prime to Terce, he read and explained the Scriptures, and later the Creed. Many already baptized Christians attended this instruction, which reminded them of their own introduction to the faith.

This lenten usage of the mother Church, visited by numberless pilgrims, no doubt partly accounts for the vast extension of morning reading which can be observed soon afterwards among the ascetics of various regions. It also casts light on the meaning of the practice. 'At all times', Benedict will say in the next chapter, 'the monk's life should maintain lenten observance' (49:1). Monks do all year round what the Christians present in Jerusalem do during Lent: they recall the truths of the faith by reading the Bible. In monasteries, the Holy City's annual reorientation workshop becomes a kind of ongoing formation. Each day, the monk returns to the study of the divine word which is his life.

The three continuous hours during Lent represent the oldest usage; the two hours during the other winter months are a mitigation of this. As often occurs in the history of the liturgy, the sacred period of preparation for Easter preserves the primitive custom. Why does the Rule maintain the complete reading period only during this time? The reason is that it requires a costly effort, as is shown by the supervision which Benedict organizes immediately afterwards. The Bible makes dry reading. Remaining face to face with it for three hours presupposes generosity. And we are in fact dealing with the Bible: it alone properly deserves the name 'divine reading' (*lectio divina*) which Benedict used at the beginning of the chapter, and the 'library' mentioned here is made up essentially of biblical books, with commentaries on them by the Fathers (cf. 9:8).

Several details call for our attention in this passage on Lent. First, the personal nature of the reading. Each brother performs it for himself, taking care to read his whole book straight through. This contrasts with the descriptions found in the Rule of the Master, where reading took place in groups: one monk read while the others listened. Next, the seniors who hunt down idleness and chattering correspond to a Mount Sinai custom to which John Climacus witnesses a century later: two 'supervisors' (*episkopous*) protect the time for psalmody, reading or private prayer which takes up the end of the day (*Past.* 14 Greek). Finally, we are presented with a portrait of the brother suffering from *acedia*. In taxing him with not 'applying himself to reading', Benedict uses an expression from Saint Paul (1 Tm 4:14). And when he requires that he be punished 'so as to inspire fear in the others', he has in mind another saying of the Apostle's (1 Tm 5:20), which he will quote explicitly at the end of the Rule (70:3).

22 Likewise, on Sunday all are to devote themselves to reading, except for those who have been assigned various duties.

23 However, if anyone is so remiss and lazy that he is unwilling or unable to study or read, he is to be given some work in order that he may not be idle.

24 Brothers who are sick or weak should be given an appropriate type of work or craft that will keep them from idleness without overwhelming them or driving them away. 25 The abbot must take their weakness into account.

In the Rule of the Master, reading was only one of several occupations offered on Sunday, a day of rest on which sleeping after the great night vigil was allowed (RM 75). Benedict, whose Sunday vigils are relatively brief, here shows himself more demanding: all are to spend their time reading. The Lord's day must be spent in the Lord's company. Monks were among the first to abstain from work on Sundays.

Benedict's judgment concerning the brothers unable to occupy themselves with reading is also harsher than the Master's (RM 50:76). He calls them 'lazy', a term which recalls the basic vice of humans estranged from God as it was depicted at the beginning of the Prologue (Prol 2). There the term referred to disobeying the Lord, as Adam had done. Here, laziness consists in not listening to the word of God which reverberates in sacred Scripture.

The concern not to 'drive away' a brother also calls the Prologue to mind. There Benedict was addressing the postulant (Prol 48). Here he speaks to the abbot. This preoccupation with the weak, which never leaves him—he has just expressed it in beginning the chapter (48:9)—adds a personal note to these last recommendations, in which he follows the Master very closely (RM 50:75–78).

In the previous section we recognized in passing Paul's words to Timothy: 'Apply yourself to reading' (1 Tm 4:14). When Benedict now says: 'All are to devote themselves to reading', we are reminded of another pauline expression: 'devote oneself to prayer' (1 Co 7:5). In order to allow married couples thus to devote themselves to prayer, Paul contemplated their separating temporarily. We must also separate ourselves from the cares and occupations of this world in order to be able to devote ourselves to divine reading. Happy the monk who, by the grace of God, compels himself to take such a daily and weekly 'vacation'.

XLIX

The observance of Lent

THIS FINE CHAPTER replaces three of the Master's, which followed one another under the title of 'Rule for Lent' (RM 51–53). The first two were very short; they prescribed silent community prayer in the midst of each interval between two offices, by day and by night. The third, which was much longer, regulated abstinence and fasting. The Master placed his rules for Lent where he did because the prayer between offices, with which he begins, fitted into the schedule sketched out in the previous chapter (RM 50). In Benedict's text, where the discussion of Lent also follows that of the schedule, the connection between the two does not emerge clearly.

[1] Although the monk's life should maintain lenten observance at all times, [2] however, since few have the strength for this, we recommend keeping one's life most pure during these days of Lent, [3] and washing away all together in this holy season all the negligences of other times. [4] We shall achieve this by giving up all manner of vice and by applying ourselves to prayer with tears, to reading and to compunction of heart as well as abstinence. [5] During these days, therefore, let us add something to the usual measure of our service: special

prayers, abstinence from food and drink, [6] so that each shall offer God, of his own will, with the joy of the Holy Spirit, something above the assigned measure, [7] that is, let him deny his body something in the way of food, drink, sleep, talkativeness, idle jesting, and let him look forward to holy Easter with the joy of spiritual longing.

[8] However, each shall make known what he offers to the abbot and do it with his prayer and will, [9] for whatever is done without the permission of the spiritual father will be reckoned as presumption and vainglory, not deserving a reward. [10] Therefore, everything must be done with the abbot's will.

Benedict sets aside the Master's legislative tone and addresses to the monks a spiritual exhortation inspired by Saint Leo's lenten sermons. His first sentence in particular clearly echoes the great pope's preaching (*Serm.* 39.2; 43.1; 44.2). Addressing persons in the world, the bishop of Rome urged them to take advantage of the coming of Easter to recover the purity which should characterize the life of a Christian at all times. Only a small number—we are reminded of monastic circles—preserve that paschal purity throughout the year. Of most of the faithful, the Church requires at least an annual effort at purification, in view of which the time of preparation for Easter has been instituted.

In making this exhortation his own, Benedict transfers it from the secular Church to the monastic community. There, too, the level of observance which should be constant appears reserved to a few. Most attain it only in passing, at the price of a special lenten effort. This time, which, according to Cassian, had been instituted only for seculars (*Conf.* 21.24–30), proves beneficial, indeed necessary, even for monks.

The negative effort at renouncing sin finds expression in positive acts. Benedict lists these three times. In doing so, he follows the Master rather than Leo. The regime preached by the pope to the faithful consisted in fasts and 'good works', the main one being almsgiving. Now this latter is not possible for monks as individuals. Therefore, Benedict's three lists follow the Master's pattern instead: prayer and abstinence. This pair, exactly reproduced in the second list, is also found in the first, where prayer is complemented by tears, reading, and compunction; abstinence is merely mentioned at the end. Conversely, the third list omits prayer and rounds off abstinence in food with other forms of exterior renunciation revolving around sleep, talkativeness, and joking. Benedict thus starts by detailing the first kind of lenten good works mentioned by the Master and then goes on to the second; the two are on an equal footing in his middle-of-the-road program.

The prayer to which the monks are invited is not equivalent to the Master's regulated community devotions; we find here a private and spontaneous act. The concomitant tears and compunction of heart recall Benedict's other two descriptions (20:3; 52:4). We are also reminded of the tools for good works, where confession of sins 'with tears and sighs' follows reading and prayer (4:55–57).

Tears are not an unimportant accessory of prayer, but rather a substantial enrichment, which endow it with an incomparable quality. Anyone who has experienced this transformation wonders whether they are not the normal sign of all true prayer: can a heart which speaks to God do so without the deep stirring that leads to tears? Thus it is hardly surprising that Benedict prescribes or suggests praying with tears, as though this was something to which every worshipper can and should aspire. Tears are no doubt a gift and a grace, but asking for them and working towards them is also a signal way of beginning to pray.

As for abstinence, it does not consist merely in cutting down on food and drink, as the Master provided in the second part of his 'Rule for Lent'. It also has to do with sleep, talkativeness, and joking. The first of these was subject to a few restrictions in the Master's text, but the other two were missing from his lenten agenda. There is something all-embracing about the benedictine notion of abstinence, as there is to continence in the writings of Basil (*Reg.* 9): all disorderly behavior is subject to cutbacks.

In his chapter on stillness, Benedict, following the Master, had absolutely banned all idle jesting (6:8). Here the same sort of joking is the object of special restrictions during Lent. This verifies the idea expressed in the first sentence: most monks do not ordinarily live as they should.

This last list of lenten ascetic practices is encompassed by a twofold mention of joy. First, these mortifications are offered to God 'with the joy of the Holy Spirit', after the fashion of the persecuted Christians to whom Saint Paul wrote (1 Th 1:6). Next, we look forward to Easter 'with the joy of spiritual longing'. This second calls to mind another christian value evoked by the Apostle: the 'joy of hope' (Rm 12:12). In fact, there is no greater happiness here below than to hope, that is, to expect God's promise with the certainty conferred by faith.

This spiritual longing which brings overwhelming joy has already been mentioned by Benedict among the tools for good works (4:46). There the focus was on its ultimate object, everlasting life. Now it is the Easter resurrection, which heralds and inaugurates an eternity of bliss. The chief fruits of the Spirit, who is the source of that longing, are love and joy (Gal 5:17–22).

Joy of the Holy Spirit, joy of spiritual longing: whatever it is called, in Benedict's Rule joy penetrates to the very heart of Lent. It is like the 'unspeakable delight' he promised the postulant at the end of the Prologue (Prol 49). In both cases, spiritual exultation bursts into a period dedicated to painful effort. From the Master's perspective, Lent was the image of life on earth: both led to happiness—Lent to Paschaltide and life to eternity, but in themselves they held nothing but long-suffering and austerity. While preserving their arduous character, Benedict lights them up with the joy born of love.

Another noteworthy feature appears in the introductory sentence to this third list: the monk offers his sacrifices to God 'of his own will'. Everywhere else in the Rule, 'self-will' is synonymous with disobedience and sin. Here the phrase takes on a positive meaning. Yet the conclusion to the chapter shows that Benedict had not lost sight of his teaching on obedience. Even when good, one's own will must be submitted to the 'abbot's will'. At the beginning of Lent, the Master organized a ceremony during which each brother informed the abbot of what he wished to do (RM 53, 11–15). But the purpose was not so much to obtain the superior's approval as to ensure, by means of a public statement amounting to a commitment made in front of everyone, that the abstainer would persist in his renunciation. On the other hand, the Master, in a brief later chapter, condemned any fasting and abstinence not authorized by the abbot (RM 74), as Basil had already done (*Reg.* 181). This is what we find here in Benedict's Rule.

Let us not leave this very important chapter—Lent is the model of the monk's entire existence—without noting the title of 'spiritual father', given the abbot. In the realm of the Spirit, where the joy of sacrifice and hope are to be found, the monk also has a father who holds the place of Christ, the second Adam, our father.

L

Brothers working at a distance from the oratory or travelling

[1] Brothers who are working at quite a distance and who cannot come to the oratory at the proper time—[2] the abbot having determined that this is the case—[3] shall celebrate the work of God right where they are laboring, and kneel with trembling before God.

[4] Likewise, those who have been sent on a journey are not to let the prescribed hours go by, but to observe them as best they can, not neglecting their measure of service.

THE TWO MATTERS dealt with together in this brief passage were the subject of distinct chapters in the Rule of the Master (RM 55–56). Beyond the discussion of Lent, they are connected with the schedule laid out in the previous chapter: once the conjunction of occupations and offices for brothers in the monastery has been taken care of, the same is done for those who are away at work or travelling.

The other Rule very readily dispensed monks from attendance at the choral office: any brother working more than fifty steps (seventy-five yards) away from the oratory was to stay where he was and pray by himself. The grounds for this very generous dispensation was that the monks

were to assemble in an instant and that even the slightest
tardiness was punished. Arriving on time from even a
minimal distance would have implied unwholesome haste.

Having made the sanctions for tardiness more flexible
and slowed down the process of assembling—sometimes
there are as many as two signals before an office (48:12)—
Benedict is more demanding about attendance at the
community celebration. Only those working 'at quite a distance' from the oratory are dispensed—a case not contemplated by the Master, who forbade agricultural labor, but
possible in the Rule of Benedict, who allows it (48:7). Moreover, the distance justifying a dispensation is no longer
set by the Rule, but left up to the abbot's judgment; his
permission is now required in each case.

As for travellers, Benedict brings his forerunner's detailed norms down to one simple principle: the brothers
are to do what they can; the essential objective is to celebrate the hour. For the office is not only a community
action to which a monk is bound when present within the
community. It is a personal obligation flowing from his
aim: to pray without ceasing.

Together with abstinence, Benedict included prayer in
the 'measure of service' to which we are to add during Lent
(49:5). By here reiterating the same expression (*seruitutis
pensum*), applied solely to praying the office, Benedict once
more calls to mind the slave of ancient times, who was
compelled to turn out a set amount (*pensum*) of work every
day. The office is a personal duty incumbent on each monk
as a servant of God.

This task is to be performed 'with divine trembling', as
was said earlier. Benedict also wanted the brothers to read
or chant in choir 'with trembling' (47:4). Happy the person
who perceives the greatness of God!

LI

Brothers on a short journey

[1] A brother who is sent on an errand and who is expected to return to the monastery that same day shall not presume to eat outside, even if he receives a pressing invitation—and no matter from whom—[2] unless his abbot has so bidden him. [3] Should he act otherwise, he will be excommunicated.

OF THE MANY QUESTIONS the Master dealt with in connection with the meals of travelling brothers, Benedict keeps only this one, and he simplifies it as much as his forerunner had complicated it. In the other Rule, permission to eat outside depended on several circumstances: the days of the week, the status of the person extending the invitation (monk, ordinary layman, or pious person), its more or less repeated and pressing character (in the name of charity or accompanied by an oath). A very elaborate casuistry took all these variables into account, not to mention the duration of the trip, which influenced the choice of mealtimes (RM 61).

Benedict cuts all these considerations short and leaves the matter to the abbot's discretion. Instead of being defined beforehand by the Rule, the course to be followed is decided on the spur of the moment by the superior. A written text cannot foresee everything; it is better to rely on the leader's living prudence. In principle, monks who go out only for the day do not eat outside. Exceptions are a matter of obedience. The augustinian Rule had already formulated this simple solution (*Ordo monasterii* 8). Benedict merely, and readily, adds a punishment. Such a sanction was missing both from the Master's text and from Augustine's.

The monk is not to eat outside because, having broken with society for God's sake, he is, as Evagrius says, 'separated from all and united to all' (*De oratione* 124). Paradoxically, for him union is conditional on separation.

LII

The oratory of the monastery

THIS LITTLE PASSAGE is truly an erratic block, with no apparent connection to what comes before and after it. It owes its place to the Master, whose corresponding chapter (RM 68) deals with observing silence when leaving an office; this matter is related to that of the prayer said after the office for brothers returning from a journey (RM 67). The benedictine chapter is thus indirectly and obscurely connected with the theme of going out, which has just been discussed (50–51).

[1] The oratory shall be what its name means, and nothing else is to be done or stored there. [2] Once the work of God is over, all shall leave in complete silence and with reverence for God, [3] so that a brother who may wish to pray alone and in private will not be prevented from doing so by another's inconsiderateness. [4] Moreover, if at other times someone wishes to pray alone and privately, let him go in and pray, not in a loud voice but with tears and heartfelt intent. [5] Accordingly, anyone who does not act in this manner shall not be allowed to remain in the oratory once the work of God is over, as we have said, to avoid his interfering with someone else.

Silence upon leaving the oratory: this order of the Master aimed at preventing the monks from humming psalms while going out after the office, as this would be a lack of reverence to the office and to God himself. Starting from this, Benedict constructs a brief treatise on the oratory which extends far beyond his forerunner's very limited purpose.

He borrows the initial principle from Augustine: the oratory's sacred purpose, written into its very name, must be preserved (cf. Mt 21:12–13). In the augustinian Rule, the purpose of thus ruling out all profane activity was to protect private prayer, which took place in the oratory between the hours of common prayer (*Praec.* II.2). In Benedict's the objective is the same, but the discussion of prayer between offices (4) is linked, under the influence of the Master, with that of prayer immediately after the office, when the community is leaving the sacred place.

Moreover—and this aspect is the most interesting—the obstacle to private prayer that must be eliminated is not only working in the oratory, but praying noisily in a loud voice. There was no question of this either in the Master's text or in Augustine's. It is Benedict who introduced this ban on praying out loud, while conversely recommending tears and heartfelt devotion.

We recognize here the interest in private prayer which appeared in the chapters on prayer (20) and Lent (49). Then as now, Benedict spoke in this connection of tears and of the heart. True prayer comes from the heart and brings tears. The place of prayer, which we must 'enter' for good, is the inner oratory of the soul, the regenerated heart into which the Holy Spirit pours his love. The word we must speak is the cry of this very Spirit calling on the Father and confessing the Lord Jesus in silence and tears.

'Not in a loud voice' (*non in clamose uoce*): these words could already be read in connection with human conversation, in the description of the humble monk (7:60). The same note of unobtrusiveness is appropriate in speaking to God. This was the meaning given in ancient times to the Gospel's ban on praying ostensibly and to its invitation to pray in the secrecy of one's room, with the door shut (Mt 6:5–6). The room is one's heart, the door is one's mouth. God who sees in secret also hears in silence. In contrast with the then common habit of praying out loud, silent prayer gives homage to God's loving attention.

This interpretation of the evangelical principle was all the more necessary because in Benedict's day the cenobite had no cell in which to pray secretly. In his day the oratory had become, of necessity, the place of private prayer as well as of the common office. For the community as a whole and for each of its members, it is spatially what the abbot is humanly: a sign of the Lord, the mediator between the monk and God.

LIII

The reception of guests

THIS EXTENSIVE DISSERTATION on hospitality includes notes scattered throughout four chapters (RM 65; 71–72; 79) by the Master, who did not yet have any organic treatise on the subject. But in speaking of other matters he repeatedly discussed relations with visitors, people encountered on journeys and strangers staying at the monastery. It was up to Benedict to articulate this material in a synthesis on the subject of 'the reception of guests'.

[1] All guests who present themselves are to be welcomed as Christ, for he will say: 'I was a stranger and you welcomed me'. [2] Proper honor shall be shown 'to all, especially to our brothers in the faith' and to foreigners.

[3] Once a guest has been announced, therefore, the superior and the brothers are to meet him with all the courtesy of love. [4] First of all, they are to pray together, and then they shall give one another peace. [5] This kiss of peace must be given only after praying, because of the delusions of the devil.

[6] All humility should be shown in addressing a guest on arrival or departure. [7] By a bow of the head or by a complete prostration of the body, Christ is to be adored because he is indeed welcomed in them. [8] After the

254

guests have been received, they should be led to prayer; then the superior or an appointed brother will sit with them. [9] The divine law shall be read to the guest for his edification. After that, every kindness shall be shown him. [10] The superior shall break his fast for the sake of the guest, unless it is a day of major fasting which cannot be broken, [11] while the brothers continue to observe the usual fasts. [12] The abbot shall pour water on the hands of the guests. [13] The abbot with the entire community shall wash the feet of all the guests. [14] After the washing they will recite this verse: 'God, we have received your mercy in the midst of your temple'.

[15] The greatest care and concern are to be shown in receiving poor people and pilgrims, because Christ is received in them more particularly; our very awe of the rich guarantees them special respect.

The end of this passage echoes the beginning. Both speak of receiving Christ in the person of the guest. Midway, this presence of Christ in those welcomed is recalled once again (7). The religious design—honoring Christ—which permeates the entire discussion could not be more clearly indicated.

The introduction, with its Gospel quotation (Mt 25:35), recalls the chapter on the sick, which also began by saluting Christ in the suffering brothers (36:2–3; cf. Mt 25:36 and 40). Benedict insisted then on the obligation of caring for them 'above and before all else'. Now he repeats the same term by directing that *all* guests be welcomed as Christ and that *all* be suitably honored. His major concern is indeed to 'honor all men', as he said at the beginning of the Rule (4:8), without any distinctions suggested by social rank. On the contrary, since Christ is being received, the highest honors must go to those closest to him: the 'brothers in the faith' (*domestici fidei*; Gal 6:10) who believe in him, the poor and foreigners whose destitution he shared.

Viewed as homage to Christ, hospitality is described with a fervor which recalls the *Lives of the monks of Egypt* even more than the Rule of the Master. Its first manifestation consists in praying with the guest, before giving him the kiss of peace. This priority given to prayer is justified by the fear of 'diabolical delusions'; in fact, the monks of the egyptian desert dreaded apparitions of devils disguised as human visitors. But beyond this motivation, the prayer-peace sequence obeys a basic liturgical law: in the christian assembly, dialogue with God precedes brotherly communion—which is grounded on it—just as the mutual kiss 'seals' prayer.

This order, which is that of the summary of the Law, is required here so that the relationship between the monks and their guest may be established in God rather than at the level of worldly intercourse. Albeit no hellhound, as the Egyptians feared, the person who comes to the monastery remains a subject of the Prince of this world. The monk, likewise a sinner, must be wary of establishing ungodly ties. That would truly be a 'delusion of the devil'. The guest must not bring the world into the monastery; instead, the monastery must give God to the guest.

Once purified by prayer, hospitality is truly a welcome given to Christ. After having followed him out of the world, we recognize him in those who come from the world. A gesture of worship expresses this lively faith.

Just as prayer comes before the peace, the reading of Scripture precedes the meal. The guest is granted the supreme honor of being treated as a spiritual person, interested primarily in the word of God. As for breaking the fast on his account, this comes down to stating implicitly that he represents the Bridegroom, in whose company we may not fast (Mt 9:15). Only the memory of the Passion on 'major days'—particularly Wednesdays and Fridays—overrides this awareness that Christ is there.

The washing of feet, a mark of hospitality dear to the early Church (1 Tm 5:10; cf. Lk 7:44–45) also calls the Lord to mind. Saint Martin, who bestowed it on some of his visitors, added to it the washing of hands, as Benedict requires (Sulpicius Severus, *Vita Mart.* 25.3). The psalm verse which follows (Ps 47:10) states once more that God has been welcomed in the guest. One needs to have seen the abbot and all the brothers kneeling at the feet of a postulant, as they formerly did at clothings, to appreciate the greatness of this Holy Thursday ritual.

[16] The kitchen for the abbot and guests shall be separate, so that guests, who arrive at unpredictable hours—and they are never lacking in monasteries—need not disturb the brothers. [17] Each year, two brothers who can do the work competently are to be assigned to this kitchen. [18] If necessary, they shall be given help so that they can perform this service without grumbling, and conversely, when they shall have less to do, they are to go wherever other work is assigned to them. [19] And this consideration is not only for them, but applies to all duties in the monastery: [20] when necessary, they shall be given help, and conversely, when they are free, they shall obey the orders given them.

[21] As for the guest quarters, they are to be entrusted to a brother whose soul is permeated with the fear of God. [22] An adequate number of beds, with bedding, shall be available there, and the house of God shall be wisely managed by wise men.

[23] No one is to speak or associate with guests in any way unless he is bidden, [24] but if he meets or sees them, he is to greet them humbly, as we have said, and asking for a blessing, he shall continue on his way, saying that he is not allowed to speak with a guest.

Of the three additional matters dealt with in this conclusion to the chapter—the guests' kitchen, their lodgings, the brothers' conversations with them—, the first has been initiated by the instructions concerning the meal (10–11). Since the abbot sometimes eats with strangers while the brothers fast, this difference in schedule makes separate kitchens advisable. The institution is entirely Benedict's own; neither the Master nor any other writer mentions this special kitchen. The fact that it is entrusted to two brothers, who may even need help, suggests not only that guests 'are never lacking', but also that there are ordinarily quite a few of them—many more in any case than in the Master's day.

The two brothers responsible for serving them remain in charge for a year, as was the case for all duties in contemporary palestinian monasticism, which we are acquainted with through Cyril of Scythopolis (*Vita Euthymii* 17, etc.). Concern with honoring the guests is obvious once more in this appointment of competent cooks on an annual basis, in contrast to the brothers who succeed one another in serving the community according to a simple weekly rotation, without any special qualification. Another preoccupation characteristic of Benedict is that of giving help to those who need it and of keeping them from grumbling (cf. 35:3–4 and 13).

The Master had provided special quarters for guests, with beds and bedding, but his aim was chiefly to avoid having the monastery's possessions stolen by dishonest visitors. It was also with a view to overseeing these dangerous gyrovagues that he entrusted the guesthouse to two brothers, who remained in charge only a week (RM 79). There is nothing common between Benedict's permanent guestmaster and these mere week-long custodians. The brother imbued with the fear of God and able to manage God's house wisely is obviously destined to serve the brothers of Christ sent by the Lord in a truly religious spirit.

The last paragraph, devoted to relations between monks and guests, is unprecedented in the Rule of the Master, but a tradition going back to Basil (*LR* 32.2; 45.1–2) and the Fathers of Lérins (*RIVF* 2.40) reserves such contacts to the superior and to those chosen by him. Like separate meals, separate conversations aim both at protecting monastic life and procuring the guests' welfare.

There is something severe about both these measures, in contrast to the enthusiasm of the welcoming ceremony. Like the Master's corresponding passages, the benedictine chapter on hospitality shifts from overflowing faith and charity to a reserved, almost distrustful attitude. The mystery of monastic life lies in this contrast between the religious fervor of the welcome and the demands of a conversion which is never completed. Only in the kingdom of God will we no longer need to fast and abstain from speech, to stay on our guard and apart from our neighbor. But such fasting and silence, such prudence and separation do in fact lead to the kingdom of God.

LIV

Should a monk receive letters or anything else?

THE PRECEDING CHAPTER ended with the prohibition of unauthorized communication with guests; the next one will recall the demands of renunciation in regard to clothing. The present passage is related to both: like *viva voce* conversations, letters and gifts are means of communicating with the outside, and accepting a proffered object is a way of appropriating it. Benedict has thus drawn from the surrounding chapters the idea of inserting this passage, which replaces instructions given by the Master on a completely different topic (RM 80).

[1] Under no circumstances shall a monk be allowed, unless the abbot says he may, to receive (or to give) letters, eulogies or small gifts of any kind, either from his parents or anyone else, or from a fellow monk. [2] Even if his parents send him something, he must not presume to accept it without previously telling the abbot. [3] If the abbot decides to accept, he has the power to give the gift to whom he will, [4] and the brother for whom it was originally sent is not to surrender to sadness, 'lest occasion be given to the devil'. [5] Whoever presumes to act otherwise shall be subjected to the punishment provided by the rule.

Benedict borrows the main body of his provisions from the augustinian Rule. In two separate passages, Augustine condemned quite distinct misdeeds, placed under the common heading 'hidden reception': receiving letters or small gifts from a woman on the sly (*Praec.* IV.11), and likewise receiving useful objects sent by one's family (*Praec.* V.3). In the first case, an offence against separation from the world and chastity was involved; in the second, a breach of common life and poverty.

Benedict brings these two passages from Augustine together and fuses them into a single law, whose sole aim is to subject all circulation of objects—either between the monastery and the outside or even within the community—to the abbot's control. Some details indicate that he felt the influence of Caesarius of Arles through the latter's paraphrase of the first augustinian text (*Reg. uirg.* 25). Like him, Caesarius added 'eulogies' (blessed tokens), which were commonly exchanged by servants of God, to Augustine's 'letters' and 'small gifts'. A famous example of this custom is the blessed bread sent Benedict by his neighbor, the priest Florentius (*Dial.* II.8.2–3).

The abbot alone can allow receiving or giving, and he alone allocates objects: these two rules simply recall chapters 33 and 34. As in the latter, Benedict here cautions against sadness at not receiving what is given to someone else. The scriptural phrase quoted to justify this warning (Eph 4:27; 1 Tm 5:14) has already been used twice (38:8; 43:8).

The monk, who is totally separated from the world, is so closely united to his brothers that what is sent him belongs to them as much as to himself. Thus the monastery offers a picture of the charity of early days: everything was common to all, and the Apostles, whose successor the abbot is, gave to each according to his needs (Ac 4:32 and 35).

LV

The brothers' clothing and footwear

THE MASTER DEALT with the brothers' clothing and total dispossession in two consecutive chapters (RM 81–82). The connection between the two matters is obvious: clothes are the main objects at the monk's disposal, those he can be tempted to appropriate. Benedict sums up the Master's two chapters in one. In his Rule, the transition from one question to the other takes place through instructions concerning beds, which along with bedding are both an appendage to clothing and a hiding place for monks bent on ownership.

1 The brothers shall be given clothing according to the nature of the place they live in and according to its climate, 2 for more is needed in cold areas and less in warmer ones. 3 This is left to the abbot's discretion. 4 However, we believe that in temperate regions a cowl and a tunic will suffice for each monk—5 a felted cowl in winter, a smooth or worn one in summer—, 6 and a scapular for work; as footwear, hose and shoes.

7 As for the color or coarseness of all these articles, the monks must not complain, but are to use what is available in the province where they live, or can be bought more cheaply. 8 However, the abbot shall see to

size, so that these garments will not be too short for the wearers, but fitted to them.

9 Whenever new clothing is received, the old shall be returned at once and temporarily stored in a wardrobe for the poor. 10 For it suffices a monk to have two tunics and two cowls, for night wear and laundering. 11 Anything more is superfluous and must be taken away. 12 The same holds for hose and everything old; it is to be returned when receiving new articles.

13 Those who are sent on a journey shall receive drawers from the wardrobe; they shall give them back on their return after washing them. 14 The cowls and tunics shall be a little better than those they usually wear. They are to receive them from the wardrobe when they leave on a journey and shall put them back on returning.

15 For bedding a mat, an ordinary blanket and a woolen one and a pillow shall suffice.

This first part, which corresponds to the first chapter of the other Rule, ranges from clothes and footwear to bedding. At the start, Benedict's thought process recalls what he said about food and drink: just as these necessarily differ from one individual to the next, clothing must likewise vary according to climate. In both cases, the Rule can indicate no more than an average, which the superior must adapt to the people or places involved.

Besides people and places, the seasons call for variations. The various requirements of day and night, life in the monastery and going out, must also be taken into account. However, these grounds for differentiation were not always acknowledged. At the beginning of monastic reflection on this matter, Basil categorically rejected them: a single garment must suffice day and night, inside and outside the monastery (*Reg.* 11; *LR* 22–23). Such radicalism may seem excessive, but it expresses an ideal of total simplicity which gives food for thought: a monk—or rather

a 'Christian', as Basil says—aims at being the same everywhere and always. He has neither several faces nor several
costumes.

To be precise, Benedict owes the principle governing the
quality of cloth to the basilian Rule: use what is available
locally, at the lowest possible price. This maxim, first formulated by Basil in connection with food (*Reg.* 9.21), was
then applied by him to clothing and footwear (*Reg.* 11.1
and 31). Like Benedict, he was also concerned with the
size of garments, which were to fit the wearer (*Reg.* 95.1).

Since the benedictine Rule makes use of Basil's in this
area, we would be well advised to examine the latter in
searching for the essential features of the habit, whose parts
Benedict is content to list. In fact, the great Cappadocian
was the first and last to draw up overall norms for the
clothing of his 'Christians', based on Scripture and following the line of the asceticism of early centuries. Later
authors will do no more than consider the elements of the
monastic habit one by one, sometimes endowing them with
a symbolic meaning which is attractive but appended (see
particularly Cassian, *Inst.* 1).

In brief, Basil wants the habit to be humble and poor, for
a Christian is to regard himself as the lowliest of all; it must
be distinctive and recognizable, so as to set the consecrated
person apart visibly; finally, it must be common to all
the brothers, so that there will be no worldly differences
between them. Clothing thus reflects the two basic characteristics of life in the brotherhood, which is both separated
from the world for love of God and communal for love of
one's neighbor. The habit must be practical as well as poor,
suitable for manual labor and other good works. As for
its distinctive appearance, Basil rightly acknowledges its
important educational function: constantly reminding the
wearer and those who see him of the holy life it signifies.
Putting it on means committing oneself, in the eyes of

everyone and in one's own, to a certain kind of behavior, forbidding oneself everything which might go against such holiness.

At the end of the present passage, Benedict insists several times on returning to the wardrobe anything which is no longer needed: old articles when new ones are received, travel outfits on coming back. As for food, he is keen on the monk's having only what 'suffices'. In both areas, in fact, he shows himself less generous than the Master.

Among these recommendations, one detail attracts our attention: after being replaced, used garments are stored in the wardrobe 'for the poor'. This has led some to conclude that the monks' dress was no different from that of seculars. In actual fact, the available documents unanimously prove that monks' garb always differed markedly from that of other people. But while it singled out the consecrated at a glance, the 'holy habit' was not so far removed from ordinary clothing as to prevent some items' being given to the destitute.

[16] However, these beds shall be inspected frequently by the abbot, because of the appropriated objects which might be found there, [17] and if someone is found with something he has not received from the abbot, he shall be subjected to very severe punishment. [18] And in order that this vice of ownership may be completely uprooted, the abbot shall give all that is necessary, [19] that is, cowl, tunic, hose, shoes, belt, knife, stylus, needle, handkerchief, tablet, in order to do away with any excuse based on need.

[20] However, the abbot must always bear in mind this sentence from the Acts of the Apostles: 'They gave to each according to his needs'. [21] Thus the abbot also is to take into account the weaknesses of the needy, not the ill-will of the envious. [22] Yet in all his judgments he must bear in mind God's retribution.

In going on to the Master's second chapter, Benedict neglects a long spiritual dissertation on dispossession and dwells only on the practical provisions at the end (RM 82:26–28). In his forerunner's text, the group leaders were to examine their men; in his, the abbot must inspect the monks' beds. Indeed, now that private cells had been done away with, beds were the last hideout for the spirit of private ownership. They may be seen serving this function in Gaul (Caesarius of Arles, *Reg. uirg.* 30; *Lives of the Fathers of Jura* 79) and in Palestine (Dorotheos, *Instr.* 11.121), as well as in Italy.

We more or less re-encounter here the condemnation of the vice of private ownership and the norms regarding the distribution of essentials which formed the subject matter of chapters 33 and 34. But this time Benedict explicitly and exclusively addresses the abbot, insisting in new terms that all the brothers' needs must be met. In Chapter 34, he cautioned the members of the community against the discontent which necessary inequalities might arouse in them. Here he cautions the abbot not to give in to such 'envy' on the part of some. The superior must beware of egalitarianism as much as of favoritism, if the charity of the early Church is to prevail (Ac 4:35).

Before leaving this chapter, let us note that it does not exhaust the subject. When Benedict later speaks of the reception of postulants, he rounds off these rules about clothing by adding the most important point of all: the habit, which is received at the end of the profession ceremony, is *res monasterii*, 'the monastery's property' (58:26–28), and marks the new brother as belonging to God's household and to God himself.

LVI

The abbot's table

¹ The abbot's table must always be with guests and
travelers. ² Whenever there are fewer guests, it is within
his power to invite any of the brothers he wishes. ³ However, for the sake of maintaining good order, one or two
seniors must always be left with the brothers.

THIS BRIEF PASSAGE exactly corresponds, in place and
content, to a slightly longer chapter of the Master (RM
84). At the abbot's table the Master had the following eat:
the seniors of the monastery—in particular the porters,
both elderly men—, visitors, and the brothers who knew
the psalter, these last in turn and at the abbot's choice.
Benedict, in line with the chapter on hospitality (53:10–11
and 16), singles out 'guests and pilgrims', who are now the
abbot's only appointed table companions; the locals simply
fill the gaps when there are fewer strangers.

This confirms what we learned three chapters earlier: in
the community, the abbot is, so to speak, especially charged
with hospitality, with a view to honoring and edifying
guests. The person who represents Christ in the monastery
shares his table with those whom the monastery receives
as Christ. In Benedict's view as in the Master's, moreover,

this table is probably in the common refectory, in spite of a widespread interpretation which has come down through the centuries. On fast days, the abbot and guests eat there earlier than the members of the community, but often all have dinner and supper together.

As for the brothers' tables, the Master wished the two heads of each group of ten to be always present to supervise their men. Benedict is less strict: 'one or two' seniors are to see to good order. While probably retaining two deans at the head of each group of ten, he does not attach as much importance as had his forerunner—here and elsewhere—to the educational task of these abbot's helpers. Might he rely more on each monk's looking out for himself in the sight of God?

LVII

The artisans of the monastery

[1] If there are artisans in the monastery, they shall exercise their trade in all humility, if the abbot permits. [2] If one of them becomes puffed up by his skillfulness in his craft, thinking that he is conferring something on the monastery, [3] he is to be removed from practicing that craft and not allowed to resume it, unless he humbles himself and the abbot so orders him.

[4] Whenever products of these artisans are sold, those responsible for the sale must not dare to practice any fraud. [5] Let them always remember Ananias and Sapphira, who incurred bodily death, [6] lest they and all who perpetrate fraud in monastery affairs suffer spiritual death.

[7] The scourge of avarice must not creep into prices, [8] but they shall always sell for slightly less than the other secular producers are able to, [9] 'so that in all things God may be glorified'.

THIS PASSAGE is the exact equivalent of a chapter of the Master (RM 85) which is barely longer. Yet, it denotes new concerns, unique to Benedict. The Master's main and nearly sole purpose was bringing sale prices down; to this he added, in closing, some precautions against the dishonesty of the vendors. These two questions are dealt with in reverse order by Benedict in his second and third paragraphs. On the other hand, the first benedictine paragraph, with its characteristic concern for humility, is entirely new. The chapter as a whole takes a new orientation from this, as appears from the title itself: instead of dealing with the sale of the products of craftmanship (RM 85:T), its subject is 'the monastery's artisans'. Benedict is more interested in people than things.

Obedience and humility: these two major virtues of the monk are brought out once more in the first lines of the text. They come before all monetary profit. The spiritual dimension comes first: the community is to lose money, if necessary, rather than lose a soul. This detachment from profit presages the lack of interest in sales, which will be brought up in closing.

In the Master's small monasteries, the artisans themselves sold what they made. In two general phrases, which allow us to discern the presence of middlemen, Benedict directs his warnings at 'all those' involved in the sale. He also innovates in conjuring up the memory of Ananias and Sapphira (Ac 5:1–11). The Master contented himself with requiring honesty and with imposing it through practical measures. Omitting the latter, Benedict makes the request more pressing by founding it on a scriptural example.

In the final description, a charitable cut in prices obviously presupposes an economic context different from our own. The days of the Master and of Benedict were not marked by affluence, as ours are, and selling inexpensively was a form not of competition, but rather of generosity. In this regard, Benedict backs down slightly from his predecessor's directions: the current price is lowered only 'a little'.

Apart from this qualification, no doubt due to the economic difficulties of the time—the terrible years of the war between Byzantines and Goths—, the benedictine Rule makes the Master's splendid abnegation its own. For the community as a whole as for each of its members, the spiritual dimension comes first. The fine scriptural maxim with which Benedict ends his chapter expresses this priority concern: 'glorifying God' (1 P 4:11). Unlike the unworthy monks ridiculed by Saint Jerome—who took advantage of their religious status in order to increase their prices (*Ep.* 22.34.2)—the true servants of God cut theirs, for there is more happiness in giving than in receiving.

LVIII

The procedure for receiving brothers

THIS LONG and singularly important chapter replaces four of the Master's which successively regulated the arrival of postulants and the disposal of their goods, the two months of reflection granted them, their commitment in the profession ceremony, and finally the year of waiting required of laymen before their clothing (RM 87–90). Benedict has made this great whole, which lacked cohesion, into a synthesis where we find most of its elements, even though they have been reordered and rounded off by many new provisions.

1 When a newcomer arrives with a view to religious life, he shall not easily be granted entry, 2 but as the Apostle says: 'Test the spirits to see if they are from God'. 3 Therefore, if the new arrival persists in knocking at the door, shows himself patient in bearing, after four or five days, the harsh treatment inflicted on him and the difficulty of entry, and persists in his request, 4 he shall be allowed to enter, and he will be in the guest quarters for a few days.

5 After that, he shall be in the novices' quarters, where they study, eat and sleep. 6 They shall be given a senior

skilled in winning souls, who shall watch over them with the utmost attention.

7 The concern shall be whether he truly seeks God, whether he shows eagerness for the work of God, for obedience, for practices of humility. 8 All the hardships and difficulties that lead to God shall be foretold to him. 9 If he promises perseverance in his stability, after a period of two months let this rule be read straight through to him, 10 and let him be told: 'This is the law under which you are choosing to serve. If you can keep it, come in; if you cannot, you are free to leave'. 11 If he still stands firm, then he is to be taken back to the above-mentioned novices' quarters, and again tested in all manner of patience.

12 And after a period of six months, the rule shall be read to him, so that he may know what he is entering. 13 And if he still stands firm, after four months this rule shall be read to him once more. 14 And if, after having conferred with himself, he promises to keep everything and to observe everything commanded him, let him be received into the community, 15 knowing that the law of the rule establishes that from this day he will no longer be free to leave the monastery, 16 nor to shake from his neck the yoke of the rule, which, in the course of so prolonged a period of reflection, he was free either to reject or to accept.

Setting difficulties in the way of future monks is a tradition as old as monasticism among both hermits and cenobites. The purpose is to 'test spirits' (1 Jn 4:1) so as to avoid admitting to God's service persons moved by a spirit other than his own. In the primitive Church, the message of prophets was thus 'proved'; its divine authenticity was tested through confrontation with faith in Christ, the incarnate Word. In the monastery, 'probation' is demanded of persons asking to be monks, that is, to follow Christ, and their will is subjected to the test of patience. For it is through patience that we participate in Christ's passion (Prol 50). Persevering unto death through patience is the very core of monastic life. The ability to lead the life can thus validly be recognized by the perseverance with which the candidate for a time endures the difficulty of entry.

This time of waiting and testing underwent variations. In Egypt, according to Cassian, it lasted ten days or more (*Inst.* 4.3). At Lérins, it lasted a week (*RIVF* 2.25). Benedict's 'four or five days' correspond to only half these periods, but the trial retains its former roughness ('harsh treatment', literally 'insults'), which the Master seems to have relinquished.

'To persist in knocking' denotes an obstinate petitioner whose prayer is answered by God (Lk 11:8). Entering God's house cannot be achieved other than by entering his fatherly heart. He loves this persistent request, which he elicits by taking a long time in satisfying it.

After the 'few days' spent in the guesthouse, the candidate moves to separate premises. These 'novices' quarters' are an innovation of Benedict, as is the senior in charge of watching over them. The novice no longer stays at the monastery gate in the custody of the porter, as in the egyptian monasteries described by Cassian, or in the parlor, as in Caesarius' monastery at Arles, but in a special dwelling place, with an instructor who takes special care of him and his fellows. This novice master's role, which the Rule of the Master ascribed to the abbot himself, requires, according to Benedict, the ability to 'win souls', an expression which calls to mind the Gospel (Mt 18:15) and especially Saint Paul (1 Co 9:19–22). Just as Paul transformed himself in order to be all things to all people, the senior must adapt himself to each novice in order to win him, imitating the abbot who labors in directing souls and in bowing to the monks' multiple character differences (2:31).

'Studying' (literally 'meditating'), 'eating, sleeping': most of the novice's existence takes place apart from the brothers, whom he encounters only at the office and perhaps at manual work. The purpose of this separation is to make the step of profession—the real entry into the community—a more important and desirable one. Until then, the novice must still feel like a free stranger, not admitted and not committed. Being a monk entails deciding to remain one forever. In this sense, there is and there can be no such thing as a monk on a trial basis. While the experience which precedes profession thus remains limited, the decisive import of that commitment is all the clearer for it: it and it alone gives access to monastic life.

Just as the novice's existence has been summed up in three verbs, likewise the eagerness which he must evince has three objects: the work of God, obedience, and practices of humility (literally: 'opprobrium'). This threefold agenda bears some analogy to the ladder of humility, in which the first step consists in being attentive to God, and the next in various forms of obedience and then of abasement. Only the last steps, relative to outward behavior, are missing here, perhaps simply so as not to go beyond the figure of three, that perfect measure which conditions many of this chapter's provisions.

In describing the ideal novice, Benedict also seems to remember the basilian Rule, which had already asked that candidates be examined for a 'vehement desire for the work of God' and the readiness to do everything commanded them, even things regarded as 'opprobrium' in the world (*Reg.* 6–7). In going from Basil to Benedict, the phrase 'work of God' changes meaning: for Basil, as for Saint Paul (1 Co 15:58), it referred to the full scope of the divine service; for Benedict, it surely refers, here as in the rest of the Rule, to the office, the greatest divine act, without excluding the secret prayer which must ceaselessly prolong it.

As for 'opprobrium', on the other hand, nothing suggests that Benedict's notion differs from Basil's. He simply had in mind the not very choice tasks required by daily life in community. This final object of the novice's concern is made up of the humble and necessary jobs enjoined by his superiors, rather than of artificial humiliations.

Prayer, obedience, humility: these three main criteria of a good novice are the signs of one and the same will which 'seeks God'. A common expression in the Old Testament, this formula occurs at least once in the New, in connection with the obscure and irrepressible dynamism which moves the entire history of mankind (Ac 17:27). 'Seeking God' is also the deep and unifying motive which sustains each monk's activity. Without this basic desire, any and all virtuous practices shrivel and degenerate. With it, no effort is tiring, no difficulty is insurmountable.

For God, we are ready to undergo 'all hardships and difficulties'. And in fact, this is how we 'go to God'. The cross is on the shoulder of anyone who follows Christ, and Paul, who had learned this by experience, spoke of the 'many tribulations through which we must enter the kingdom of God' (Ac 14:22). Following his example, the monastery's superiors—the abbot in the Rule of the Master, the senior in Benedict's—foretell the trials of this journey, not without giving a glimpse of the fullness of happiness and hope to which it leads (cf. Prol 49).

These realistic predictions are supported by the reading of the Rule, which uncovers the demands and asperities of monastic life. It is read three times at irregular intervals: after two, six, and then four months. This uneven division of the year is peculiar to Benedict but originated with the Master, who placed commitment by profession at the end of a two-month period. Although it does not have the same solemn and final character, the 'promise of perseverance in stability' (*de stabilitate sua perseuerantia*) which Benedict has the novice make is a genuine anticipation of profession, in which the first promise will be precisely that of 'stability' (58:17).

The soldier's *stabilitas* consists in 'standing' (*stare*) in spite of the enemy who attempts to cut him down, and in 'holding his ground' instead of running away. This warlike vocabulary, which Saint Cyprian makes abundant use of in his exhortations to martyrs, reappears whenever Benedict depicts the novice face to face with the demands of the Rule and 'still standing firm'. These successive decisions to 'stand firm' prefigure and prepare the great commitment to standing firm one's whole life long which will be made at profession.

The second reading of the Rule does not give rise to a particular commitment. On the contrary, the third is followed by a 'promise' having two terms: keeping everything prescribed by the Rule and obeying all the superiors' commands. This twofold commitment, made in private, will be publicly renewed in the act of profession: these will be the promises of 'good life and morals' and of 'obedience'.

[17] Before being received, he shall promise before all, in the oratory, stability, good life and morals, and obedience, [18] before God and his saints, so that, if he ever acts otherwise, he shall know that he will be condemned by the one he mocks. [19] He is to state his promise in a petition drawn up in the name of the saints whose relics are there, and of the abbot in charge. [20] He shall write this petition with his own hand, or, if he does not know how to write, another shall write it at his request, and the novice shall put his mark to it and with his own hand lay it on the altar. [21] After he has put it there, the novice himself shall begin the verse: 'Receive me, Lord, according to your word, and I shall live, and do not disappoint me in my expectation.' [22] The whole community shall repeat the verse three times and add: 'Glory be to the Father'. [23] Then the novice brother shall

prostrate himself at the feet of each monk, that they may pray for him, and from that day he is to be counted as one of the community.

24 If he has any possessions, he should either give them to the poor beforehand, or make a formal donation of them to the monastery, without reserving himself anything at all, 25 since from that day he will not even have power over his own body.

26 Then and there in the oratory, he is to be stripped of his own garb that he is wearing and clothed in the monastery garb. 27 The clothing taken from him is to be put away and kept safely in the wardrobe, 28 so that, should he ever agree to the devil's suggestion and leave the monastery—which God forbid—he may be stripped of the monastery garb before he is cast out. 29 But that petition of his which the abbot took from the altar should not be given back to him, but kept in the monastery.

Of the three solemn promises made in the oratory on the day of profession, only the second is somewhat difficult to interpret. Let us note first that this *conuersatio morum* was replaced for centuries by *conuersio morum*, which was translated or rather transposed as 'conversion of manners'. In actual fact, *conuersatio* is not a 'conversion' but a way of life. The word, used ten times by Benedict, can be translated in most cases by 'religious life' (cf. 58:1), sometimes by 'behavior' or 'asceticism'.

This 'religious life' can be led in many different ways: in some cases it is 'wretched' (1:12), in others 'holy' (2:1); beginners bring to it a sometimes naive fervor (1:3) and each monk has his own more or less generous manner of practising it (22:2). But the most important fact is its dynamic character: it has a 'beginning' and a 'perfection' (73:1–2), between which extends an indefinite career of 'progress' (Prol 49; cf. 63:1).

The second term of the formula (*morum*, 'of morals') simply reiterates and reinforces the first, more or less as in the expression 'life and morals'. Promising *conuersatio morum* thus amounts to committing oneself to living the religious life. But since this is a dynamic process, an undefined movement toward perfection, we commit ourselves to entering into that movement in order to let it carry us as far as God wills. In practice, the Rule defines the 'beginnings of religious life' to be practised here and now and throughout our life, so as to 'have at least some decency of morals' (73:1).

The object of promising 'good life and morals' is therefore the observation of the Rule, conceived as the foundation of a monastic life which will develop, with God's help, in the light of Scripture and of the teaching of the Fathers (73:2–9).

Preceded by stability and followed by obedience, *conuersatio morum* is linked to both. The monk first promises to 'stand firm' on the spot his whole life. But staying there is not enough to achieve this purpose. To 'stand firm' is to persevere in a certain way of life, the one led in the monastery and defined in the Rule. Obedience to the superior is the most general trait of this monastic behavior, for the abbot is the interpreter and keeper of the Rule.

A place: the monastery. A law: the Rule. A live authority: the abbot. We recognize here the three elements by which Benedict, following the Master, defined cenobitism (1:2). In binding himself to them by a solemn commitment, the new cenobite recapitulates the successive promises of his novitiate: after two months, he promised stability; at the end of the year, observance of the Rule and obedience to his superiors.

Stamped this way with the number three, which haunts Benedict throughout this chapter, the promise is recorded in a written deed which the novice lays on the altar. This gesture was already prescribed by the Master, as was the recitation of the verse that follows: 'Receive me . . .' (Ps 118:116). In both Rules, the prayer of the community seals the commitment, which is no mere act of the human will, but a work of grace which finds its origin and end in God. It is the Spirit of God which led the postulant to the monastery. It is his Word, both a call and a norm, which prompts the offering and the expectation of the professed. The divine promise envelops the human promise.

Entering the community is accompanied by a renunciation of all ownership. This can take two forms, the first inspired by the Gospel (Mt 19:21) and the second by the Acts of the Apostles (Ac 4:32). Here as earlier (33:4), Benedict connects dispossession with obedience: since he no longer has power over his own body (cf. 1 Co 7:4), a monk may still own an object exterior to him.

The stripping away of personal clothing brings dispossession to its utmost limit. It brings to mind Jesus on Calvary, but also the hour at which the baptized person is stripped of the old man and puts on Christ. The monastic habit represents Christ. The monk is reminded at every moment by this 'monastery garb', which he wears constantly and which does not belong to him, that he no longer belongs to himself, but has become God's property.

LIX

Sons of nobles and sons of poor people who are offered

[1] If a nobleman offers his son to God in the monastery, if the child is very young, his parents shall draw up the petition mentioned above, [2] and they shall wrap this petition and the child's hand in the altar cloth with the gifts, and offer him thus.

[3] As to his property, either they shall make a sworn promise in this petition that they will never give him anything nor afford him the opportunity of ever possessing anything—neither personally, nor through the guardian whom they might appoint, nor in any way at all—, [4] or else, if they are unwilling to do this and are bent on offering something as alms to the monastery so as to win their reward, [5] they shall make a donation of the property they wish to give to the monastery, keeping the revenue for themselves, if they so desire. [6] And thus all avenues shall be barred, so that the child may not be left with any notions that might deceive him for his own ruin, God forbid! This is what we have learned by experience.

[7] Poorer people shall do the same. [8] As for those who have nothing at all, they shall simply write the petition and offer their son with the gifts in the presence of witnesses.

AFTER HIS FOUR CHAPTERS on the admission of postulants, the Master added a very long one devoted to the special case of sons of noble families not yet in possession of
the considerable wealth they were to inherit from their parents. Addressing the parents, Benedict's predecessor urged
them to settle their son's material situation either by giving
his entire share to the poor, or by dividing it between the
poor, the family, and the monastery, or by not bequeathing
him anything at all.

The benedictine text, which is nearly ten times shorter,
remains dominated by the Master's major concern: the
young noble must be totally dispossessed so as not to be
tempted to return to the world. But Benedict innovates in
two ways. First, instead of the case of an adolescent who
spontaneously decides to become a monk, he considers that
of a child offered by his parents. Next, he generalizes: to
noble candidates, he adds those from other social back-
grounds.

The first of these changes led to the creation of a ritual for
the offering of children. We re-encounter the written deed
of the previous chapter, but instead of being placed on the
altar by the professed himself, this 'petition' is wrapped in
the altar cloth, along with the child's hand, by the parents.
By specifying that both document and hand are joined to
the eucharistic 'gifts', Benedict indicates the time and the
liturgical setting of the action: it takes place at the offertory
of the Mass. The person of the child is ritually associated
with the bread and wine, the body and blood of Christ.

This indication may also apply to the profession of adults,
in which time was not determined by the preceding chapter. In any case, the conjunction of the monastic commitment and the eucharistic sacrifice is highly significant, and
it is easy to understand why it has become the general
norm. Becoming a monk means strengthening and deepen-
ing the relationship with the dead and risen Christ

established once and for all at baptism. What better way is there of signifying this renewal than by inserting the action into the Eucharist, which proclaims the Lord's death and resurrection?

The relation between monastic commitment and baptism must be kept in mind in considering the point we find difficult in this chapter: the fact that the child is consecrated through the sole will of his parents, who pledge his entire existence without his consent. Although the history of the first christian centuries offers many examples of similar acts, the Church long maintained as a matter of principle that the parents' offering had to be ratified by their offspring, whether a boy or a girl, between the ages of fifteen and twenty. But a general evolution which took place in Rome between the fifth century (Saint Leo) and the eighth (Gregory II) increasingly regarded the parental act as an irrevocable commitment, to the detriment of the child's freedom.

The benedictine Rule offers some of the oldest and surest evidence of this evolution. Its rite of commitment visibly establishes a permanent state, the breach of which its other provisions simply aim at preventing. The child is not afforded the slightest possibility of choice, despite what Saint Basil's Rule prescribed.

Outrageous as it is in our modern eyes, and was already in the view of the early Church, this refusal to take freedom into consideration becomes more understandable if we think of infant baptism, by which most of us became Christians without so choosing. No doubt the choice of celibacy and asceticism is not as vital as that of faith, but faith is no less personal than they are. Yet in both cases a person's religious fate is decided by someone else; the person concerned has only to ratify the commitment made in his stead, in the hope of receiving, along with this calling conferred through a third party, the grace of faith offered to all or the special charism of virginity.

LX

Priests who wish to dwell in the monastery

[1] If a member of the priestly order asks to be received into the monastery, he should not meet with agreement too quickly. [2] However, if he persists absolutely in his pleading, he must know that he will have to observe the full discipline of the rule [3] and that there will be no mitigation in his favor, according to Scripture: 'Friend, what have you come for?' [4] However, he may occupy the place after the abbot's and give blessings and conclude the prayers, provided the abbot so bids him; [5] if not, he shall not presume anything at all, knowing that he is subject to the punishments of the rule, and he shall rather give everyone an example of humility. [6] And whenever there is question of an appointment or of any other business in the monastery, [7] he shall regard as his own the place that corresponds to his entry into the monastery, and not that granted him out of respect for his priesthood.

[8] As for clerics, if one of them, similarly moved by the same desire, wishes to join the monastery, he shall be ranked somewhere in the middle, [9] provided, however, that they also promise to keep the rule and observe stability.

CONTINUING HIS REVIEW of special vocations, Benedict here deals with priests and clerics; the next chapter will be devoted to unknown, or stranger, monks. The Master already provided for priests' living in the monastery, but he did so in another place and from a very different perspective: instead of following the chapters on recruitment, the one on priests preceded them (RM 83) and was connected instead with the advice on hospitality. In fact, priests were received only as guests; the legislator's main concern was to keep them from meddling in the government of the community and to oblige them to perform manual labor.

Unlike his forerunner, Benedict admits priests as members of the community and applies to them—more considerately—the method of probation set out for ordinary vocations. In their case there is no mention of waiting at the door or insults, nor of a novitiate year with formal demands to choose; but they must overcome an unwilling reception, insistently renew their request, and agree to submit to the Rule in everything. More specifically, as is said in closing with regard to clerics, they must promise to keep the Rule and observe stability. We here recognize the promises of *stabilitas* and of *conuersatio morum* (58:17), the latter obviously including obedience to superiors.

Subjection to the Rule, mentioned three times, is accompanied by another condition for admission: acceptance of a community rank determined basically by date of entry, even though the priest or cleric is granted a fairly lofty place of honor. These remarks on rank, alternating with appeals to keep the Rule, herald the chapter which Benedict will soon devote to rank in community (63).

Priests can thus be granted a special place and allowed to carry out the sacred functions which belong to the superior: give blessings, conclude the prayers (*missas tenere*, an expression which can also mean 'to celebrate Mass'). Like the Master, Benedict readily acknowledges their priestly

dignity. But as in the Rule of the Master, they are denied any special authority independent of the abbot's. We
have here a truly remarkable situation: by joining a society
whose sole law is that of Christ, the minister of Christ
loses all power and submits to a superior who may not be
invested with priesthood.

Nothing can better evince the mysterious nature of the
monastery and its relation to the Church. As a 'school
of Christ', the monastery is both a part of the universal
Church and an entity distinct from the secular Church,
subordinate to it and superior to it. While receiving the
word of God and the sacraments from the Church and
its hierarchy, as well as the baptized who come to it and
the acknowledgment which authenticates its leaders, the
monastery's task is nevertheless to teach and institute a
perfect way of life which Christians and their shepherds
cannot lead in the world. In this 'school' of evangelical
perfection, authority belongs entirely to a representative of
Christ whose mission is to teach, to live the Gospel, and to
see that it is lived in its full force, so as to recreate around
himself the group of the Twelve around Jesus, the Church
of Jerusalem surrounding the Apostles.

After preaching the faith, instilling the foundations of
christian life, directing the assembly of the faithful, the
priest-turned-monk becomes a disciple of Christ in a new
way, learning the perfect christian life among those who
strive to lead it. Hence the self-effacement required of him
in the 'school of Christ'. Already called upon, like all ministers of the Lord, to make himself all the smaller because
he was greater, he is now urged by Benedict to provide
everyone with an example of humility. This is why he
came to the monastery: to live out this characteristic trait of
Christ and of Christians. As a collaborator of the apostolic
order, he is asked the question which Jesus, when entering
his Passion, put to one of those he had chosen: 'Friend,
what have you come for?' (Mt 26:50).

LXI

Unknown Monks: How they are to be received

[1] If an unknown monk arrives from distant provinces, if he wishes to stay in the monastery as a guest [2] and is content with local custom as he finds it, and does not trouble the monastery by his pointless demands, [3] but is simply content with what he finds, he shall be received for as long a time as he wishes. [4] If he should make some reasonable criticism or remark, with humble charity, the abbot shall prudently consider whether the Lord did not send him for this very purpose.

[5] If later on he wishes to remain for good, he shall not be refused this wish, especially as there was time enough to judge his life while he was a guest. [6] If he showed himself demanding or full of vices while a guest, not only he should not be joined to the body of the monastery, [7] but instead he should be politely told to leave, lest his wretched ways vitiate others. [8] If he does not deserve to be dismissed, not only, if he so asks, he shall be received and made a member of the community, [9] but he shall even be urged to stay, so that others may learn from his example, [10] and because in all places we serve the same Lord, we serve under the same king.

IN TWO CONSECUTIVE chapters, the Master dealt with unknown brothers who asked for hospitality. Following an early christian maxim (*Didachè* 11–12) taken up by the monks of Egypt (*Vitae Patrum* V.10.97), he limited to two days the duration of hospitality properly so called. Once this time was over, the guest had to earn his living through work as the members of the community did; otherwise he was asked to leave (RM 78). Lodged in separate premises and constantly supervised by two attendants, guests could either request admission into the community—in which case they followed the common channel—or prolong their stay, provided they earned their keep (RM 79).

Like those the Master devoted to priests, these chapters on unknown monks were placed before the section on recruitment and mainly concern hospitality. Benedict, on the contrary, deals with these two categories of persons after the chapter on novices and from the angle of integration into the community. Moreover, he deeply renews the subject by doing away with some points—the Master's two days are replaced by an indefinite period, the manual work requirement and supervision disappear—and by placing himself on a higher plane, from which the matter is considered in a more general and spiritual way. He is interested above all in the good or bad influence which the monastery and the unknown monk may exert on one another. The community may expect that the guest will not only refrain from disturbing its peace, but will even make profitable remarks and eventually join it for its greater edification. On his side, the unknown monk, in settling down, finds the benefit of stability, and along with it a clearer awareness of the one thing that is necessary: the Lord and his service, wherever one is.

This beautifully formulated final sentence obviously recalls the beginning of the Prologue. But there Benedict spoke only of 'serving the Lord Christ, the true king' (Prol 3); the verb (*militare*) referred to a soldier's public service. Here the image is heightened by *seruire*, the private service of the slave, while the word referring to the Lord (*Domino*) also calls to mind the master of a household, rather than a king.

Another echo of the early pages of the Rule may be perceived in the good advice given the abbot: he is to consider whether the guest's admonitions might not come from the Lord. Already, in dealing with the council, Benedict prescribed that everyone be allowed to voice his opinion, because 'often the Lord reveals what is better to the younger' (3:3). Soon, in connection with rank in community, we will reencounter this spirit of a faith which is able to recognize in every human being, whatever his status, a potential messenger from God. Here, moreover, Benedict notes the sign which indicates the possibility of divine intervention: the reasonable, humble, and charitable way in which the guest offers his suggestions. We are again reminded of the chapter on counsel, where the brothers were asked to give their opinion humbly. Humility is the mark of God.

[11] Further, if the abbot sees that he is worthy of it, he may set him in a somewhat higher place. [12] In fact, not only a monk, but also the members of the priestly and clerical orders mentioned above may be set by the abbot in a place higher than that of their entry, if he sees that their life warrants it.

[13] However, the abbot must take care never to receive a monk from another known monastery permanently without his abbot's consent or without letters of recommendation, [14] for it is written: 'Do not do to another what you do not want done to yourself'.

The unknown monks who join the monastery do not seem to be subject to the ordinary system of probation described three chapters earlier. Like priests, they enter the community without special formalities. Also, like priests and clerics, they may be given a place higher than that of their entry. In reiterating what he said earlier regarding the rank of clerics, Benedict moreover modifies the grounds for promotion: instead of 'respect for the priesthood' (60:7), they now consist in the quality of 'life'. This new motivation is very much in line with a chapter where the prevailing concern is one of influence and example.

Since the Master did not establish any set rank among the brothers within the community, he could hardly have dealt with the place to be assigned the unknown monk. Neither did he mention the question addressed by Benedict in his final note: relations with the guest's original monastery. In actual fact, the all-too-numerous monks who dropped by the Master's guesthouse seem to have been mostly gyrovagues devoid of hearth and home.

Thus the benedictine Rule alone is concerned with the ties remaining between the guest and the community from which he comes. But this is no new concern. For centuries churches had been careful to preserve good mutual relations by requiring that visiting faithful, and especially clerics, provide written evidence that they were in communion with their bishops. Making this custom their own, abbots had begun to give similar certificates to the monks they sent out. In 506, the council of Agde had made this obligatory. Just as, and even more than, the Church, the monastery is a communion of faith and love; the order of charity must prevail between monasteries as between Churches, that order whose law is the golden rule of both covenants (Mt 7:12; Tb 4:16).

LXII

The priests of the monastery

[1] If an abbot asks to have a priest or a deacon ordained, he shall choose among his men one worthy to exercise the priesthood. [2] As for the one so ordained, he shall be on guard against conceit or pride, [3] and shall not presume to do anything besides what the abbot commands him, knowing that he shall be all the more subject to the punishments of the rule. [4] And he shall not forget obedience and the discipline of the rule just because he is a priest, but he shall make more and more progress toward God. [5] He shall always regard as his own the place that corresponds to his entry into the monastery, [6] except when it comes to the service of the altar, and unless the whole community chooses and the abbot wishes to give him a higher place because of the merit of his life; [7] however, he must know how to keep the rule established for deans and priors.

[8] Should he presume to act otherwise, he shall not be regarded as a priest but as a rebel. [9] And if after many warnings he does not improve, let the bishop himself be brought in as a witness. [10] Should he not amend even then, and his faults become notorious, he shall be dismissed from the monastery, [11] but only if

his obstinacy is such that he will not submit or obey
the rule.

THIS CHAPTER, which has no equivalent in the Master,
is no longer part of the section on recruitment; instead it
complements what was said there on priests and clerics
received into the community (60). In fact, the instructions
concerning clerics come up here again point by point. The
two chapters are as close in content as in place.

Thus, the monastery does not simply receive members of
the clergy to become monks. It can also ask the bishop to
ordain one of its members. This is a considerable innovation over the Master's purely lay communities. It ensures
the monastic community a permanent means of celebrating
the Eucharist, and thereby an autonomous ecclesiastical
status. Instead of attending Mass in the parish church,
as the Master's brothers did, or bringing secular clerics
to the monastery, as nuns or some monks were forced to
do, Benedict's disciples number among themselves ministers who provide them with the sacraments. The monastic
'school' thus comes to resemble a Church.

This developement tended to become general in the sixth
century. Aurelian of Arles, one of Benedict's contemporaries, ratified it in his own Rule, and the Emperor Justinian codified it in one of his laws (*Nou.* 133.2). Next to its
obvious advantages, it does, however, entail a risk: that of
dividing authority by setting up against the abbot a priest
who misuses his sacred powers. This disadvantage, often
avoided by having abbot and priest be one and the same
person, greatly concerned Benedict, who faced up to it by
advising the ordained monk to be submissive and humble.

Chosen for his ability to 'exercise the priesthood' (Si
45:19), the priest must not rest on this acknowledgment
of his merits, but rather 'make more and more progress
toward God', following the advice given by Saint Cyprian
to the 'confessors' of his day. Those who had braved death

for Christ's sake enjoyed great prestige, but their behavior in times of peace was not always on a par with the courage they had shown under persecution. The bishop of Carthage thus invited them to 'make more and more progress toward the Lord' (*Ep.* 13.6), instead of being content with their victory in the struggle of faith. By his priestly dignity, the ordained monk resembles these prominent Christians. Like them, he must honor his lofty position by constantly striving to draw nearer to God.

The monk-priest's humility will be evident in particular through his attachment to the rank which is his on account of his entry date. Higher rank obviously falls to him when performing his sacred ministry, and can also occur as a result of promotion 'because of the merit of his life'. This is the reason indicated in the previous chapter (61:12), instead of the 'respect for the priesthood' mentioned earlier (60:7).

The monk-priest's duties are restricted to the 'service of the altar': he presides at the eucharistic assembly. In Benedict's monastery, the Eucharist seems not to have been a daily event—nothing is said of it in connection with the schedule—, but it certainly took place on Sundays and feast days. On ordinary days, the monks probably received communion during a brief communion service annexed to the office preceding the meal, as directed by the Rule of the Master. This relative rarity of Mass does not indicate a lack of appreciation for it, quite the contrary. Reserving it to Sundays removes it from the daily routine and exalts both the Lord's day and his mystery.

In Benedict's time, priests and deacons were ordained for this liturgical service of the monastery. Their number was therefore determined by the requirements of the community liturgy. Only in the course of the following centuries did monk-priests multiply because of the daily celebration of private masses on many altars—usually at the request of the faithful, who sought intercession for themselves and their dead.

LXIII

Community rank

1 They shall keep their rank in the monastery as determined by date of entry and merit of life, and as the abbot decides. 2 However, the abbot is not to upset the flock entrusted to him, and he shall not make any unjust arrangement, as if enjoying unrestricted power, 3 but he shall always reflect that he will have to give God an account of all his judgments and actions. 4 Thus when the brothers come for the kiss of peace and for Communion, when they lead psalms or stand in choir, they shall do so in the order decided by the abbot or already existing among them. 5 And absolutely everywhere, age shall neither determine rank nor be an impediment, 6 since Samuel and Daniel, when still children, judged elders.

7 Therefore, except for those whom the abbot, as we have said, shall promote advisedly or demote for specific reasons, all the rest shall be as they entered: 8 for instance, the one who came to the monastery at the second hour of the day will regard himself as junior to the one who arrived at the first hour, whatever his age or dignity. 9 However, children are to be disciplined in everything by everyone.

BY ITS ROOTS in the Rule of the Master, this chapter is linked to the next, where the abbatial succession is regulated. For the Master did in fact closely connect the matter of community rank (RM 92) with the choice of a new abbot (RM 93). He made no mention of the brothers' places within their groups of ten, but directed that no set order be established between those groups, to avoid letting the leader of any of them rank second to the abbot and thus make him appear as his chosen successor.

Unlike his forerunner, Benedict deals with rank for its own sake, and far from mingling the brothers, he arranges them in a well-defined order based on the date of their entry into the community. There is nothing original about such an arrangement—it can be found as early as the beginnings of cenobitism in the pachomian congregation, and in Benedict's time in the writings of Fulgentius of Ruspe—, but it signals a reaction against the Master's principles. While the decanal system so dear to the Master holds a very modest place in the benedictine Rule, the latter carefully regulates and makes use of community rank. For Benedict, the monastic community is no motley crowd, nor an army subject to military discipline, but a spiritual family in which each member has an acknowledged age and an appointed place.

This age is reckoned from the date of religious birth, no account being taken of the years before that. To justify such a cancellation of natural seniority, Benedict quotes the cases of Samuel (1 K 3:11–18) and Daniel (Dan 13:44–62). But age according to the flesh is not the only factor abolished; social status is also obliterated. In this connection, Benedict could quote here, as he did in the chapter on the abbot, the words of Saint Paul declaring that all the baptized are one in Christ: there is no longer any slave or free man (Gal 3:28; Col 3:11).

By this denial of social distinctions, at the root of which is the renunciation of property, the monastic 'school' makes into an operational and tangible reality an equality which remained potential and mystical in the Church. After baptism, which in principle abolishes former categories, Christians remain divided into adults and children, rich and poor, masters and servants. After profession, monks are truly emancipated from these natural or artificial classifications and grouped according to uniquely spiritual criteria: the date of entering religion and the merit of their life, the latter being evaluated by that representative of Christ, the abbot.

Based on intense faith, which counts all qualifications other than belonging to Christ as nothing, this new order does not, however, blindly negate the visible realities instituted by Providence. According to the final words of the text, special measures, specified further on, are allowed for the care of children. In many instances, the Rule has also provided for the special needs of children and the elderly, as well as of those who are more delicate on account of their former status. This realism tempers the ideal make-up of a society where everything is defined simply in relation to the service of the Lord.

[10] The young shall, therefore, honor their seniors, and the seniors shall love their juniors. [11] As regards the names by which they adress one another, no one shall be allowed to call another simply by name, [12] but the seniors shall call the juniors by the name of brothers, while the juniors shall give their seniors the title of *nonni*, which means 'Reverend Father'. [13] As for the abbot, since he is believed to represent Christ, he shall be titled lord and abbot, not for any claim of his own, but out of honor and love for Christ. [14] But for his part, he must reflect on this and behave so as to be worthy of such honor.

[15] Whenever the brothers meet, the junior is to ask the senior's blessing. [16] When a superior comes by, the subordinate shall rise and offer him his seat. And the junior

shall not presume to sit down again until his senior bids him, [17] that they may do as is written: 'Vie with one another in honoring one another'.

[18] In the oratory and at table, small children and adolescents shall keep their rank in good order. [19] But outside or anywhere else, they shall be supervised and kept in line until they are old enough to understand.

On the basis of seniority, Benedict establishes a charter of fraternal relations which he will complete in the last chapters of the Rule. Nothing similar could be found in the Master's text. A strictly personal concern urged Benedict to complement the purely hierarchical structure of the Master's community—where only the monk's relationship with God through his superiors mattered—with what we may call 'horizontal' relations among the brothers. Yet these in turn are organized into a hierarchy: although spoken of in terms of 'honoring one another', the duties of seniors and those of juniors are not identical, but are conditioned by their respective ranks.

Respect on the part of the juniors, love on the part of the seniors: these two basic attitudes already formed the subject of a pair of tools for goods works (4:70–71). They remind us of the reciprocal obligations of men and women, parents and children, in the exhortations in the Letters of Captivity (Eph 5:22–23 and 6:1–4; Col 3:18–21). Neither honor nor love are unilateral however. When the seniors call their juniors 'brothers'—rather than 'sons', which would correspond to their own title of 'fathers'—they grant them a sign of religious respect. And when the juniors in turn title their seniors 'father', affection mingles with 'reverence'. This is clear in the note on the abbot, who is called 'lord' in honor of Christ and 'abbot', that is, 'father', in love of Him.

In spite of these elements of reciprocity, which to some extent justify the expression 'honor one another', the Rule lays the emphasis on the respect which subordinates owe their superiors. In addition to titles, two signs of consideration are prescribed: asking a blessing (with a simple word, *benedic*, which the senior answers by calling on God: *Deus*), and rising from one's seat and offering one's place. The first is as old as the Bible; it implies seeing all human beings, seculars included (53:24), as blessed creatures and bearers of divine grace. The second is also a biblical custom (Lv 19:32), adopted by the Christians of ancient times: the 'hoary head' of Leviticus is succeeded by 'bishops and priests' in the writings of Saint Cyprian (*Test.* 3.85), while the council of Agde (canon 65) bids each category of clerics to honor the higher order in this way.

In addition to these distant sources, the code of fraternal relations explicitly refers to the words of Saint Paul: 'Vie with one another in honoring one another' (Rm 12:10). The religious courtesy of monasticism is a legacy of the early Church. The first Christians addressed one another as 'brothers', as Christ himself had suggested (Mt 23:8), and at the end of the age of persecution Lactantius could explain to pagans who found this custom surprising: 'We address one another as brothers solely because we believe that we are all equal' (*Inst.* 5.15.2). A little later, the constantinian peace led to the loss of this characteristic appellation, but monks took it up and faithfully preserved it. It proclaims that we are all children of God.

LXIV

The ordination of the abbot

¹ In ordaining the abbot, the guiding principle shall always be to establish the person chosen by the whole community, unanimous in the fear of God, or even by some part of the community, no matter how small, in accordance with sounder judgment. ² The one to be ordained shall be chosen for the merit of his life and the wisdom of his teaching, even if he ranks last in the community.

³ Even if the entire community should concur in choosing a person who goes along with its vices—God forbid— ⁴ and if to any extent these vices come to the knowledge of the bishop to whose diocese the place belongs and of the abbots or Christians in the area, ⁵ they must prevent the conspiracy of the wicked from prevailing, and they shall set a worthy administrator in charge of God's house, ⁶ knowing that they shall receive a good reward for this, if they do it with a pure intention and out of zeal for God, just as on the other hand they would commit a sin if they neglected to do it.

IN THE RULE of the Master the choice of a new abbot—a choice conditioned by ruling out any kind of community rank—belonged to his predecessor. When about to die, the abbot, in the presence of the brothers, named the monk he had found superior to all in observance and virtue. The bishop was immediately invited to come to the monastery and sanction this choice by liturgical rite (RM 92–93).

Benedict's system of succession is completely different. The former abbot has no part in it at all. It is up to the community to choose its leader through an election. But this choice remains subject to the judgment of the bishop who liturgically 'ordains' the person elected. Neighboring abbots also have their say, and the faithful themselves may intervene. Like an episcopal consecration, an abbatial blessing is an action of the Church which concerns the entire people of God.

The contrasting systems advocated by the Master and by Benedict correspond to the contemporary practices of the Church of Rome. Between 498 and 530 Rome suspended the traditional rule of election, whose enforcement had given rise to serious disorders. The Master's legislation was formulated in the course of this period, during which each pope chose his own successor, whereas Benedict's coincides with the re-establishment of elections in Rome in 530 or 532.

While acknowledging that the community has the right to elect its shepherd, Benedict attaches only relative value to this legal rule. A poor choice, even if unanimous, must be nullified by higher authorities, who may then impose another candidate. Moreover, the electoral procedure remains totally undetermined. The majority, whether absolute or relative, may not lay down the law. The choice of a minority may be preferred—by the bishop, obviously—if it seems better. In sum, Benedict does not leave matters up to any ready-made rule, which would automatically pick the new abbot. His concern is not to set an unchanging legal criterion, but to obtain by any possible means the appointment of an authentic vicar of Christ.

For the monastery is a house of God. When Benedict speaks of 'setting an administrator' (or 'steward') 'in charge of it', he is using the very terms of the Gospel: 'Who is the faithful and wise steward whom the Lord shall set over his household?' (Lk 12:42; see also Ps 104:21). The same evangelical image recurs at the end of the chapter. As Christ's servant, set over his co-servants and at their service, the abbot performs a sacred task which, like that of the deans (21:4), requires holiness of life and the ability to teach.

Community rank, to which Benedict otherwise attaches such importance, must not play any part here. Religious seniority is not a qualification for first place, any more than natural age comes into consideration in establishing rank. In the preceding chapters, the Rule gave the superior the power to modify a monk's rank on account of his holy life. Here total freedom is left to God.

> [7] As for the abbot who has been ordained, he must always reflect on the burden he has received and on the one to whom he will have to 'give an account of his stewardship'. [8] Let him know that he must 'serve rather than rule'. [9] He must therefore be 'learned' in the divine law—so as to know and have the wherewithal to 'bring forth the new and the old'—chaste, sober, merciful. [10] And let 'mercy always prevail over judgment', that he may obtain the same treatment for himself. [11] 'Let him hate vices and love the brothers.' [12] Even in reprimanding them, let him act prudently and 'avoid excess', for fear of breaking the vessel by rubbing too hard at the rust. [13] He shall never lose sight of his own frailty, and he shall remember 'not to crush the broken reed'. [14] By this we do not mean that he should allow vices to flourish, but that he should prune them away with prudence and charity as he sees best for each individual, as we have already said. [15] And he shall strive 'to be loved rather than feared'.

[16] Let him not be excitable and anxious, let him not be extreme and obstinate, let him not be jealous and oversuspicious, for he would never be at rest. [17] He shall show foresight and consideration in his orders, and whether the task he assigns concerns God or the world, he shall be discerning and moderate, [18] bearing in mind the discretion of holy Jacob, who said: 'If I drive my flocks harder, they will all die in a single day'. [19] Therefore, drawing on this and other examples of discretion, the mother of virtues, he must so arrange everything that the strong have something to yearn for and the weak nothing to run from.

[20] And above all, let him keep this rule in every particular, [21] so that when he has served well, he will hear the Lord say to him, as to the good servant who gave his fellow servants grain at the proper time: 'In truth I tell you, he shall set him over all he owns'.

According to the Rule of the Master, the former abbot, at the end of the abbatial ordination, was to give the new abbot the rule of the monastery, presented as the 'law of God', with a brief admonition inviting him to take care of the souls for which he would have to account on the last day (RM 93:15–23). Benedict says nothing of this ordination ceremony, but he also addresses an admonition, much longer than the Master's, to the new superior. He thus draws up a second abbatial directory—one very different from the first, which was largely derived from the other Rule.

This new portrait of the abbot is studded with augustinian maxims. Beginning with the first sentence, Benedict echoes Augustine's Rule, which requires the superior to reflect constantly on the account he will have to give to God (*Praec.* VII.3). But Augustine had in mind the account to be given 'for souls' (Heb 13:17). Benedict replaces this scriptural formula with that of the gospel parable in which the dishonest steward prepares an account 'of his stewardship' (Lk 16:2). We know how the steward went about it.

The abbot too, as we shall soon see, must make friends by not pressing the master's debtors.

Before coming to this, Benedict gives him another watch-word drawn from Augustine (*Serm.* 340.1): 'Serve rather than rule'. He then goes back to the Gospel and evokes the 'scribe learned in the kingdom of heaven, who draws from his treasury both new things and old' (Mt 13:52). In a monastery, as in a church, the first service expected from the leader is that he dispense the word of God.

The Pastoral Letters also require the bishop to be 'learned' or a 'teacher', and Benedict also borrows from them the next two qualities on his list: 'chaste' and 'sober' (1 Tm 3:2; Tt 1:7–9 and 2:2–5). To this he adds mercy. This last virtue will now form the subject matter of a wide-ranging exposition on how to correct the brothers (10–15). Here we encounter the dishonest steward's behavior.

For, according to a saying of Saint James (Jm 2:13) which recalls one of the Beatitudes (Mt 5:7), the abbot must be more merciful than just in order to be judged mercifully himself. 'Hate vices, love men', said Augustine (*Praec.* V.10). The love shown the brothers will return to its giver; as Augustine further says, the superior must be 'loved rather than feared' (*Praec.* VII.3).

Between these two maxims on charity, Benedict twice advises 'prudent' correction; the first time he complements this term with a proverbial expression: 'avoid excess'. This *ne quid nimis*, ascribed to Solon of Athens (Sidonius Apollinarius, *Carm.* 15.47), had in any case received its latin formulation from Terence (*Andria* I.1.34). This profane saying is combined with a scriptural quotation recalling the Servant of Isaiah and Christ: by taking care 'not to crush the broken reed' (Is 42:3; Mt 12:20), the abbot will imitate the Merciful One *par excellence*. In advising that the abbot prune away vices according to each individual's disposition, Benedict refers back to what he himself said in the first abbatial directory (2:26–29 and 32).

This exposition on mercy in reproof ends the comments on the last of the positive qualities listed earlier. Benedict now cautions the abbot against six failings, joined two by two. The first is again borrowed from Isaiah's portrait of the Servant (Is 42:4). Through this *non turbulentus* ('not excitable'), we again glimpse Christ and his peace. Like him, his representative must find rest for himself and procure it for others.

A reference to two new qualities—the first of which has already been required of the abbot in the chapter on counsel (3:6: 'with foresight')—introduces a second exposition, devoted to the orders given the brothers. The key word in this advice is 'discretion', understood as 'measure' or moderation. 'Mother of virtues', as Cassian had already called it (*Conf.* 2.4.4), this quality consists in following a middle way, equally removed from two opposite excesses: too much and too little. But since, among those who seek God, the first of these excesses is more frequent than the second, *discretio* has come to mean—unilaterally—the avoidance of intemperate austerity, immoderate demands, and excessive zeal.

Benedict recommends here discretion in this limited sense, as Cassian already had at the end of his second Conference. He puts it under the patronage of an Old Testament saint, wily Jacob, whose answer to Esau is very freely quoted (Gn 33:13). This benedictine concern for the weak, who must not 'run away', was expressed from the very beginning of the Rule (Prol 46) and is characteristic of all of it.

In closing, Benedict recommends observing the Rule. Just as in the Master's text the outgoing abbot gave it to the incoming, here its author enjoins the superior to keep it. A rule (*regula*) is nothing without a leader who interprets and enforces it, but neither is the leader anything without the rectitude and firmness of this law based on the Gospel.

A few words from the latter serve as a conclusion. Like the good servant in the parable (cf. Mt 25:21), the abbot, once he has served well (cf. 1 Tm 3:13), will be rewarded by the Master (Mt 24:45–47). Although Benedict here has mainly the first Gospel in mind, his reference to 'grain' comes from the parallel text in Luke (Lk 12:42) and recalls the beginning of the chapter (64:5; cf. Lk 12:42). But this eschatological conclusion is especially reminiscent of the end of the first abbatial directory. There Benedict, following the Master, led the abbot to hope for a spiritual benefit in this life: the amendment of his faults. Here he opens the gates of eternity up to him.

LXV

The monastery's provost

THE MONK whom Benedict names 'provost' (*praepositus*) is the second superior, today called the 'prior'. This obviously necessary assistant to the abbot appeared from the start. Among the Pachomians there were 'seconds in command', not only in all the monasteries but also in every house. Like the heads of monasteries and houses, they were appointed by the superior general of the congregation. Saint Basil also directs the head of the fraternity to have a substitute who can replace him when he is away (*LR* 45.1).

In spite of this general custom, the Master opposed the nomination of a second-in-command for fear his dignity would lead him to become self-satisfied and negligent. The office could be held only accidentally: when a new abbot had been ordained to succeed the old one who, instead of dying, revived. Even then, this second-ranking abbot was to remain humble, submissive, and obedient on pain of being demoted and put back in to the ranks (RM 93:43–90).

While sharing the Master's distrust for the office of second in command, Benedict did not adopt his predecessor's original legislation. Not without reservations, he reverted to the common practice and accepted the installation of a provost, provided he was appointed by the abbot and remained entirely subordinated to him. The beginning of the chapter very clearly indicates the serious disadvantages of another way of doing things only too widespread in surrounding monasticism:

> [1] Too often in the past, the ordination of a provost has given rise to serious conflicts in monasteries. [2] For some of them, puffed up with an evil spirit of pride and thinking of themselves as second abbots, usurp tyrannical power, foster conflicts and sow discord in their communities, [3] especially in places where the provost is ordained by the same bishop and the same abbots who ordain the abbot. [4] It is easy to see how absurd this is: as soon as he is ordained, he is given grounds for pride, [5] as his thoughts suggest to him that he is exempt from the authority of his abbot, [6] since 'you too were ordained by those same men who ordained the abbot'. [7] This leads to envy, quarrels, slander, rivalry, discord, depositions, [8] and, abbot and provost being thus opposed, their souls are inevitably in danger as long as such discord lasts, [9] and their subordinates go to their ruin, because they flatter those who side with them. [10] The responsibility for this dangerous evil belongs primarily to those who initiated such a disorder.

We have abundant evidence of the tensions that did indeed arise between abbots and their seconds-in-command. Such interpersonal conflicts need not surprise us: they belong to the nature of things. But the benedictine Rule assigns them a particular cause, stemming from an institutional flaw. The previous chapter already let us glimpse the part played by the bishop and neighboring abbots in the ordination of a new abbot. We now learn that these outside authorities sometimes appointed a provost as assistant to the abbot. As we may remember, Pachomius and his successors named both the heads of monasteries or houses and their seconds-in-command. In the sixth century, Gregory the Great attested to these twin appointments in his correspondence and—curiously enough—in his *Life of Saint Benedict*: in founding the monastery at Terracina, the saint is said to have 'ordained' its abbot and its provost simultaneously (*Dial.* II.22.1).

In painting this distressing picture of the quarrels between provost and abbot, Benedict seems to be remembering two passages from Saint Paul: 'envy, slander, discord' among the disorders threatening the Church at Corinth (2 Co 12:20); and 'envy, brawls, jealousy, discord' among the works of the flesh listed elsewhere (Gal 5:20–21). To such scourges there is no remedy other than the Spirit and its fruits: charity, joy, peace and the rest.

[11] It thus seems advisable to us, for the preservation of peace and charity, that the abbot run the monastery according to his own judgment. [12] If possible, all the services of the monastery shall be managed through deans, as we have already established, according to the abbot's provisions. [13] Thus, several persons being in charge, no one individual will yield to pride. [14] If the place so requires or if the community reasonably and humbly so requests and the abbot judges advisable, [15] the abbot shall choose whom he wills with the counsel of the God-fearing brothers, and he himself will ordain him as his provost.

[16] This provost, however, shall respectfully carry out whatever his abbot commands him, without doing anything against the abbot's orders or will, [17] for the more he is set above the rest, the more careful he must be to keep what the rule commands.

[18] If this provost is found to be full of vices or if, led astray by conceit, he grows proud, or if he is convicted of contempt for the holy rule, he shall be warned verbally as many as four times. [19] If he does not amend, he is to be punished as required by the discipline of the rule. [20] If even then he does not improve, he shall be

deposed from his rank of provost and replaced by someone worthy. [21] If even after all that he is not peaceful
and obedient in community, he should even be expelled
from the monastery. [22] The abbot shall reflect, however,
that he must give God an account of all his judgments,
lest the fire of envy or jealousy burn his soul.

While hoping that the deans will be enough for the management of the community, Benedict allows the appointment of a prior. After exhorting him to remain submissive,
Benedict considers the possibility that he might not and
provides for his punishment, deposition and replacement,
and, indeed, for his ultimate eviction. This pitiful chain of
events is reminiscent of the penal code. In the details, we
come across many features of the chapters on deans (21)
and on priests (62).

Throughout this quarrel Benedict constantly sides with
the abbot and regards the provost simply as prideful and
rebellious. He knows, however, that the fault may lie on
both sides, as his last sentence shows. In the second directory addressed to the abbot, he had already cautioned
against jealousy (64:16). Concern for the abbot's frailty is
a distinctive note of the benedictine Rule as compared to
the Master's.

In this distressing passage, where human misery appears
only too hardily, a few expressions have a comforting spiritual ring. The community's 'humble and reasonable' request brings to mind the chapters on the cellarer (31:7)
and on unknown monks (61:4). The 'God-fearing brothers'
whose advice the abbot asks in choosing his second-in-
command recall not only the abbatial election, where the
same fear directed the unanimous choice of the community
(64:1), but the expression once more denotes the religious
atmosphere, permeated with the divine presence, in which
the life of the entire monastery, as well as that of individuals, unfolds. Finally, here and in the penal code (23:1),
the words 'holy rule' are worthy of note. Canonized like

this, the Rule itself enters the religious sphere enveloping every monastic reality. Shortly before Benedict, Caesarius of Arles, in his rule for women, had already used such terms (*Reg. uirg.* 62.2; 64.5).

Besides these spiritual notes, what touches us in this chapter is the openness Benedict shows toward an institution which he barely favors. As we have already seen in connection with the office (18:22), he is not attached to his own views. The Rule deserves to be called 'holy' because its author himself abides by the command which he gives three times over to those who must express an opinion: to think and speak 'reasonably and humbly'.

LXVI

The porters of the monastery

[1] At the door of the monastery a wise old man is to be placed, one who knows how to take a message and give a reply, and whose age keeps him from roaming about. [2] This porter is to have his lodging near the door, so that visitors will always find him there to answer them. [3] And as soon as someone knocks or a poor man calls out, he shall answer *Deo gratias* or *Benedic*, [4] and with all the gentleness that comes from the fear of God, he shall hasten to answer with the warmth of charity. [5] If this porter needs help, let him be given a younger brother.

[6] As for the monastery, it should, if possible, be so constructed that within it all necessities, such as water, a mill, a garden and various crafts are found inside the monastery, [7] so that the monks will have no need to roam outside, for that is not at all good for their souls.

[8] We wish this rule to be read often in the community, so that no brother may put forth the excuse of ignorance.

IN AN EARLY VERSION, this was doubtless the Rule's final chapter. Two facts which tally suggest this. First, the final sentence on the reading of the Rule, which sounds like a conclusion. Next, the placement of the Master's corresponding chapter, at the end (RM 95). Like his predecessor, Benedict must initially have ended his legislative work with these instructions regarding the door and the doorkeeper—a very natural way of closing both Rule and monastery. Then new questions must have led him to insert six extra chapters before the epilogue.

In placing an elderly brother at the door, Benedict partially follows the Master, who entrusted the charge to two old men. But besides bringing the number down to one—a cutback that may be made up for by adding a younger brother—the benedictine Rule has as a distinctive feature the aptitudes required in the porter: wisdom, competence, maturity. 'Wisdom' is a generic quality already required of the cellarer (31:1) and guest master (53:22). 'Knowing how to take a message and give a reply' is especially necessary at the door. Benedict attaches great importance to this, as shown by the fact that these words are repeated as the text goes on. This is the main difference between him and his forerunner. For the Master, the porters' job consisted merely in opening and closing the door, which was always to be kept shut. For Benedict, the role is a distinctly human one: answering whoever calls.

This promptness in answering is described with striking insistence. As in the chapter on guests, we perceive here the spirit of faith, the respect for all human beings, and the special love for the poor with which Benedict was consumed. The porter's first word is a thanksgiving or a request for a blessing, both of which immediately acknowledge God in the human person arriving. Gentleness and warmth, fear and love: the religious and human quality of this eagerness could not be more intensely marked.

In the following paragraph, Benedict remembers both the Master and the *History of the Monks of Egypt*. The latter sang the praises of the exemplary monastery of Abbot Isidore, whose impenetrable fence enclosed everything the monks needed: well, gardens, orchards and the rest (*Hist. mon.* 17). Along with the Master, Benedict inserted a mill on to the list, and added the crafts on his own. For all three writers, the purpose of this self-sufficiency was to avoid going out. Roaming about outside the monastery is not in the monks' best interest, any more than in the porter's. As the Master aptly puts it: 'Shut up inside with the Lord, the brothers will, so to speak, be in the heavens, cut off from the world because of God' (RM 95:23).

As the Rule's primitive conclusion, the final note was probably followed by the epilogue (73). This way of ending a body of monastic legislation—by directing that it be read often—goes back to Augustine, who wanted his read every week (*Praec.* VIII.2). The Master had his Rule read continuously in the refectory. The benedictine Rule, which is three times shorter, is less suited to occupying mealtimes in this way. Benedict, whose text lacks precision on this point as on many others, simply asks that it be read 'often'. The three readings during the novitiate year (58:9–13) give concrete expression to this norm. Thanks to it, not only can no one be unaware of the law, but moreover everyone becomes permeated with words that convey God.

LXVII

Brothers sent on a journey

HERE BEGINS what may be called the appendix of the Rule: half a dozen brief chapters added to that on the porter, initially the last. The first of these additional matters is quite naturally travel: after discussing the door, Benedict deals with going through it on the way out and on the way back. He thus makes up for an oversight. The Master had indicated the rites for exiting and returning in the middle of his work (RM 66–67). In reiterating these indications here, the Rule adds others—whether borrowed from other parts of the Master's text, inspired by other writers, or original— to make up a little survey on trips.

[1] The brothers who are leaving on a journey shall ask the abbot and community to pray for them, [2] and all absent brothers shall always be remembered at the closing prayer of the work of God. [3] As for brothers returning from a journey, on the very day of their return, at all the canonical hours, at the conclusion of the work of God, they shall prostrate on the floor of the oratory [4] and ask all to pray because of their faults, for fear of having been caught off guard on the way by seeing or hearing some evil thing or idle talk. [5] And no one shall presume to relate to another what he saw or heard outside the monastery, because that causes the greatest harm.

⁶ If anyone does so presume, he shall be subjected to the punishment of the rule. ⁷ Likewise whoever presumes to leave the enclosure of the monastery and to go anywhere and do anything at all, however unimportant, without an order from the abbot.

Between their departure and their return, each marked by a prayer, the absent brothers are remembered at every office. This commemoration had already been prescribed by the Master, with an interesting explanation: since the absent monk is sacrificing himself in the service of the community, he is entitled to its explicit intercession; lacking that, the spiritual benefit of the office would be his alone, since he makes it possible by providing for everyone's material needs (RM 20:4–9).

In repeating his forerunner's directions, does Benedict have this principle of solidarity in mind? He may be thinking instead of the risks faced by travelers. In any case, this is the reason he gives next for the prayer for those returning. This motivation, which is new, confirms the negative judgment passed on going out in the preceding chapter. We were told there that it was 'not at all good for the souls' of the monks. We now learn why: it leads to their seeing and hearing unedifying things. Saint Roman, founder of the Jura monasteries, knew this well: he would hasten back so as not to undergo such pollution (*Lives of the Fathers of Jura* 50).

The ban on relating things seen and heard outside the enclosure follows the same line of thought. On this point, Benedict may be remembering Saint Pachomius (*Praec.* 57 and 86). But Pachomius did not punish breaches of that prohibition. The final sanction Benedict adds here, as he does at the end of so many chapters, affords him an opportunity of generalizing. To inopportune tales, he adds going out without permission and all manner of unauthorized initiatives. This generalization is reminiscent of one of Saint

Basil's Short Rules (*Reg.* 80 = *SR* 120), but also of the benedictine chapter on Lent (49:10). Benedict finds independence so hateful that he is always quick to proscribe it. This stain on the human heart is no less fearsome than the other.

LXVIII

If impossible tasks are assigned to a brother

[1] If a brother is assigned burdensome or impossible tasks, he shall receive the order from the one commanding with complete gentleness and obedience. [2] If he sees that the weight of the burden is altogether too much for his strength, he shall explain to his superior, patiently and at the appropriate moment, the reasons for his inability, [3] without any pride, resistance or spirit of contradiction. [4] If after his explanations the superior's order is maintained without his changing his mind, let the subordinate know that it is good for him to act thus, [5] and out of charity, trusting in God's help, he shall obey.

A PASSAGE from the Rule of the Master reveals that sending brothers on a journey—a thankless and exhausting mission—sometimes elicited a refusal or grumbling (RM 57:14–16). This might explain the placement of the present chapter. It follows the one on going out, one of the difficult assignments which could occasion moral dilemmas. Here, however, Benedict owes nothing to the other Rule; his chapter is entirely independent of the Master.

The structure of the passage is simple and clear. Each of the three sentences begins with an hypothesis and ends with an order. We thus witness the unfolding of a brief

317

three-act drama: the difficult command and its reception; the acknowledgment of impossibility and the explanation given the superior; the upholding of the command and its performance. At each stage, Benedict indicates, by means of two or three positive or negative terms, how the monk is to think and act. The chapter as a whole is remarkably constructed. It may be the most accomplished composition in the Rule.

The problem had already been formulated by Saint Basil, who had been asked whether it was permissible to refuse a task. After listing the reasons against this, he concluded his negative answer by saying that, if one is convinced of having a good reason to ask for a dispensation, all one can do is to indicate it to the superior, leaving the decision up to him (*Reg. 69 = SR 119*).

This passage of the basilian Rule inspired the unknown author of the *Admonition to a Spiritual Son* ascribed to Saint Basil. Exhorting his disciple to receive all orders willingly, even those beyond his strength, he suggests that he make known the reason for his inability so as to be dispensed (*Admon. 6*).

Benedict seems to have read his two predecessors, the real and the pseudo-Basil. But after drawing inspiration from both, he added an original hypothesis and conclusion. Instead of stopping at the explanation (Basil) or simply foreseeing an ensuing dispensation (Pseudo-Basil), he considers instead that the order may be upheld and thus leads the drama of obedience to its heroic outcome.

This little chapter, which is new in relation to the basilian line from which it derives, appears even more novel if we compare it to the tradition of egyptian monasticism. There, too, also superiors were known to give impossible orders, but these were intentional trials, deliberately imposed to test the obedience of some monk. The only response expected of the latter was the immediate and blind performance of the command.

Unlike these sublime feats, several of which are related by Cassian (*Inst.* 4.24–29), the obedience described by Benedict advances gradually, modestly, getting to the bottom of things. It is far more like that of Christ, who first breathed out the anguish of his soul in prayer and then obeyed, for the love of God and men, unto death.

LXIX

Let no one in the monastery presume to defend another

THIS CHAPTER and the next form a pair: protecting and striking are two opposite but equally improper acts, both of which encroach on the authority of the person in charge of correcting. Nowhere did the Master contemplate them. Why does Benedict discuss them? Perhaps because he had found them mentioned in his reading, particularly in Saint Pachomius, but probably because life had led him to encounter failings of this kind, to which he reacted strongly.

> [1] Care must be taken that no one in the monastery, on no occasion, presume to defend another monk or, so to speak, act as his protector, [2] even if there is some bond of kinship between them. [3] In no way shall the monks presume to do this, because it can be a very serious source and occasion of conflict. [4] Whoever transgresses this rule is to be severely punished.

Defending a brother who has been punished means undermining the right to correct, which belongs to the abbot. In the Master's circle, the latter seems to have enjoyed undisputed power. This was no longer the case with Benedict; he felt obliged both to lecture the abbot and to reinforce his authority. Although he is not mentioned here, it is his prerogatives which are at stake.

This drop in the abbot's prestige, which made it necessary to confirm his role, is doubtless not unrelated to the reestablishment of the traditional rank of seniority done away with by the Master. By granting each monk a right of precedence over those who entered after him, Benedict has given the brothers a certain share in the abbot's dignity. Called 'father' like the abbot, the seniors might be tempted to take their position too seriously and to exercise some sort of patronage over the juniors. This abuse of power is akin to the provost's, denounced by Benedict in one of the previous chapters.

Sometimes defending a brother has a more earthly cause, which the Rule itself indicates: family ties. Like age and rank, kinship is an attribute of the old man which we renounce in becoming monks. Cassian celebrates the detachment of a father who unflinchingly witnessed the ill-treatment inflicted on his son, who had entered the monastery along with him (*Inst.* 4.27).

Saint Pachomius concludes his third collection of rules by severely reproving and punishing this misdeed of 'defense' (*Iud.* 16). After him, the same offence was denounced by his successor Horsiesius (*Lib.* 24) and by Saint Basil (*Reg.* 26 = *SR* 7), both of whom saw it as a case of 'scandal' in the evangelical sense of the word (Mt 18:6): instead of helping the culprit recover through penance, the 'defender' worsens his fall. Benedict, who also speaks of *scandala*, means by this the 'conflicts' caused by the misplaced protector. Inasmuch as it supports sin, defending a brother who has been punished amounts to false charity. Inasmuch as it destroys the order and peace of the community, it is an offence against charity.

LXX

Let no one presume to strike another at will

¹ Every kind of presumption is to be avoided in the monastery, ² and we decree that no one shall have the right to excommunicate or to strike any of his brothers unless he has been given the power by the abbot. ³ But 'offenders shall be reprimanded in the presence of all, that the rest may fear'. ⁴ As for children under the age of fifteen, all shall take care to control and supervise them, ⁵ but reasonably and with moderation.

⁶ If anyone presumes anything against an adult without instructions from the abbot or flares up without discretion against children, he shall be subjected to the punishments of the rule, ⁷ for it is written: 'Do not do to another what you do not want done to yourself'.

LIKE THE MISDEED discussed previously, the one targeted here is liable to occur in a community structured according to seniority. Seniors can be tempted to punish their juniors even more than to shield them. In both cases, Benedict upholds the abbot's exclusive right of correction: no one may oppose it, no one may usurp it. Saint Pachomius had already noted that no one in the monastery might reprimand a brother unless authorized to do so by the superior (*Inst.* 5).

Inflicting excommunication or corporal punishment without mandate is thus a serious offense which calls for public sanctions. Part of the phrase from Saint Paul quoted by Benedict in this connection (1 Tm 5:20) has already been used in the Rule (23:3; 48:20). In discipline as in everything else, the monastic community is modeled on the primitive Church. The abbot plays the roles of the Apostle and his successor, of Paul and Timothy.

By his present ban on striking others, Benedict completes his great charter of fraternal relations based on community rank. The earlier chapter mentioned children twice (63:9 and 18–19). Benedict now returns to the subject. He agrees with the Master in setting the age limit at fifteen (RM 14:79), but the supervisory mission he grants the adult monks is a novelty. By it, an educational role is assigned to all the brothers, not only to members of the hierarchy—abbot and deans—as in the Master's text.

This disciplinary task must be performed 'reasonably and with moderation', like everything else. We are reminded in particular of the 'moderation' required of the cellarer (31:12), of the 'humble and reasonable' language which an unknown monk is to use in making remarks (61:4). But an adult who corrects a child especially needs 'discretion'. Once again, this virtue likens him to the abbot, of whom Benedict makes the same demand (64:17–19). The educational activity of the brothers leads them to participate in that of their superiors.

In closing, Benedict recalls the golden rule of Scripture (Mt 7:12; Tb 4:16), which he likewise quoted at the end of the chapter on unknown monks. In his Rule as in the Master's, this maxim appears high on the list of tools for good works (4:9 = RM 3:9). But he alone reiterates it outside that theoretical catalogue, in connection with some practical matter. The present chapter, which began in a legal perspective, thus ends on a note of charity. We have gone from respect for the abbot's rights to the duty of loving even while correcting.

In this also the adult brother is identified with the abbot, who must 'hate vices but love the brothers'. Besides, isn't 'loving one's juniors' inscribed at the heart of the charter of fraternal relations?

LXXI

Let them obey one another

¹ Not only in relation to the abbot are all to practise the good of obedience, but the brothers shall moreover obey one another, ² knowing that by this way of obedience they will go to God. ³ Thus, aside from the orders of the abbot or of the provosts he has established, which may not be superseded by those given in a private capacity, ⁴ in every other instance all juniors shall obey their seniors with all charity and concern. ⁵ If someone is found objecting, let him be reprimanded.

⁶ Moreover, if a brother receives some reprimand from the abbot or any of his seniors for any reason whatsoever, trifling though it may be, ⁷ and if he senses that any senior is mildly angry at him or upset, however slightly, ⁸ immediately and without delay he shall prostrate on the ground and make satisfaction, stretched out at his feet, until the disturbance is calmed by a blessing. ⁹ Whoever refuses to do this shall be subjected to corporal punishment, or, if he is obstinate, he shall be expelled from the monastery.

LIKE THE TWO preceding ones, this chapter completes the system of fraternal relations based on seniority which was established in Chapter 63. There Benedict outlined rules of courtesy. Here he deals with two other points: obedience and satisfaction. While speaking of 'mutual' obedience, he in fact institutes a form of obedience grounded on hierarchy, unilaterally paid by juniors to their seniors. Only in the next chapter will marks of honor and obedience become fully reciprocal, thanks to the disappearance of this mention of rank.

Even now, however, there is something 'mutual' about obedience: instead of being reserved to the abbot and his officers, it is due from any brother to any other monk senior to him. This extension endows it with a universal scope: all common life is placed under its control. It matters little whether the senior may be more or less qualified to give an order. Independently of the objective quality of what he commands, obedience is always 'good' for the subject, because it leads him to practice self-renunciation and humility, imitation of Christ and charity.

A maxim forcefully expresses this incomparable value of obedience: it is the way by which we go to God. We are reminded both of the journey earlier proposed to the novice—'the hardships and difficulties that lead to God'— and of the great perspective outlined at the beginning of the Prologue—'returning through the labor of obedience to him from whom you had drifted through the sloth of disobedience'. We now see this immense and undetermined perspective crystallize into a multitude of specific actions, which fill the monk's entire existence.

As in the third step of humility, as also in connection with obedience in impossible things, Benedict indicates by a word why the monks obey one another: out of love. Saint Basil, quoting Scripture, had already invoked this motive: we must obey and serve one another, he said, because Christ directed us to do so by command and example (Mt 20:26–28) and because the Apostle said 'in the charity of the Spirit, serve one another' (Gal 5:13). Obeying does in fact mean adopting the attitude of a servant, and this, at the

Last Supper, was offered us as an example of the highest love. To this brief question of Basil (*Reg.* 64 = *SR* 115) we may add Cassian's Conference 16, which provides a long and beautiful commentary of our chapter.

The second part of this chapter is somewhat unexpected, for the title gives no hint of it. It is obviously linked not only to the charter of fraternal relations, but also to the two chapters just written by Benedict. It also deals with correction, but instead of the excommunication and thrashing mentioned in the previous chapter, mere verbal reprimands are involved here. After denying the seniors the right to punish without special authorization, Benedict here acknowledges that they may reprove.

This acknowledgment remains implicit, however, for the passage is addressed not to the seniors but to the juniors. It is they who are invited humbly to receive any reprimand made by their elders. In so doing they will imitate, within the framework of their community structured according to rank, the admirable humility evidenced by many a desert Father celebrated in the Apophthegms (*Vitae Patrum* V.15.88–89). Humility is disarming. It quiets all the commotion of anger.

LXXII

The good zeal which the monks must have

[1] Just as there is an evil zeal of bitterness which separates from God and leads to hell, [2] there is also a good zeal which separates from vices and leads to God and everlasting life. [3] This, then, is the zeal which monks must practice with most fervent love: [4] they shall 'vie with one another in honoring one another'; [5] they shall bear one another's weaknesses of body and behavior with the utmost patience; [6] they shall earnestly compete in obeying one another; [7] no one shall pursue what he judges better for himself, but rather what seems better for someone else; [8] they shall practice disinterested brotherly charity; [9] they shall lovingly fear God; [10] they shall show their abbot sincere and humble charity; [11] 'they shall prefer absolutely nothing to Christ'. [12] May he lead us all together to life everlasting!

PRIOR TO THE FINAL chapter, an epilogue which doubtless originally followed the chapter on the porters, Benedict concludes the appendix to the Rule (67–72) with this admirable passage, which may be regarded as his masterpiece. Reverting to the initial perpective of the Prologue, he traces a new journey toward God. The way is no longer called 'obedience' (Prol 2; 71:2), but rather 'zeal', and the translation of this ancient biblical term is given immediately: to be zealous is to love. Evil and good, bitterness and love, God and the vices, hell and everlasting life: human beings are invited to choose between these opposites. And just as at the beginning of the Prologue the call for a return to God was followed by a presentation of Christ, the true king, here also the monks on their way to God and everlasting life are given Christ, whom they prefer to everything, as their guide.

Between the first and last sentences of the chapter, which obviously echo one another, Benedict describes good zeal in eight short maxims. This list is somewhat reminiscent of the great catalogue of 'tools for good works' derived from the Master, but the number of precepts is remarkably diminished. Besides cutting down by more than nine tenths, the new list is much more homogeneous. Leaving personal asceticism aside, it concentrates on relations among the brothers, which lead to the brothers' relations with God. Love for him and for his Christ, which headed the 'tools', here comes only toward the end, in accordance with the image of making one's way toward God. The chapter on good zeal offers a literary depiction of the reality brought about concretely through good zeal: both move toward God and life everlasting.

While moving thus from human beings to God, the series on the effects of good zeal also progresses in the actions to be performed. From expressions of charity we go on to charity itself, twice named toward the end or indicated by the equivalent terms: love, affection, preference. Lovingly practised, good zeal ends in love. This ascent toward charity, crown of the spiritual structure, calls to mind the ladder of humility.

Actions inspired by charity and acts of charity properly so called: these two halves of the list are both introduced by a quotation from the same verse of the Letter to the Romans. 'In brotherly charity, love one another, vie with one another in honoring one another', wrote Saint Paul (Rm 12:10). Reversing the order of the two precepts, Benedict first writes: 'They shall vie with one another in honoring one another', then, fifth on the list, he directs them to practice 'brotherly charity'.

As we may remember, this pauline recommendation to 'honor one another' served as a conclusion to the charter of fraternal relations (63:17). Here it is taken as the starting point of good zeal. Beginnning where Chapter 63 left off, the present chapter takes an important step forward—not only because it complements honor with patience, obedience and the rest, but also and especially because it crosses the boundaries within which 'mutual' courtesy and obedience were until now shut up. In the framework of a community structured according to seniority, respect and obedience are not reciprocal, but one-way: the junior accords them to the senior. These restrictions based on rank, which were clearly marked in Chapters 63 and 71, disappear here: the monks are simply invited to honor and obey one another. Seniority and its practical consequences are not abrogated, certainly, but this order laid out by the rule breaks down under the pressure of love and zeal, which know no barriers.

This mystical transcendence of community rank brings to mind what we observed in Chapter 63. Baptism, we noted then, mystically annuls the natural and social differences between human beings—all become one in Christ—but this spiritual unity remains invisible. Christians, like their fellow human beings, remain set off from one another by the concrete situations which determine their relations. Only in the monastery are age, wealth, and social status no longer taken into account. These differences are effectively done away with and replaced by a new order, based on the time spent in God's service. But this purely religious order is nonetheless an order, analogous to the former one in that it distinguishes between persons and assigns them differing rights. This differentiation disappears at the end in the chapter on good zeal. Just as the old order was mystically obliterated in baptism, so the new order itself is transcended by a final surge of pure spirituality.

Besides the verse from the Letter to the Romans which introduces its two parts, Benedict's list calls on another principle dear to Saint Paul: seeking not one's own advantage but that of others (1 Co 10:24 and 33; Ph 2:4). Further on, the maxim 'they shall prefer absolutely nothing to Christ' is borrowed from Saint Cyprian (*De orat. dom.* 15)—a very fine passage from which Benedict no doubt drew inspiration in composing this whole chapter. In particular, it includes the sequence: brotherly charity - love of God - love of Christ. In making it his own, Benedict has introduced love of the abbot. Placed significantly between God and Christ, the abbot is regarded as God's representative and introduced into the theological sphere.

The passage from Cyprian which this chapter on good zeal imitates is a commentary of the third petition of the *Our Father*: the great martyr bishop attempted to say in a few sentences what is meant by the 'will of God' which must be done on earth as in heaven. He did not speak of 'zeal', good or evil. Where did Benedict find such a notion? The Master, toward the end of his Rule, mentions 'zeal for good', which should create a genuine spirit of competition between the brothers (RM 92:51). But the idea is far older. It can be found already in Saint Paul (1 Co 12:31; 14:1), Saint Clement (*Ep. ad Cor.* 9), and especially in the *Life of Saint Anthony*. When the young man Anthony, bent on renunciation, began to practice asceticism, he took a senior monk as his model and 'rivaled with him in good actions' (*V. Ant.* 3.3).

To rival: this is what the word *zelus* originally meant, and although Benedict does not emphasize this aspect of zeal, it should not frighten us. Inscribed into the social nature of human beings, a healthy spirit of competition is a noble and necessary thing. Christians and monks instinctively imitate their brothers and try to do as well as they do, indeed even better. Monastic life is not synonymous with timidity and mediocrity, but with inexhaustible generosity in search of unending greatness.

LXXIII

The observance of all justice is not prescribed in this Rule

¹ We have written this rule, moreover, so that by observing it in monasteries we may evince at least a certain degree of moral decency and the beginnings of religious life. ² But for whoever hastens on to the perfection of religious life, there are teachings of the holy Fathers whose observance leads man to the very heights of perfection. ³ Indeed, what page, what phrase authored by God in the Old and New Testament is not the truest of guides for human life? ⁴ What book of the holy catholic Fathers does not resoundingly summon us along the true way until we reach our Creator? ⁵ Then, what are the *Conferences* of the Fathers and their *Institutions* and their *Lives*, as well as the Rule of our holy father Basil, ⁶ if not tools of virtue for obedient monks of good conduct? ⁷ But as for us, slothful, of ill conduct and negligent as we are, they make us blush with shame.

⁸ Whoever you may be, then, who are hastening toward your heavenly home—with Christ's help, keep this little rule for beginners which we have finished writing; ⁹ and only then, under God's protection, will you reach the loftier summits of teaching and virtues we have just mentioned. Amen.

THE CHAPTER on porters, and with it the first draft of
the Rule, ended by directing that the Rule should be read
often in community (66:8). The present epilogue is doubtless linked to that initial conclusion, from which it was
separated by the insertion of the appendix (67–72). After
directing that the Rule be read to the brothers, Benedict
explains why he wrote it. In so doing, he indicates the place
of his work within christian literature and sheds light on
the significance of monasticism—which is nothing but the
implementation of divine revelation in both Testaments,
the fulfillment of the Gospel and of catholic Tradition.

By stating that the Rule does not contain 'all justice',
the title reproduces Christ's words to John the Baptist (Mt
3:15). Further on, the sentence which concludes the first
paragraph (7) echoes Daniel's confession: 'Shame on
us . . . !' (Dan 9:7–8). These are the only scriptural reminiscences in the chapter. But all of it is a recommendation of
Holy Scripture, presented as the highest norm for human
life and placed above all the books of the Fathers, 'catholic'
or monastic, which merely repeat and explain its teachings.

Compared to these writings emanating from God himself
and from his saints, the Rule is presented by its author as a
paltry little work which does not lead very far. Perfection
must be sought elsewhere. Observing the Rule merely pro-
cures 'a certain degree of moral decency and the beginnings
of religious life'. It is a 'little rule for beginners'.

Should these judgments be seen as mere protestations
of humility, virtually mandatory and more or less sincere,
such as those commonly found in the writings of ancient
times, particularly those of Christians and monks? In actual
fact, they are inspired less by personal modesty than by a
deep awareness of the distance separating contemporary
monasticism from its origins and models. Twice before,
Benedict has forcefully voiced the conviction that 'we', the
monks of today, 'are slothful, ill behaved, negligent'. Both

in connection with the recitation of the psalter (18:25) and with the consumption of wine (40:6), he contrasted—as he does here—the fervor and austerity of the monks of old with the laxity of his own generation.

In this context of decadence, the Rule appears as a safety catch which can prevent lapsing further and as a minimum beginning with which recovery may take place. This transcending of the Rule is suggested not to communities, but rather to persons. As at the beginning and end of the Prologue, Benedict here addresses the individual monk: 'whoever hastens on to perfection . . . Whoever you may be, then, who are hastening toward your heavenly home. . . .'

On the basis of the Rule and its community observances, generous individuals are invited to aim endlessly at perfection. Perfection is no added luxury, but the very end to which Christ calls us: 'Be perfect, as your heavenly Father is perfect' (Mt 5:48); 'If you wish to be perfect . . .' (Mt 19:21). No one can save himself the trouble of seeking it. And it is to be found not in the Rule, but beyond it, in the 'teachings of the holy Fathers'.

In recommending a higher literature to which his own work is but a modest introduction, Benedict clearly sets himself off from the Master. The latter readily referred to the Fathers, but without putting such a distance between them and himself. Convinced that he was following their standards and remaining at their level, he presented his Rule as an all-embracing survey which seemed sufficient unto itself.

The difference between the two authors may be due to several causes. First of all, Benedict is aware of a recent flagging in observances, particularly in the area of fasting and vigils. Secondly, through the apophthegms just translated by the roman clerics Pelagius and John, he has rediscovered the lofty demands of primitive monasticism.

Finally, in his genuine humility and his thirst for perfection, he is inclined to leave himself behind in order to seek edification from the great monks of old.

The Rule of the Master did not refer to a higher literature; it was careful to root monastic life in ordinary Christianity by marking its connections with baptism and with the Church. Such views are lacking from the benedictine Rule, which in contrast is concerned with bringing regular observance to completion by a flight toward loftier 'heights'.

After Scripture and the catholic Fathers, of whom Benedict has already spoken in connection with the office (9:8), these sublime writings are in particular the *Conferences* of the Fathers and their 'Lives', already mentioned in connection with the reading before Compline (42:3). The *Institutes* are added here. We recognize the titles of Cassian's two great works: the cenobitic *Institutes* and the anchorites' *Conferences*. As in Chapter One, Benedict closely unites the two forms of monastic life, communal and solitary. The apophthegms, which he surely had in mind, primarily when speaking of 'Lives', came from eremitical circles, like Cassian's *Conferences*. They are no less relevant and beneficial to cenobites.

This reading list, which reflects an open cenobitism, ends with the Rule of Saint Basil, called like the heroes of the apophthegms, 'our holy Father' (18:25). By what he said earlier, Benedict does not seem to have adopted the condemnation of solitary life formulated by the great cappadocian legislator in the third Question of his Rule (*Reg.* 3 = *LR* 7). He nonetheless recommends this distinguished work, from which he borrowed just as he did from Cassian. Rather than being eclectic, his attitude is one of unreserved openness to all of monastic tradition.

'Hasten on to perfection. . . . Hasten toward one's heavenly home. . . .' The first of these goals is to be found here below, the second in the hereafter. Perfection is not to be found in this world, as the saying goes, but it is indeed in this world that we laboriously strive for it. It is our first spiritual goal, still an earthly one, short of the final end which is the kingdom of heaven. Better than anyone, Cassian explains the connection between this immediate 'goal' and that transcendent 'end' (*Conf.* 1). The last page of the Rule directs our gaze toward both. After leading us, in the previous chapter, to hope to enter everlasting life, it now reminds us that this heavenly home is the term of our present striving after perfection.

Table of Abbreviations

RB   The Rule of Saint Benedict. Latin-English edition: RB 1980. Collegeville, Minnesota: Liturgical Press, 1980. Critical latin edition by Adalbert de Vogüé and Jean Neufville, *La Règle de saint Benoît*, Sources chretiennes 181–186. Paris: Editions du Cerf, 1971–1972.

RM   *The Rule of the Master*. PL 88. Critical latin edition by A. de Vogüé, *La Règle du Maître*, Sch 105–107. Paris: Cerf 1964–1965. English translation by Luke Eberle OSB, Cistercian Studies 6. Kalamazoo: Cistercian Publications, 1977.

AA SS   *Acta Sanctorum*

ACW   Ancient Christian Writers

CC   Corpus Christianorum. Turnhout, Belgium: Brepols.

CSCO   Corpus Scriptorum Christianorum Orientalium

FCh   Fathers of the Church series.

MGH   *Monumenta Germaniae Historica.*

PL   J.P. Migne, *Patrologia cursus completus . . . series Latina.* 221 volumes.

SCh   Sources chrétiennes. Paris: Les Éditions du Cerf,

Works Cited

Augustine of Hippo (354 - 430)

C. Faust. *Contra Faustum Manichaeum* (Against Faustus the Manichaean). CSEL 25 (1885) 83–112 and PL 43:111–128.

Ordo monasterii *Ordo monasterii* (Regulations for a Monastery). Translation by Raymond Canning OSA, *The Rule of Saint Augustine*. London: Darton Longman Todd - New York: Doubleday Image, 1984, 1986. Critical edition by Luc Verheijen, *Règle de saint Augustin*, 1: Tradition manuscrite. Paris 1967: 148–152.

Praec. *Praeceptum* (Rule). Edited by Verheijen, *Règle de saint Augustin* 1: Tradition manuscrite, pp. 417–437.

Serm. *Sermon*. Latin editions: PL 38–39. CCSL 41. English translation in Nicene and Post Nicene Fathers, vol. 6.

Basil (+379)

Admon. Admonition to a Spiritual Son (Ps-Basil). PL 103; P. Lehmann, *Die Admonitio S. Basilii ad filium spiritalem*, Sitzungsberichte der Bayerischen Akademie der Wissenschaft, Philologische-historische Klasse 7 (1955–1957). Translation: H.W. Norman, *The Anglo-Saxon Version of the Hexameron of St. Basil and the Saxon Remains of St. Basil's Admonitio ad*

Filium Spiritalem, with a Translation. London 1848.

LR — *Regulae fusius tractatae* (The Longer Rules). PG 31. A. Gribomont, *Histoire du textes des Ascétiques de Saint Basile,* Bibl. du Museon, 32. Louvain, 1953. ET: Clarke, *The Ascetical Works of St. Basil.* London: SPCK, 1925; NPNF, 2nd series (1895) volume 8. Fathers of the Church, volume 9 (1950) 223–337.

Reg. — *Regula.* Latin version by Rufinus. Ed,. Klaus Zelzer, CSEL (Vienna)

SR — *Regulae breuius tractatae* (The Shorter Rules). PG 31; Gribomont, *Histoire du textes.* ET: Clarke, *The Ascetical Works of St. Basil.*

Caesarius of Arles (+ 542)

Reg. uirg. — *Regula sanctarum virginum* (Rule for Nuns). PL 67; G. Morin, CC 103–104; SCh 345. Translation by M.C. McCarthy, *The Rule for Nuns of St. Caesarius of Arles.* Washington: Catholic University of America Press, 1960.

Cassian, John (+435)

Conf. — Conferences (*Conlationes*). PL 49; CSEL 13, 17; SCh 42, 54, 64. English translation by Boniface Ramsey OP, *The Conferences of John Cassian,* Cistercian Studies Series 136–138, and in the Nicene and Post Nicene Fathers, Series 2, volume 11.

Inst. — Institutes (*De institutis coenobiorum*). CSEL 13 (1886); SCh 109. Translation

Nicene and Post Nicene Fathers, Series 2, vol. 11; forthcoming by Boniface Ramsey OP from Cistercian Publications.

Clement of Rome (fl. 150)

Ep. ad Cor.   Letter to the Corinthians (*Epistola ad Corinthios*) or First Epistle. PG 5; F.X. Funk and K. Bihlmeyer, *De apostolischen Väter*, 2nd edition. Tübingen 1956. English translation in Ancient Christian Writers 1 (1961); Fathers of the Church 5, Library of Christian Classics.

Cyprian of Carthage (c. 200- 258)

De orat. dom.   *De dominica oratione* (On the Lord's Prayer). PL 4; CSEL 3. CC 3A.

Test.   *Testimonia*, or *Ad Quirinum* (Testimony or To Quirinus). PL 4. CSEL 3. Translation Ante Nicene Fathers 25; FCh 36; ACW.

Cyril of Scythopolis

Vita Euthymii   Life of Euthymius. Edited E. Schwartz, *Kyrillos von Skythopolis*. Texte und Untersuchungen 49:2. Leipzig, 1939. Translated by R.M. Price, *Lives of the Monks of Palestine*, Cistercian Studies Series 114.

Didachè

Edited F.X. Funk, *Patres Apostolici* I. Tübingen 1907; SCh 248. Translation: E. J. Goodspeed, *The Apostolic Fathers: An American Translation*. New York 1950.

Dorotheos of Gaza (sixth century)

Inst.   *Instructiones* (Instructions). SCh 92. Translation: *Dorotheos of Gaza: Discourses and Sayings*, Cistercian Studies Series 33.

Egeria (Etheria)

Peregrinatio: CC 175; SCh 21. Translation: Ancient Christian Writers 38; J. Wilkinson, *Egeria's Travels to the Holy Land*. Warminster: Aris and Philips 1981.

Eugippius

V. Seu.   *Vita Severini* (Life of Severinus). MGH *Auctores* 1/2 (1877). Translation: FCh 55.

Evagrius (345–399)

De oratione   (On Prayer). PG 79. Translation by John Eudes Bamberger ocso, *Evagrius Ponticus: Praktikos and Chapters on Prayer*, Cistercian Studies Series 4 (1970).

Gregory the Great (+604)

Dial.   *Dialogorum libri IV* (Dialogues). PL 77; A. de Vogüé, SCh 251, 260, 265 (1978, 1979, 1980); U. Moricca, *Gregorii Magni Dialogi Libri IV* (Rome 1924); SCh 251, 260, 265. English translation: Fathers of the Church 39; Book two (The Life of St Benedict) *The Life of Saint Benedict*. Liturgical Press: Collegeville.

Moralia   *Moralia in Iob* (Morals on the Book of Job). PL 75–76; CC 143, 143A, 143B; SCh 32, 212, 221.

In I Reg.   *In librum primum Regum expositionum libri vi* (Commentary on the First Book of Kings). PL 79; SCh 351.

Hippolytus

        Apostolic Tradition: Edited B. Botte, *Liturgiewissenschaftliche Quellen und Forschungen*. Münster 1966. Translation by Gregory Dix: *The Apostolic Tradition of Hippolytus*. London 1937.

Hist. mon.

        Historia monachorum in Aegypto (Histories of the Monks of Egypt). PL 21; A.-J. Festugière, *Édition critique du texte grex*, Subsidia Hagiographia 34. Brussels 1961. Translation by Norman Russell, *The Lives of the Desert Fathers*, Cistercian Studies Series 34.

Jerome

    Ep.   *Epistolae* (Letters). PL 222; CSEL 54–56. Translation ACW 33.

John Climacus (+c. 649)

    Past.   *Ad Pastorem* (To the Shepherd). PG 88. Translation by Lazarus Moore, *St. John Climacus, The Ladder of Divine Ascent*. Boston: Holy Transfiguration Monastery, 1978. Pp. 231–250.

Lactantius c. 250 - c. 325)

    Inst.   *Lactantius: Institutiones divines II*, ed. P. Monat, SCh 337. Translation: *Lactantius: The Divine Institutes Books 1–7*, FCh 49.

Lausiac History

> Palladius, *Historia Lausiaca*. PG 34;
> PL 74; C. Butler, *The Lausiac History
> of Palladius*, Texts and Studies 6:1–2
> (2 volumes). Translation: ACW 34.

Life of Anthony

> Athanasius, *Life of Anthony
> (Vita Antonii)*. PG 26; PL 73;
> H. Hoppenbrouwers, *La plus ancienne
> version latine de la vie de S. Antoine par
> S. Athanase: Étude de critique textuelle*.
> Nijmegen: Dekker & Van de Vegt,
> 1960. Translation ACW 10; *Athanasius*,
> Classics of Western Spirituality. New
> York: Paulist.

Lives of the
Fathers of Jura

> *Vita patrum Jurensium*. SCh 142.

Origen

Hom. on Joshua *Homiliae in Iesu Nave* (Homilies on
Joshua). PG 12, GCS 30, SCh 71. ET:
R.B. Tollington, *Selections from the
Commentaries and Homilies of Origin*,
London: SPCK, 1929.

Pachomius

G[1]

> *First Greek Life*. F. Halkin, *Sancti
> Pachomii Vitae Graecae*, Subsidia
> Hagiographica 19. Brussels 1032.
> Translation by Armand Veilleux,
> *Pachomian Koinonia 1: The Lives of Saint
> Pachomius*, Cistercian Fathers Series
> 45. Kalamazoo, 1980.

Inst.

Precepts and Institutes. CSCO 159. Translation by Armand Veilleux, *Pachomian Koinonia* 2: *Pachomian Rules and Chronicles,* Cistercian Studies Series 47. Kalamazoo 1981. 169–174.

Iud.

Precepts and Judgements. A. Boon, *Pachomiana latina. Règle et épîtres de s. Pachôme . . . ,* Bibliothèque de la Revue d'histoire ecclésiastique 7 (Louvain 1932) 63–70. Translation by A. Veilleux, *Pachomian Koinonia* 2:175–179.

Lib.

Liber Orsiesius. L.-T. Lefort, *Oeuvres de s. Pachôme et de ses disciples,* CSCO 159. Louvain 1956. Translation by Veilleux, 2:197–219.

Praec.

Praecepta (Precepts). Boon (see Iud.). Translation by Veilleux, 2:145–174.

SBo

The Bohairic Life of Pachomius. L.-T. Lefort, *S. Pachomii vita bohairice scripta,* CSCO 89 (1925). Translation by A. Veilleux, *Pachomian Koinonia* 1: 23–265.

Pass. Anast.

Passion of Saint Anastasia *et al.* H. Delehaye, *Étude sur le Légendier romain* BHL 1795, 118, 8093,401.

Pass. Seb.

Passion of Saint Sebastian. PL 17. AA SS Jan. 2:629–642.

2RF

> *Regula ii Ss. Patrum* (Second Rule of the Fathers): PL 103; PG 34. Translation: *Early Monastic Rules*. Collegeville: Liturgical Press 1982.

RIVF

> *Regula iv Patrum* (Fourth Rule of the Fathers): J. Neufville, 'Règle des iv Pères et seconde règle des Pères', *Revue Bénédictine* 77 (1867) 47–106. Translation: *Early Monastic Rules*.

Sextus (third century)

Ench.

> *Enchiridion* (Sentences), translated by Rufinus. Edited and translated by Henry Chadwick, *The Sentences of Sextus*, Texts and Studies, New Series, 5. Cambridge 1959; and by R.A. Edwards and R.A. Wild, *The Sentences of Sextus*. Chico, California: Scholars Press, 1981.

Sidonius Apollinarius (+ c. 487)

Carm.

> *Carmina* (Poems). PL 58 and MGH auctores antissimi 8 (1887). Translation by W.B. Anderson, *Sidonius, Poems and Letters*, Library of Christian Classics 1 (1937) and 2 (1965).

Vitae patrum

> *Vitae patrum* (Lives of the Fathers), *Verba Seniorum*, Sayings of the Fathers, Latin version by Pelagius and John. PL 73. J.C. Guy, *Rescherches sur la tradition grecque des Apophthegmata*

Patrum, Subsidia Hagiographica 36. Brussels 1962. Translation by Owen Chadwick, *Western Asceticism*, Library of Christian Classics. Philadelphia, 1958.

Scriptural Index to the Commentary

Index of Ancient Authors

Personal Names

Latin Words

CISTERCIAN PUBLICATIONS, INC.
TITLES LISTING

—CISTERCIAN TEXTS—

THE WORKS OF BERNARD OF CLAIRVAUX

Apologia to Abbot William
Five Books on Consideration: Advice to a Pope
Homilies in Praise of the Blessed Virgin Mary
The Life and Death of Saint Malachy the Irishman
Love without Measure: Extracts from the Writings of St Bernard (Paul Dimier)
On Grace and Free Choice
On Loving God (Analysis by Emero Stiegman)
The Parables of Saint Bernard (Michael Casey)
Sermons for the Summer Season
Sermons on Conversion
Sermons on the Song of Songs I–IV
The Steps of Humility and Pride

THE WORKS OF WILLIAM OF SAINT THIERRY

The Enigma of Faith
Exposition on the Epistle to the Romans
Exposition on the Song of Songs
The Golden Epistle
The Mirror of Faith
The Nature of Dignity of Love
On Contemplating God, Prayer & Meditations

THE WORKS OF AELRED OF RIEVAULX

Dialogue on the Soul
Liturgical Sermons, I
The Mirror of Charity
Spiritual Friendship
Treatises I: On Jesus at the Age of Twelve, Rule for a Recluse, The Pastoral Prayer
Walter Daniel: The Life of Aelred of Rievaulx

THE WORKS OF JOHN OF FORD

Sermons on the Final Verses of the Songs of Songs I–VII

THE WORKS OF GILBERT OF HOYLAND

Sermons on the Songs of Songs I–III
Treatises, Sermons and Epistles

OTHER EARLY CISTERCIAN WRITERS

The Letters of Adam of Perseigne I
Alan of Lille: The Art of Preaching
Baldwin of Ford: Spiritual Tractates I–II
Gertrud the Great of Helfta: Spiritual Exercises

Gertrud the Great of Helfta: The Herald of God's Loving-Kindness
Guerric of Igny: Liturgical Sermons I–[II]
Idung of Prüfening: Cistercians and Cluniacs: The Case of Cîteaux
Isaac of Stella: Sermons on the Christian Year, I–[II]
The Life of Beatrice of Nazareth
Serlo of Wilton & Serlo of Savigny: Works
Stephen of Lexington: Letters from Ireland
Stephen of Sawley: Treatises

—MONASTIC TEXTS—

EASTERN CHRISTIAN TRADITION

Besa: The Life of Shenoute
Cyril of Scythopolis: Lives of the Monks of Palestine
Dorotheos of Gaza: Discourses and Sayings
Evagrius Ponticus: Praktikos and Chapters on Prayer
Handmaids of the Lord: The Lives of Holy Women in Late Antiquity & the Early Middle Ages (Joan Petersen)
The Harlots of the Desert (Benedicta Ward)
John Moschos: The Spiritual Meadow
The Lives of the Desert Fathers
The Lives of Simeon Stylites (Robert Doran)
The Luminous Eye (Sebastian Brock)
Mena of Nikiou: Isaac of Alexandra & St Macrobius
Pachomian Koinonia I–III (Armand Vielleux)
Paphnutius: A Histories of the Monks of Upper Egypt
The Sayings of the Desert Fathers (Benedicta Ward)
Spiritual Direction in the Early Christian East (Irénée Hausherr)
Spiritually Beneficial Tales of Paul, Bishop of Monembasia (John Wortley)
Symeon the New Theologian: The Theological and Practical Treatises & The Three Theological Discourses (Paul McGuckin)
Theodoret of Cyrrhus: A History of the Monks of Syria
The Syriac Fathers on Prayer and the Spiritual Life (Sebastian Brock)

WESTERN CHRISTIAN TRADITION

Anselm of Canterbury: Letters I–III (Walter Fröhlich)
Bede: Commentary on the Acts of the Apostles
Bede: Commentary on the Seven Catholic Epistles

CISTERCIAN PUBLICATIONS, INC.
TITLES LISTING

Bede: Homilies on the Gospels III
The Celtic Monk (U. O Maidín)
Gregory the Great: Forty Gospel Homilies
The Meditations of Guigo I, Prior of the
    Charterhouse (A. Gordon Mursell)
Peter of Celle: Selected Works
The Letters of Armand-Jean de Rancé I–II
The Rule of the Master
The Rule of Saint Augustine
The Wound of Love: A Carthusian Miscellany

CHRISTIAN SPIRITUALITY

Abba: Guides to Wholeness & Holiness East &
    West
A Cloud of Witnesses: The Development of
    Christian Doctrine (David N. Bell)
The Call of Wild Geese (Matthew Kelty)
Cistercian Way (André Louf)
The Contemplative Path
Drinking From the Hidden Fountain
    (Thomas Spidlík)
Eros and Allegory: Medieval Exegesis of the
    Song of Songs (Denys Turner)
Fathers Talking (Aelred Squire)
Friendship and Community (Brian McGuire)
From Cloister to Classroom
The Silent Herald of Unity: The Life of
    Maria Gabrielle Sagheddu (Martha
    Driscoll)
Life of St Mary Magdalene and of Her Sister
    St Martha (David Mycoff)
Many Mansions (David N. Bell)
The Name of Jesus (Irénée Hausherr)
No Moment Too Small (Norvene Vest)
Penthos: The Doctrine of Compunction in the
    Christian East (Irénée Hausherr)
Rancé and the Trappist Legacy
    (A.J. Krailsheimer)
The Roots of the Modern Christian Tradition
Russian Mystics (Sergius Bolshakoff)
Sermons in A Monastery (Matthew Kelty)
The Spirituality of the Christian East
    (Tomas Spidlík)
The Spirituality of the Medieval West
    (André Vauchez)
Tuning In To Grace (André Louf)
Wholly Animals: A Book of Beastly Tales
    (David N. Bell)

—MONASTIC STUDIES—

Community and Abbot in the Rule of St
    Benedict I–II (Adalbert De Vogüé)
The Finances of the Cistercian Order in the
    Fourteenth Century (Peter King)
Fountains Abbey & Its Benefactors
    (Joan Wardrop)

The Hermit Monks of Grandmont
    (Carole A. Hutchison)
In the Unity of the Holy Spirit (Sighard
    Kleiner)
The Joy of Learning & the Love of God:
    Essays in Honor of Jean Leclercq
Monastic Practices (Charles Cummings)
The Occupation of Celtic Sites in Ireland by
    the Canons Regular of St Augustine and
    the Cistercians (Geraldine Carville)
Reading Saint Benedict (Adalbert de Vogüé)
The Rule of St Benedict: A Doctrinal and
    Spiritual Commentary (Adalbert de
    Vogüé)
The Rule of St Benedict (Br. Pinocchio)
Serving God First (Sighard Kleiner)
St Hugh of Lincoln (David H. Farmer)
Stones Laid Before the Lord (Anselme Dimier)
What Nuns Read (David N. Bell)
With Greater Liberty: A Short History of
    Christian Monasticism & Religious
    Orders (Karl Frank)

—CISTERCIAN STUDIES—

Aelred of Rievaulx: A Study (Aelred Squire)
Athirst for God: Spiritual Desire in Bernard of
    Clairvaux's Sermons on the Song of
    Songs (Michael Casey)
Beatrice of Nazareth in Her Context
    (Roger De Ganck)
Bernard of Clairvaux & the Cistercian Spirit
    (Jean Leclercq)
Bernard of Clairvaux: Man, Monk, Mystic
    (Michael Casey) Tapes and readings
Bernard of Clairvaux: Studies Presented to
    Dom Jean Leclercq
Bernardus Magister (Nonacentenary)
Christ the Way: The Christology of Guerric of
    Igny (John Morson)
Cistercian Sign Language (Robert Barakat)
The Cistercian Spirit
The Cistercians in Denmark (Brian McGuire)
The Cistercians in Scandinavia (James France)
A Difficult Saint (Brian McGuire)
The Eleventh-century Background of Cîteaux
    (Bede K. Lackner)
A Gathering of Friends: Learning &
    Spirituality in John of Forde (Costello
    and Holdsworth)
Image and Likeness: The Augustinian
    Spirituality of William of St Thierry
    (David N. Bell)
An Index of Authors & Works in Cistercian
    Libraries in Great Britain I (David N.
    Bell)

CISTERCIAN PUBLICATIONS, INC.
TITLES LISTING

The Mystical Theology of St Bernard
(Etiénne Gilson)
Nicolas Cotheret's Annals of Cîteaux (Louis J. Lekai)
A Second Look at Saint Bernard (Jean Leclercq)
The Spiritual Teachings of St Bernard of Clairvaux (John R. Sommerfeldt)
Studiosorum Speculum (Louis J. Lekai)
Towards Unification with God
(Beatrice of Nazareth in Her Context, 2)
William, Abbot of St Thierry
Women and St Bernard of Clairvaux
(Jean Leclercq)

MEDIEVAL RELIGIOUS —WOMEN—

Lillian Thomas Shank and John A. Nichols, editors

Distant Echoes
Peace Weavers
Hidden Springs: Cistercian Monastic Women
(2 volumes)

—CARTHUSIAN— TRADITION

The Call of Silent Love
Guigo II: The Ladder of Monks & Twelve Meditations (Colledge & Walsh)
Interior Prayer (A Carthusian)
Meditations of Guigo II (A. Gorden Mursell)
The Way of Silent Love (A Carthusian Miscellany)
The Wound of Love (A Carthusian Miscellany)
They Speak by Silences (A Carthusian)
Where Silence is Prayer (A Carthusian)

–STUDIES IN CISTERCIAN– ART & ARCHITECTURE

Meredith Parsons Lillich, editor
Volumes II, III and IV are now available

—THOMAS MERTON—

The Climate of Monastic Prayer (T. Merton)
The Legacy of Thomas Merton (P. Hart)
The Message of Thomas Merton (P. Hart)
The Monastic Journey of Thomas Merton (P. Hart)
Thomas Merton Monk & Artist (Victor Kramer)
Thomas Merton on St Bernard
Toward an Integrated Humanity
(M. Basil Pennington ed.)

CISTERCIAN LITURGICAL —DOCUMENTS SERIES—

Chrysogonus Waddell, ocso, editor

Hymn Collection of the Abbey of the Paraclete
Institutiones nostrae: The Paraclete Statutes
Molesme Summer-Season Breviary (4 volumes)
Old French Ordinary & Breviary of the Abbey of the Paraclete: Text & Commentary
(2 volumes)
The Cadouin Breviary (2 volumes)
The Twelfth-century Cistercian Hymnal
(2 volumes)
The Twelfth-century Cistercian Psalter
The Twelfth-century Usages of the Cistercian Lay brothers
Two Early *Libelli Missarum*

STUDIA PATRISTICA —XVIII—
Volumes 1, 2 and 3

❖❖❖❖❖❖❖❖❖❖❖❖❖

Editorial queries & advance book information should be directed to the Editorial Offices:

Cistercian Publications
Institute of Cistercian Studies
WMU Station
Kalamazoo, Michigan 49008
Tel: (616) 387-8920 ❖ Fax: (616) 387-8921

Cistercian Publications is a non-profit corporation. Its publishing program is restricted to monastic texts in translation and books on the monastic tradition.

North American customers may order these books through booksellers or directly from the warehouse, (address below):

Cistercian Publications
St Joseph's Abbey
Spencer, Massachusetts 01562-1233
Tel: (508) 885-8730 ❖ Fax: (508) 885-4687

British & European Orders:

Cistercian Publications
Mount Saint Bernard Abbey
Coalville, Leicester LE67 5UL
Fax: [44] (1530) 81.46.08

❖❖❖❖❖❖❖❖❖❖❖❖❖

A complete catalogue of texts in translation and studies on early, medieval, and modern monasticism is available, free of charge, from Cistercian Publications.